Computers in Language Learning

John Higgins and Tim Johns

Collins ELT · London and Glasgow

Collins Educational
8 Grafton Street
London W1X 3LA
© John Higgins and Tim Johns, 1984

10 9 8 7 6 5 4 3 2 1

First published 1984

Phototypeset by Tradespools Limited, Frome,
Somerset

Printed in England by Hazell, Watson and Viney Ltd.

ISBN 0 00 370623 0

Contents

Acknowledgements

We have been fortunate in that our topic has aroused a great deal of interest and we have been able to travel widely and discuss CALL (Computer Assisted Language Learning) with a variety of people. Where we can trace the origin of a specific idea, we acknowledge it in the notes to each chapter.

In addition, we need to acknowledge the debt we owe to a number of our colleagues, in particular Jeremy Fox of the University of East Anglia, and Harold Fish, Ian Sedwell and John Sinclair of the University of Birmingham, all of whom read and commented on early drafts of the manuscript or discussed the ideas in it. Peter Skehan of London University, Chris Jones of London, Chris Harrison of the British Council, Sue Fortescue of Eurocentres, Carole Lowe of the British Council in Munich and Bernard van Lierop of Wolverhampton have all provided us with ideas or with feedback based on materials they used. Muriel Higgins has defined the BOOH factor (see Chapter 3.10) for us, an idea of great simplicity and power, as well as providing some actual program scenarios. Her readings of the manuscript have been helpful and professional.

4

Introduction

Readership
This book is designed for language teachers who want to know, even if only in a general way, how computers can be used in their profession. It is not intended to be a general introduction to the subject of computing. We assume that readers are aware of what computers look like and how they are used. We also assume that readers will either have had some access to a machine and read the instruction manual that comes with it, or have read a general introductory text on computing (see notes to Chapter 1), or seen one of the many computer journals on sale in newsagents.

We will therefore not attempt to define and explain the common jargon of computing, and will describe only those features of the hardware which are relevant to the language teacher. However, we hope we have avoided taking too much for granted and that most of the book will be fully intelligible to those readers who count themselves as computer novices.

Languages
Both the authors are teachers of English as a foreign language (EFL). We have worked in Britain and overseas, teaching a variety of levels from beginner to advanced. Most of our experience, however, has been with older children and adults, rather than at the primary level, and this may show in the range of materials and activities described in the book.

Although most of the illustrations are for the teaching of English, almost all the programs can be used for teaching other languages by replacing the language content – and one program for teaching French is included in the listings in Chapter 5. In Chapter 3 some work being done for French, German and Italian teaching in British and European schools is described. While the authors' own professional concern is with the teaching of English to speakers of other languages, the approaches suggested in this book are, in many cases, equally applicable to the teaching of English as a first language.

Outline of the book
Chapter 1 looks at the assumptions underlying the use of computers to teach language: assumptions about the nature of teaching, the nature of language and the nature of learning. The last section gives an account of some major ideas in the development of computer-assisted learning (CAL) which are relevant to computer-assisted

language learning (CALL).

Chapter 2 looks at the way in which people communicate with computers, describing the available input and output devices and indicating how they may affect the presentation and practice of language.

Chapter 3 looks at the many roles that a computer can play in the classroom, and describes a number of CALL programs and the thinking behind them. (Note the now standard British practice of distinguishing between **program**, a set of machine instructions, and **programme**, a timetable or scheme of work.)

Chapter 4 looks at the uses of the computer outside the classroom, in linguistic research, in artificial intelligence research related to language, in the storage and updating of teaching materials and texts, and in testing. (School administration and timetabling are not included because they are not specific to language learning and are adequately covered elsewhere.)

Chapter 5 is an introduction to some programming techniques relevant to language teaching, illustrated by a number of complete program listings with annotations and notes on conversion.

Computer language

The examples in Chapter 5 are all in the form of BASIC used by the Sinclair Spectrum (a modified version of which is sold in the USA as the TS2000). In many cases the programs listed will run, with a few changes, on the simpler and cheaper ZX81 (known in the USA as the TS1000). Sinclair BASIC was chosen because, for the next year or two, the ZX81 and the Spectrum are the machines that the computer novice wanting to experiment is most likely to have access to. Their price is low enough to encourage both schools and individual teachers to use them. It makes sense not to spend too much at first. It is easy enough to invest in a larger and more permanent piece of equipment later, using one's early experiences to make an informed choice.

Software

At present there is very little commercially-produced software for the EFL learner and only a little for learners of other languages. This is likely to change quite rapidly in the next few years as the equipment becomes more readily available to language teachers. Of course, there is already a good deal of material which the language teacher can use occasionally, although it was not written in the first place for language teaching purposes. Language teachers may be, in this respect, the poor relations of teachers of science, maths and economics. Within a year or two though, material writers will start producing what language teachers need. We hope that this book will help stimulate the process.

Computer programs described in this book are by John Higgins or Tim Johns, unless another author is named.

1 Underlying assumptions

1.1 Teachers, learners and computers

Before considering whether computers can aid the language learning process, we need to have a clear idea of what activities are involved in teaching and learning languages. For all their speed and accuracy, computers are mere machines. They can replicate human activity – but only if the activity can be comprehensively and unambiguously described. Is teaching such an activity?

Although there may be differences from one culture to another, as a rule teacher activities include the following:

1 Manager of routines By routines we mean all those activities determined in advance that are designed to assist in language learning, ranging from drills and exercises to role-play, songs and games, and the way in which they are integrated into an overall programme. By talking of teachers as managers, we mean that they have the responsibility for seeing that the activities are carried out effectively. That responsibility includes the central role of initiating and giving feedback in the standard classroom interaction:

Teacher Who knows what I'm holding? John?
Student A pen?
Teacher Well done. It's a pen.
          or No, not quite. Who else would like to have a go?

It includes the wider responsibility of monitoring student progress and adjusting the pace of presentation, and the emphasis on different aspects of the routine, in response to evidence of success or failure. Teachers have a wide range of supports, including syllabuses, textbooks, and their own lesson plans, in order to ensure that the overall routine of the programme and the separate routines of each individual activity are effective and consistent.

2 Responder As well as being managers of routines, teachers have a responsibility to abandon routine and create activites, tasks and situations 'on the spot' in response to the interests, needs and initiatives of their students. Routine is necessary to create a sense of security and direction for both teacher and students; response is necessary to create the elements of expectation and involvement. Both are essential in effective teaching.

3 Facilitator Here the responsibility is to create an environment in which students will want to learn a language and will find the learning itself interesting and enjoyable. The teacher's activities as facilitator might include hanging up posters, arranging recitals of pop records in the lunchbreak or making sure that the classroom library has some cowboy stories in the target language for Tom who is bored by texts in the Reader about happy families at the seaside.

4 Model   Teachers of languages are usually the only model available to students for genuine communication in the language being learned, as opposed to the stilted pseudo-communication of drills and dialogues. This communication can occur naturally in the context of classroom management ('Who left the door open?') and in casual chat about whatever crops up ('Did you see England play football on TV last night?').

5 Informant   This is a very important potential activity of the language teacher. It involves a reversal of the usual pattern in routine teaching, in which the teacher is the initiator and the learner is the responder. The student becomes the initiator, setting the problems to the teacher: 'Why do people in language X say this and not that?', 'How would you say this in language X?' and so on. We say that this is a potential activity of the teacher, since the usual teaching situation, one teacher working with thirty or more students and needing to go through the lessons in the textbook, works against students taking the initiative. When teachers complain that their students are passive and will not ask questions, they often overlook the pressure of classroom conditions towards passivity.

Looking at the potential of a machine as a teacher in the light of this analysis, two points stand out. On the one hand, it is impossible for a machine to replace a human being totally in any of these roles. There is a warmth and immediacy in contact with another human being which no amount of electronics could ever replace. This is true even when the teacher is acting the role of routine manager. In the early days of language laboratories, when mechanised drill-and-practice was seen as the panacea for all language learning problems, many teachers discovered that if they read a drill over the console microphone to a class, it seemed to be more effective than if the same drill was played from a tape-recorder. Such basic things as eye contact and smiles between teacher and students, and moment-by-moment control of pacing, turned a dry exercise into something closer to communication. In that sense, it is over-ambitious to see the computer as a teacher. On the other hand, early work in computer-assisted instruction has tended to be under-ambitious in the role assigned to the machine in that it has *only* been seen as a provider of drill-and-practice. In this book we wish to suggest that the machine may be able to assist the teacher across the whole range of teaching activities.

Robotisation

There are two arguments for justifying the use of the computer in mechanised drill-and-practice. The first, and stronger, claim is that the introduction of computers can, by analogy with the robotisation of the factory assembly line, save manpower and thus save money: through computer-controlled drill-and-practice students will easily and efficiently acquire mastery of skills in a foreign language without needing a human teacher, except to keep an eye on the process. This is a view which, understandably, arouses a good deal of hostility among language teachers, a hostility which underlies a good deal of the distrust with which they view the introduction of machines of any kind into the classroom. The second argument, which is a weaker version of the same claim, is that the computer can take the drudgery out of teaching by doing all the boring, repetitive work, leaving to the human teacher the more creative aspects of the job. This is an argument which is rather more attractive to teachers and is not one with which we would wish to take issue. The computer is an obedient beast and will readily take on the role of drudge if required to.

Other roles

In this book we shall not give much prominence to the computer's role as drudge, or to the sort of program that it entails. Our own concern is to suggest that the computer can best assist teachers if it is seen not as a replacement for their work but as a supplement to it, and that its potential should be explored across the whole range of activities involved in teaching. In Chapter 3 the role of the computer is considered not only as routine teacher but as 'creator', as 'informant', as 'environment' and even as a source of fun. In these sections we shall not only be looking to justify the advantages that come from using a computer in such ways, but also discussing the changes of attitude or approach that must accompany such use. The learners must be, to some extent, in tune with the medium before they can benefit from it.

De-mystification

We strongly believe that language teachers should try to acquire some understanding of how computers work, how they can be applied in language teaching, and how they are programmed. Very few of the present generation of mid-career language teachers have had an opportunity to acquire this knowledge. They did their professional training at a time when computing expertise resided mainly in departments of mathematics. If you wanted to use a computer for a specific project, you called on the services of professional programmers and presented them with your problem and your data. In due course the programmer presented you with the solution. What happened in between was a mystery.

Computing began to seem less mysterious with the introduction, in the late seventies, of free-standing microcomputers which individuals could afford. When you switch on a microcomputer, it displays the message 'Ready', not the complicated rigmarole of passwords and account numbers which confronts the user of a mainframe terminal. The breaking down of one barrier quickly led to the breaking down of others, as non-mathematicians discovered that using and programming the machine were far easier than they had thought. In place of lengthy professional training, people started teaching themselves from books, or attending evening classes. Nowadays computers are to be found in schools at all levels, being handled by teachers who have no formal qualifications in computing, and in a great many homes, where they are used by both children and adults.

Language teachers' attitudes

A particular reason why language teachers have tended to be bypassed by the microcomputer revolution is that computer specialists and computer hobbyists have never found it easy to demonstrate any value for the computer in language learning. Programs written by amateurs tend to consist of vocabulary tests, and professionally produced programs are usually in the drill-and-practice format and cover inflexional morphology or sentence structure. When these are demonstrated, the usual reaction from language teachers is that they contain nothing which cannot be done already with pencil and paper, and that the gains (in individualisation or motivation) do not justify the expense and trouble. There is also some disquiet that such programs deal exclusively with word or sentence level meaning and ignore context and discourse features. Naturally enough, language teachers tend to put the blame on the machines. What they fail to realise is how unaware the computer specialist is likely to be about what happens inside a language classroom and how language teaching has changed in the last twenty years. This situation will be put right only when there are enough language teachers with substantial classroom experience who also understand computers and can use their professional knowlege to exploit the machine's potential.

Mathematical bias

Some of the blame must be laid at the door of the computer specialists who write books and run training courses, since they tend to be from a mathematics background and therefore perpetuate the myth that the computer is primarily a calculating device. They often set exercises which involve calculating mortgage repayments or doing centigrade to Fahrenheit conversions, which a computer does no better than a good pocket calculator. A computer is a device for storing, retrieving and manipulating symbols, and those symbols do not need to be numbers. There are very few introductory computing courses in which the tasks set involve the manipulation of text, and yet that is what most language teachers would ask for if they knew it was available. In fact text manipulation, in the shape of word-processing, is probably the commonest current application of all but the largest computers. It is certainly the area in which language teachers are most likely to be interested.

The human factor

One anxiety that is often expressed is that computers will de-humanise instruction, either in a practical, economic fashion by depriving human teachers of employment, or in a spiritual sense by turning learners into automata who will learn to respond in a mechanical fashion. The computing profession and popular journalism must take some responsibility for these fears, since they arise from various myths about the nature and potential of computers which have been current over the last twenty years. The student isolated in a cubicle following programmed courses all day is an unfortunate stereotype, arising from the tendency to ascribe to the machine all the authority and control which traditionally we have allowed the teacher. Seymour Papert wrote in 1980:

> In many schools today, the phrase 'computer-aided instruc-tion' means making the computer teach the child. One might say the computer is being used to program the child. In my vision the child programs the computer and, in doing so, both acquires a sense of mastery over a piece of the most modern and powerful technology and establishes an inti-mate contact with some of the deepest ideas from science, from mathematics, and from the art of intellectual model building.

Papert's ideas have been influential, and nowadays the mechanistic image of computerised teaching is more common outside the classroom than in it.

The language laboratory

The other common misgiving one hears is the fear that the computer will turn out to be as much of a disappointment as the language laboratory. The language laboratory was oversold during the fifties and sixties, and the tapes available for it at that time were generally rather unimaginative and based on sentence manipulations. The underlying learning theory was behaviourism and the underlying linguistic theory was structuralism, both of which were in the process

11

of being challenged and, to a great extent, discredited. The great mistake, in retrospect, seems to have been installing the machines in large, unwieldy assemblages which were very expensive, and skimping on the costs of training and software development. To quote the sense of a remark heard from the floor at a recent conference:

> The language laboratory was a marvellous individualising machine. So what did we do with it? We made it up into batches of twenty, stuck it in a locked room, and made each class go there for an hour a week to do the same work at the same time.

However, not all labs were used so unimaginatively, and they did provide teachers with experience of handling tape well before personal tape-recorders became widespread in people's homes. Teachers experimented with songs and authentic listening tasks, and so were ready for the real breakthrough in the late sixties when cassette recorders became generally available. Nowadays very few courses are sold without accompanying recordings, and the majority of teachers use recorders, occasionally at least. The technology of the recorder no longer frightens teachers or learners, and the machines are quite properly seen as aids, not threats.

The cheap microcomputer is still not as easy to use as the cassette recorder, but it is rapidly becoming as familiar in the form of the games-playing machine. The lessons we can learn from the language laboratory experience are not to impose computers on staff who have not been prepared or trained to use then, to put more money and effort into developing software than into acquiring hardware, and to use small, flexible units rather than large, centrally-controlled installations. Computers then become aids under the control of teachers and learners; they are slaves, not masters.

Speech

Yet another objection one often hears from teachers is that using a written channel for communication will inhibit fluency in speech, and that we should therefore wait for computers which can 'talk'. We shall have more to say about synthesised speech and voice decoding in Chapter 2.4, but meanwhile it is worth examining the force of this argument. Real life face-to-face interactions between human beings are all conducted in speech (or possibly in sign language). Writing is reserved for a particular kind of interaction where the participants are separated in space and time (i.e. letter writing), or else for completely different purposes: story-telling and other forms of entertainment, record-keeping and reference. Teachers, however, and particularly language teachers, already use a rather hybrid medium in which written language is made the cue for an immediate spoken response, 'Please read the first sentence', 'What's the answer to question two?', etc. Therefore a conversation in writing is perhaps less of a novel idea in the classroom than it is elsewhere. If the prompts on the screen merely replace the teacher's spoken instructions, then very little exposure is lost, and the rest of what is on the screen has the same function as what is on the page of the book that the teacher is telling the students to read. In the same way as the book page, it can stimulate thought or discussion and thus engender spoken language just as a textbook does. Many people are apprehensive about using bigger and better talking computers in education, precisely because the computers may speak instructions and take over more of the teacher's role, with the lessons consisting of ever more elaborate tutorial sequences. In fact, no computer in any classroom that we know of has done anything to diminish the amount of spoken language in that classroom.

1.2 Language and learning

It is usually easy to identify one language as being distinct from another. If one reads or hears an extended piece of language, one can usually say with some certainty, 'That's Swahili' or 'He's speaking German', and in a polyglot conversation one can usually mark the exact points that a speaker switches from one language to another, provided one of the languages is familiar to the listener. A language consists of a set of lexical items and a system of syntactic and phonological/graphological rules, and a linguist needs only a small sample to be able to determine whether the sample conforms to one set rather than another. The lexical inventory tends to be treated as dominant. If a speaker uses only English words but puts them into German word order, we will usually think of him as speaking 'bad English' rather than 'bad German'. Both the lexis and the syntax are dominant over phonology. A speaker who uses German sounds in rendering English sentences is speaking 'English with a German accent', not 'German with English grammar and lexis'.

The aim of teaching English lexis, syntax rules and phonology is to yield a linguistic competence: the ability to produce and recognise sentences which conform to the system called 'English'.

Communicative competence

The judgment as to whether something is or is not 'English' is independent of meaning, and could be made whether the language being used is sensible or not. In normal use, however, we expect language to be meaningful, and often make great leaps in our efforts to interpret what we hear. Consider a very ordinary exchange like the following:

A: Where the hell have you been?   *B:* It started to rain.

13

The use of the swearword shows that the first speaker is of equal or superior rank to the second speaker, and, although his question begins 'Where', he is demanding an explanation for lateness rather than information about a place. The second speaker answers the implied rather than the overt question. To interpret the answer we need to know that people do not relish walking in the rain, and may assume that the second speaker has come from another building and lacks a car, an umbrella or a raincoat, probably all three.

In programming computers to interact with humans in natural language, one of the major difficulties is the problem of providing the machine with enough knowledge of the world to make this kind of interpretive leap, something which humans take very much for granted. The ability to produce both appropriate utterances and appropriate interpretations of utterances is known as communicative competence. It can be developed in the classroom, but is often left to be 'picked up'. It normally operates within larger boundaries than the single sentence.

Writers on CALL have asserted that the computer can enhance *linguistic* competence but can do nothing to develop *communicative* competence, but this view is open to question. There are a number of activities in Chapter Three which are designed to develop a feeling for how the forms of a foreign language are used in communication.

Learning

Deciding how to teach a language is conditioned by one's view (which need not be explicit) of what language consists of and what kind of creature the learner is. Is language a body of knowledge which can be learned by conscious memorisation and recall? A set of behaviours which can be internalised by heavy repetition and drilling until it is automatic? Or a system which we humans are in some sense 'designed' to learn, so that we can absorb it from wide exposure? There is some justification for all of these views, and some danger in clinging to any one of them to the exclusion of the others. Good teachers probably always have used and always will use a mixture of explication, drilling, and exposure, deciding whether a particular feature of language is one that should be explained rationally, hammered in by repetition, or inferred and absorbed from authentic samples of language in use.

Syllabuses

Teachers have nearly always assumed that it is possible to enumerate a language syllabus as a list of language features which can be taught discretely – namely lexical sets, grammar patterns, skills. If everything in the syllabus could be taught properly, then the language would be learned when the syllabus was completed, allowing for appropriate revision cycles. This leads to a chain of command in which the syllabus tells the teacher what to do and the teacher tells the learners what to do.

The standard shape for a lesson to take under this scheme is **PPA**, standing for **Presentation, Practice** and **Activity**. If the lesson topic, as determined by the syllabus, is, for instance, a grammar pattern, this works well at the beginning. It is easy to present the past continuous tense and to practise the past continuous tense in the form of drills and dialogues. The problem arises when you reach the stage of Activity, which should indicate some free use of what has been learned. But how can one tell a student to go out and 'use the past continuous tense'? All practice of grammatical patterns tends to be controlled, and there is, therefore, a danger that students, associating the pattern with its drill context, will fail to transfer their learning to real life.

Notional/Functional syllabuses
In the last fifteen years we have seen a good deal of experimentation with notional/functional syllabuses, which take meanings as the basis for the list of items to be learned, drawing in the grammar and vocabulary which are needed to realise each meaning. Where this has been introduced into teaching it has greatly enriched the Activity phase of PPA, since it is more sensible to tell a student to 'offer a cup of coffee' than to tell him or her to 'use the past continuous tense'. At the same time it has complicated the Presentation and Practice, since it is typical of notions and functions that they do not correspond neatly to teachable items in grammar or vocabulary. There are many different ways of offering, and many of the grammar patterns which can be used to make offers can also be used for different purposes. Thus a 'notional drill' is almost inconceivable. This has led to what amounts to a reversal of PPA into a new technique christened 'deep-end strategy'. Here the teacher assigns the class a task to carry out with their available linguistic resources, sees how they get on, provides remedial teaching to cover their inadequacies, and may finally ask them to repeat the original task or a similar one in order to assess their progress. The grammar syllabus does not exist before the course, but is created out of the students' needs.

Acquisition and learning
For some time it has been recognised that there are two processes at work when language is learned, a **learning** process which concerns itself with conscious manipulation of the linguistic code, and an **acquisition** process which tries to interpret the language which is heard and seen, and to store those parts of the language system which the learner can account for.

15

A number of studies were carried out in the sixties and seventies on young children acquiring their first language, and these tended to show that certain language features were mastered at a particular age and in a relatively predictable order. Since the language that children are exposed to is highly diverse, this led to speculation that there is a 'natural order' or 'inner syllabus', that children will only be able to acquire command of a phonological or grammatical feature when they are ready for it, when it finds a place in the jigsaw puzzle of language that is being built up in their minds. Research into errors made by second language learners suggests that something similar may be occurring in second language acquisition. Some errors tend to occur at certain stages of learning, regardless of the teacher, the syllabus, or, indeed, of the learner's language background.

The implications of this are developed to what some people regard as an extreme position by Stephen Krashen. Krashen suggests that what is 'learned' and what is 'acquired' in language are used separately by the brain, and that there is very little exchange between the learning store and the acquisition store. He further maintains that only the acquisition store can initiate spontaneous conversation or creative use of language. The learning store can be used for mental translation, and will act as a monitor on the discourse produced by the acquisition store, allowing errors to be corrected. A learner whose learning store is well filled but whose acquisition store is empty will be capable of laborious 'language-like behaviour' but not of using language.

The implication of this for the teacher is that he or she must provide a rich enough linguistic environment to enable acquisition to occur, an environment which contains not just uncontrolled foreign speech but also a good deal of 'caretaker speech', speech which, like that of mothers to small children, contains more repetition, more simplification and more talk about what is visibly present than full adult speech.

Anyone learning a language should be exposed to as much language as possible which is at the threshold of his or her understanding but which can be interpreted by using visual or commonsense clues. Krashen describes this language as 'i + 1' (standing for one step beyond intelligibility). He sees the teacher's central duty as providing a sufficient quantity and diversity of language for all members of a group to be exposed to enough 'i + 1' to feed their own acquisition mechanisms, and ensuring that the language is sufficiently interesting and relevant to hold the learners' attention. He sees no need for teachers to undertake the kind of rule exposition, exercises and drilling which are traditionally part of the language classroom. He does not even see any necessity to make the learners speak, and provides evidence of people learning successfully after lengthy silent periods during which there was no sign that they were learning anything at all.

Krashen does, perhaps, underestimate the power of motivation and purpose, since prodigious feats of language learning through conscious application have been recorded, for example among missionaries learning an exotic language for the specific purpose of establishing a church or a hospital, and using no better learning tools than a bilingual Bible and a dictionary. These, though, are exceptional cases, and against them must be set the millions of learners who have spent hundreds of hours in classrooms studying a language and have passed examinations, but emerged with no useful grasp of the language at all. An acquisition-oriented classroom would probably have served them far better.

Krashen's theory has been discussed at some length because we believe it will be influential and because it has already had a bearing on people's views of the value of computers in language learning. The computer, some say, serves only the conscious process of learning, and can do nothing to facilitate acquisition. Once again, we hope to be able to show that this view is wrong, and that the computer is quite flexible enough to serve a variety of learning theories. It may also, eventually, provide us with experience and evidence to test the validity of some existing theories, and change the way we teach even when we are not using a computer.

1.3 Computer-assisted learning

The earliest electronic computers were created for and financed by military users, in America to calculate trajectories for artillery and in Britain to decode enemy ciphers (although the latter project remained classified for many years and was therefore never exploited). The next applications were in commerce and government administration. Educational uses did not begin until the fifties. Computers and computing time were in those days very expensive resources, and it was only universities that could afford to become involved. Universities, however, having students who are well above average in intelligence and motivation, have rarely been concerned with or felt the need to develop their own teaching methodologies. This is particularly true of language teaching, where universities (with certain exceptions) have generally concentrated on vocabulary, formal grammar and translation, while the rest of the profession has moved into situational and functional teaching and, more recently, into a range of approaches emphasising learner autonomy. The advocates of computer-assisted learning, particularly in the USA, have always stressed the individualisation of instruction, the fact that the learner can work at his or her own pace. However, as long as the programmed learning paradigm dominated, pace was the only element that was individualised. The learner was not free to make significant choices about the sorts of activities undertaken, or the order in which they would be tackled.

Writing-assisted learning

In 1971 Arthur Luehrmann published a paper called '*Should the computer teach the student or vice versa?*' In it, he asks us to imagine an early civilisation which has just discovered reading and writing. A new R & W industry springs up to meet the needs of government and commerce, and soon it turns its attention to education. So far education has been an expensive provision, reserved for the elite, in which master teachers deliver lectures which they have learned by heart from an older generation of master teachers. The R & W experts propose that there should be a new kind of teaching functionary, the 'reader', whose job it would be to transcribe the master teachers' lectures and read them aloud to classes of less privileged students in remote areas. The reader, not having to memorise the lectures, would need far less training than a master teacher. The proposal is controversial and the government institutes a long-term evaluation. Luehrmann offers both a sad ending and a happy ending to his scenario. The sad ending has the new 'Writing-assisted Learning' accepted and adopted on a wide scale. The happy ending has the scheme turn out to be of doubtful value, but the finding is irrelevant by the time it is published. The reason? Some master teachers have learned to read themselves, and have started to teach their students to read. Luehrmann is not talking about language learning, but the implication that we should not be using the new technology merely to carry out the same tasks that we demanded of the old applies as strongly to language as to any other subject.

Learning paradigms

In 1977 a team of researchers at the University of East Anglia, headed by Stephen Kemmis, published the results of an extensive evaluation of ten different CAL projects. The report was called '*How Do Students Learn?*', and suggests that there are three, possibly four, distinct learning paradigms within which CAL can be justified. The first of these the authors call Instructional, which covers the drill-and-practice and tutorial styles. The authors say of it that it 'involves the belief that the knowledge students need to acquire can be specified in language and learned by the transmission and reception of verbal messages'. In other words, it makes the subject matter central to decisions on how the subject is to be taught.

The second paradigm, Revelatory, is applied to learning which concentrates on discovery and vicarious experience through simulation and data-handling. '. . . this view of learning emphasises closing the gap between the structure of the student's knowledge and the structure of the discipline he is trying to master. . . . We call it "revelatory" because these key ideas are more or less gradually revealed to the learner.'

The third paradigm, labelled Conjectural, emphasises active know-

18

ledge, manipulation and hypothesis testing. 'People who work within this paradigm tend towards the view that knowledge is created through experience and evolves as a psychological and social process.'

Kemmis and his colleagues offer a fourth paradigm, Emancipatory, but suggest that it does not have the same status as the other three. In their discussion they point out that what students do can be divided into 'authentic labour (valued learning)' and 'inauthentic labour (activities which may be instrumental to valued learning but are not valued for their own sake)'. An approach to CAL which justified itself by enhancing authentic labour or by saving inauthentic labour would fall under the emancipatory paradigm.

Like many such classifications, the four paradigms do not provide a tidy and comprehensive scheme which allows one to pigeon-hole any learning activity uniquely, but they do open up new lines of speculation and development. For some people it may come as something of a surprise that there are any uses of the computer in language learning beyond the instructional paradigm. We hope that Chapter 3 will demonstrate some of the possibilities, and stimulate people to discover others.

2 Computer input and output

2.1 The computer screen

The discussion of computer hardware in this and the following three sections is concerned principally not with the internal working of the machine, but with how the machine appears to the user, and in particular with methods of output and input. This is rather like describing a car in terms of the view through the windscreen and the operation of the controls, such as steering-wheel, clutch and brakes, rather than what is happening under the bonnet. There is a great deal of benefit to be gained by even the most casual user from an understanding of how a computer operates, and references are given in the notes to this Chapter to enable the reader to pursue this further.

Screen versus printer

Nowadays a display screen of some kind is fitted to virtually every computer or terminal. This is a fairly recent development. Up to five years ago the normal way for the computer to communicate with the human user would have been via a teletypewriter, printing a line at a time, and screens (often referred to as **visual display units**, abbreviated to VDU) were an expensive luxury. Now it is the printer which is sometimes regarded as the expensive luxury, though we will have more to say on that in Chapter 2.3. A good many programs written in the seventies were obviously designed for teletype output and look decidedly laborious when implemented on modern equipment.

Writing to screen

On most mainframe terminals and on many microcomputers the normal way to write new information on a screen is on the bottom line. When the line is full, the whole contents of the screen jumps up one line, and anything written on the top line is lost. In effect, the screen is behaving like the roll of paper fed into a teletype printer. This is known as **scrolling**, and is in contrast to **paging** where information is written from the top to the bottom of the screen. When the screen is fuil and the user indicates that he or she is ready, the screen blanks out and new information is written from the top again. This is much more like the action of a human writer. It does not, however, always suit the human reader, who normally turns a page keeping a finger ready to flick back if necessary and re-read the end of the previous page. A 'flick-back' facility can be provided on a computer if necessary, for example the previous page can be restored when a special key is pressed or the page can be wiped in sections, leaving the bottom section in view while new information appears at the top. Nevertheless, such makeshifts cannot conceal the fact that the computer is not a suitable medium for the presentation of long texts which must be read consecutively.

Screen size

The cheapest computers are sold without a screen, and play through a domestic TV set (colour or monochrome). More expensive machines use built-in monitors which give sharper picture quality. A built-in screen is usually designed for a single user, and is not larger than 14 inches (using diagonal measurement). External screens can be in any of the sizes in which TVs are made, from 5 inch portables to 26 inch console sets. Naturally, for group or class use, the larger the better. Even a 26 inch screen displaying text is not easy to read from further than ten feet, so this places an effective limit on the numbers of students who can use a computer at one time. What is common to virtually all screens is that they have a horizontal format. Only certain expensive word-processing systems use a vertical screen that has the same proportions as a book page.

Colour

When switched on, most machines display white or green or amber letters on a dark background. It is usually possible to reverse this. Dark letters on a light background are known to be more legible (with black on yellow being the most legible, hence its use on car number plates), but when a user is sitting close to the computer for any length of time, the glare from a bright screen can be uncomfortable. This is why the less tiring light-on-dark mode is usually selected. Some research evidence suggests that, for prolonged use, amber letters on a dark background cause least fatigue. If a program is to be used by a group, the obvious choice is black on white, since no individual will be close to the screen for long, and students at the edge of the group need the clearest possible image. If a program is designed for individual use, it is best to offer the user the choice of black-on-white or white-on-black wherever possible. Colour is available on many computers, being a strong selling point with 'hobby computers' which will be used mainly for games. If the computer uses colour but is connected to a black-and-white television set, the output usually appears as shades of grey, though not necessarily showing the same gradations or contrasts as the colour signal. Colour needs to be used warily. It can have value in highlighting new or important information, but text printed in colour on a coloured background is always less legible – sometimes marginally and sometimes markedly so – than monochrome text. It is worth remembering, too, that some degree of colour-blindness is quite common, especially among males.

Screen format

The computer treats the screen as a grid of cells, in each of which it can print one character. The vertical dimension of the grid (the number of 'lines') varies between nineteen and twenty-five, with twenty-four being typical. The horizontal dimension (the number of 'columns') may be twenty-two, thirty-two, forty, sixty-four or eighty. Some machines provide the facility to switch between forty and eighty or thirty-two and sixty-four columns. Thus different machines provide between 450 and 1900 character positions on a screen, which roughly corresponds to between sixty and 270 words of text. A forty-column screen would permit a maximum of about 130 words of text, compared with 300 words on a typical book page, or 500 words on a typed A4 handout. Of course, one is not always using the screen for text, and, for certain purposes, one can create specially enlarged letters which use up far more of the screen but are legible from further away. The more character positions there are, the more flexibility you have with layouts, but you have to pay the penalty of reduced legibility at a distance. The common forty by twenty-four screen is probably the best compromise.

Characters

The characters that can be displayed in the character positions constitute the **character set**, and this varies greatly from machine to machine. Each character is composed of a pattern of dots or **pixels** within a grid, the size of the grid depending on the shape of the screen, 8×8 (pixels) and 8×10 being the most common.

All computers will provide a set of upper case letters, numbers and common punctuation. Most machines nowadays also provide lower case letters, essential for any educational application which involves the presentation of extended text. While it is possible to design a perfectly adequate upper-case character set within the limitations of an 8×8 format, there are problems with lower case, and it becomes necessary to sacrifice either elegance or legibility; for example, p and y have to be printed without full descenders.

A more general bar to the legibility of text on the screen is that, since each letter occupies a complete grid, there is no proportional spacing: i takes up the same space as m, as it does on a typewriter. One of the authors of this book has, however, written a machine-code routine which will allow the screen display of proportionally-spaced text by the Sinclair Spectrum, and there is no reason why the same approach cannot be taken for other machines which allow pixel-by-pixel plotting to screen.

Foreign character sets

For many languages the standard English character set will not be sufficient. Some machines (notably the Newbrain, among cheaper microcomputers) offer alternative character sets containing standard accents and other diacritics for European languages, plus Greek or Russian alphabets, while computers manufactured in Japan often allow the user to switch between an English and a Katakana character set.

Another approach is to allow the user to define his or her own character set. The Sinclair Spectrum, for example, allows twenty-one user-defined graphics in addition to those provided as standard, while, with a little more programming expertise, the full standard alphanumeric set of ninety-six characters may also be redefined, giving a total of 117. There are some languages, such as Chinese, which offer a more serious challenge to the microcomputer in the presentation of text on screen. To show a Chinese character with anything approaching adequate resolution a 16×16 grid is necessary, and the information needed to plot 10,000 characters on such a matrix would take up 300 kilobytes of memory. Until recently, the standard random-access memory supplied with microcomputers was sixteen kilobytes and the limit on expansion sixty-four kilobytes, which would seem to put the teaching of Chinese out of reach of the microcomputer except with a severely restricted set of characters or only using the standard pinyin transliteration. The fall in the cost of memory, and the development of computers with far more than 64K of memory, has, however, broken through this barrier: the Newbrain, for example, which uses the standard 8-bit Z80 processor, can be expanded to over 2000 kilobytes of memory. That such an apparently modest computer could, if required, tackle written Chinese demonstrates the enormous computing power available to language learners and teachers if they care to learn to use it.

2.2 The keyboard

With very few exceptions, computer keyboards use the standard typewriter layout, known as the QWERTY keyboard after the six letters at the beginning of the top row. Ironically this layout was designed to slow the typist down and minimise key clashes in the days of early mechanical typewriters. There has been such a great investment in training in the use of this layout that hardly any manufacturers now dare offer a more efficient keyboard. The novice will have to scan virtually the whole keyboard every time a letter is to be entered, and entering long words or sentences can be a very laborious process, aptly described as 'hunt and peck'. In fact this stage does not last very long, and regular users quickly become quite rapid two-finger typists, even without specific training. It is worth bearing in mind, however, that when a computer is being used for the first time or only very occasionally, programs should be chosen in which the user's input is as short and simple as possible.

Keyboard mechanisms are either pressure pads (known as 'touch-sensitive keyboards') on very cheap machines; raised rubber pads similar to those found on calculators; or moving keys like those of an electric typewriter. Proper moving keys provide the best feedback to the fingers, and are worth having if one can afford them. Many machines have an auto-repeat feature on some or all keys, which means that holding down the key for longer than half a second or so makes it repeat its action rapidly. This, again, may give the inexperienced user problems, but is soon mastered. What new users will need, however, is to be told how to amend faulty input, since this is not always clear.

Cursor control

While one is working at a keyboard, there is usually a flashing symbol on the screen, the **cursor**, which shows where the next character to be typed will appear. A computer keyboard needs several extra keys to control the cursor, which usually makes it more complex than a typewriter keyboard, incorporating at least some of the following keys:

CARRIAGE RETURN (sometimes labelled RETURN or CR or ENTER or NEWLINE) which is used to shift the cursor to the beginning of the next line or to mark the end of a piece of data entry.

HOME, which returns the cursor to the top left-hand corner of the screen.

CLEAR, which blanks out the screen and returns the cursor to the top left.

Arrow keys, which move the cursor one position in the direction of the arrow.

DELETE (or DEL or RUBOUT) which erases the last character typed and moves the cursor back to that position.

In addition to these there are several other keys with special functions:

BREAK, which will interrupt a program.

GRAPHICS (or GR) which calls up one of the pre-formed character graphics in place of the letter which has been typed.

REVERSE (or RVS or INVERSE or INV) which makes the character print black on white if the rest of the screen is white on black, or vice versa.

Having so many keys may seem to complicate training the user to handle the keyboard, but it remarkable how quickly people seem to acquire confidence with regular use and minimal training. However, if there is some way of making a program 'crash' by pressing the wrong key, in particular the BREAK key, then it is almost inevitable that a novice, or a mixed group containing novices, will find it. If the user is prompted to type in a number, you can be certain that a novice will enter capital letter 'O' in place of figure zero, which the computer regards as quite distinct.

The responsibility for making programs 'crash-proof' and 'user-friendly' is the programmer's, but he or she may not always have carried it out properly. Perhaps the commonest hiccup is the program which asks for input and assumes that the user will know when to mark the end of the entry with CARRIAGE RETURN. The beginner never does. Sometimes the program should provide all the necessary prompts and help, and sometimes it is necessary to assume the presence of a human supervisor, who may be a teacher or a more experienced fellow student. The programmer should always know which it is to be, and provide accordingly.

2.3 Peripherals

In addition to screen and keyboard there are numerous other devices which can be used for man/machine communication. In this section we describe some of the ones which are most likely to be relevant to teaching applications, although in many cases they will be ruled out on grounds of expense or incompatibility with the available computer.

Input devices

1 **The concept keyboard** or **bit pad** usually takes the form of a flat pad, at least twelve inches square, which is pressure-sensitive, and an overlay showing what the effect will be of touching any segment. Either the whole area or part of it can be turned into a conventional keyboard by making particular squares correspond to letters and numbers, but a commoner use of the device is to make areas correspond to movement commands, *Left*, *Right*, *Forward*, etc. Something similar, but with large orange buttons on a wooden surface, has been used for programming in the LOGO language with primary school children. The control panel of the BIGTRACK toy is a form of concept keyboard. One sees something similar in the cash tills used by certain fastfood restaurants, where the buttons on the till do not carry numbers but little pictures of the food item, say chips, hamburger, hot dog or cup of coffee. Pressing the button will cause the current price of the item to be rung up automatically, thus eliminating some keying-in errors. The true concept keyboard, however, is programmable, so that it can be used in different ways to suit each program. It has obvious value when used with young children or with the visually handicapped since, when there are only a few possible inputs, each one can have a large area of the keyboard.

25

2   The touch screen is particularly associated with PLATO, a large scale computer assisted instruction network, developed in the United States. This is a form of concept keyboard which uses the screen itself as the keyboard. A flexible, transparent, plastic screen with a grid of gold filament on its inner surface is superimposed on the normal screen, standing just clear of it. When it is pressed, it picks up the static discharge from the TV screen and registers the co-ordinates of the point touched. The great advantage of this is that the screen itself can display the meanings which will be assigned to whatever part one touches, and can change them from frame to frame. One can use drawings or diagrams rather than words, and can make some approximation to continuous movement.

3   Joysticks and **Paddles** are familiar in the context of TV games, and are the simplest form of what are known as **analogue to digital (A to D) converters**. Computers can only use digital input: whole numbers within the range that they can handle. In the real world, however, many values are infinitely variable, such as pressure, direction, speed or temperature. A to D converters take changing values provided by the pressure of a finger, say, and convert them to numbers which are passed to the computer. This is so rapid that, given fine resolution on the screen, the illusion of smooth continuous movement is preserved.

4   Graphics tablets and **Digitisers** are a more elaborate form of A to D converters which make use of a trailing arm in order to register position on a surface. Thus one can draw or trace an outline with a stylus and have the drawing displayed instantaneously on the screen. In place of the stylus one can use a light-reading cell which can scan a black-and-white picture and reproduce it in digital form as a dot pattern on the screen.

5   The light pen uses a light-reading cell to either read or change what is on the TV screen. One can use it as a pointer, in the same way as one uses the touch screen. It has the advantage over the touch screen that it is very much cheaper. Alternatively one can use it instead of a graphics tablet for direct drawing onto the screen. The Open University has experimented with a system they call CYCLOPS, in which a network of people linked by telephone can communicate drawings and diagrams to each other instantly by using a light pen.

Output devices

6   Printers are now rather rarer than VDUs, and some users will dispense with them on grounds of cost. However, any serious programmer will require a printer for development work, and a printer can be used very effectively in conjunction with a VDU to do the following jobs:

a) to print out briefing sheets which particular students will want to consult during the run of a program without showing them to other members of the group, for example in role play activities.

b) to print out 'panels' of information needed during the program, for example the rules of a game, which are too big to be displayed conveniently on one screen.

c) to record what is on the screen at any one time, which could be drawings or text, and could be the starting point for classwork or a composition exercise.

d) to print out individualised records at the end of a session with the computer. This can take the form of a summary of what has happened (as, for example, with a computer simulation), or of points learned and/or of mistakes to avoid at the end of a training session, or simply a nicely printed 'certificate of achievement'. For children the motivational effect of computer-produced certificates is known to be high.

The printer is, of course, indispensable in any administrative application, and would certainly be required if the computer was being used for storage and updating of teaching materials, for instance.

7   Plotters are specialised printers which use actual pens, often with a choice of colour, in order to produce drawings or diagrams from digitally stored data.

8   The turtle is a small mobile robot which moves in response to program commands, and will mark its trail with a pen if instructed to. It has been extensively used in primary schools in order to introduce children to spatial concepts and elementary geometry, and is the subject of Seymour Papert's influential book '*Mindstorms*' (see notes to Chapter 1). It does not, of course, 'teach' any language, but, like many other devices, it is a potential stimulator of language in a group.

9   Sound generators exist on many cheap microcomputers nowadays, producing either a single tone which can be modulated for pitch and duration, or, on some machines, up to three tones which can also be modulated for volume. They will play tunes or produce convincing imitations of familiar sounds such as telephone bells or ambulance sirens, beside generating the sound effects familiar in arcade-type games.

Networking

A typical microcomputer is a free-standing unit which is self-contained, in contrast to a mainframe where each user works from a terminal, linked by cable or telephone line to the computer itself and shares it with dozens or hundreds of other users. The advantage of sharing is the ability to call on vast amounts of data stored centrally. The disadvantage is the loss of control over one's own screen. Most mainframe terminals have far less graphics capacity than most micros. One can enjoy the best of both worlds with some form of networking, in which a number of micros can be connected in such a way as to share the use of expensive peripherals, in particular disc-drives for mass storage of information and programs. It is also possible, for example through Micronet 800, a division of British Telecom's Prestel service, to join a large network which provides access to banks of materials and texts. There is, of course, no guarantee that everything made available through the network will be of value to the user, but some access to a network is indispensable for the applications we consider in Chapters 4.1 and 4.2. The danger would come if networking was used to impose central control in an autocratic fashion, with the teacher or one machine taking up a central monitoring role, like that adopted by the teacher at a language laboratory console. The small, cheap microcomputer has done a great deal to remove the 'big brother' associations of the mainframe, and it would be a pity to sacrifice this.

Linking

Computers can control other machines. A form of computer, with a permanently 'burned in' program, is nowadays used in nearly all automatic washing machines, central heating systems and burglar alarms. Making a computer stop and start a tape-recorder is quite easy, and the facility is already provided on some machines for use with those cassette recorders which have REMOTE sockets. This has obvious relevance to language teaching. Work which combined voice prompts on tape with keyboard inputs and screen checking of the answers was being done in America in the mid sixties. The Atari Conversational French, German, Spanish and Italian courses use the same technique in their home-study approach, using a recorder which can read pulses recorded on a parallel track in order to know when to stop or start. Leicester Polytechnic and the Tandberg Corporation have developed an installation which they call AECAL (Audio-Enhanced Computer-Assisted Learning) making use of a specially designed recorder which divides the tape into several hundred sectors and accurately and rapidly finds a particular sector. This allows the program to branch to a particular part of the tape, according to the student's response.

Video

What can be done for audiotape can be and has been done for videotape. Obviously moving pictures in colour and with sound can enhance certain types of language work immensely. One reservation about audiotape applies also to videotape: it is a 'serial medium'. In other words, you have to move a lot of it past the playback head in order to reach a different sector, and this takes time. The newer technology of laser-read discs, both for sound and for video, will be far easier to use, since the disc is a 'random-access medium' providing near-instantaneous access to a chosen sector.

A further advantage of these audio and videodiscs are that they are digitally coded and are therefore ideally suited to mass storage of data. A videodisc can hold text, still pictures, moving pictures and sound, and also the computer programs that will manage the integration and presentation of the other components into a total programme. One microcomputer designed to link to videodisc is already in production, and videodisc interfaces for other microcomputers can be expected. The technology is exciting and clearly has tremendous potential.

A problem may be that software that exploits its potential to the full will be difficult to develop. One advantage of CAL using stand-alone computers is that the development of software can go forward on the basis of collaboration between teacher and learner, with programs constantly being changed and modified. This process is far more difficult with videodisc. Once the materials have been assembled and the disc pressed, no further change to them can be made. There is, moreover, the considerable expense and technological difficulty of preparing the material in the first place. The danger is that videodisc materials will tend to be prepared by 'experts' and imposed from above, rather than arising from the day-to-day experience of teachers and students in the classroom. It follows that, paradoxically, videodisc CAL may be more effective if it fails to exploit the full potential of the medium, with the attention being concentrated in the first place on providing 'banks' of different types of thematically-linked source materials which teachers can exploit in their own way and for their own purposes, through their own computer programs which are external to the disc.

2.4 Speech synthesis

It is natural that language teachers should be particularly interested in the possibility of the automatic synthesis of speech by computers. Many feel it is best to wait until computers have adequate facilities for synthesis before seriously considering using them in language teaching. However, if we examine the capacities of the speech synthesisers at present available for smaller microcomputers, we find that they are not yet adequate for any serious application in language teaching.

Digitised vocabulary

Two approaches can be taken to the production of speech by a computer. The first, digitised vocabulary, represented by the Digitalker chip, involves the storage of the sounds of a limited number of whole words – typically the names of letters, numbers, *on*, *off*, *danger* and so on. This is a special case of the general technique of recording stretches of speech in digitised form, familiar in such well-publicised facilities as the talking car computer and aids for the blind at bus stops. When vocabulary is digitised, any word can be called up by its number in the list. The speech is reasonably clear but obviously machine-produced.

The main use of the Digitalker is in control applications where the user needs to obtain stereotyped information from the computer, and where it may be difficult to obtain that information visually. Recently, for example, the Digitalker was incorporated into a British space satellite to relay information from the monitoring equipment. Apart from the poor quality of the speech, the main problem with the Digitalker approach is its inflexibility. The attempt to store anything like an adequate vocabulary for language teaching would be prohibitively heavy on memory; and, while it is perfectly possible to string a series of words together to form a longer utterance, that serves only to emphasise the machine-like nature of the speech.

Phoneme synthesis

The second current approach to speech synthesis on microcomputers is phoneme synthesis, the Votrax chip being the most readily available example. This stores not words but individual sounds. To synthesis the word *dog* we send the numbers corresponding to /d/, /o/, and /g/ in sequence to the chip, while to synthesise *computer* we would send /k/, /m/, /p/, /j/, /u:/, /t/ and /ə/. The chip provides a fascinating test-bed for simple phonetic experiments, for example, the effect on intelligibility of inserting a /ə/ between the /k/ and the /m/ in *computer*, or the effect of doubling the /m/. While it has greater flexibility than the Digitalker in that any word can be built from its constituent phonemes, the quality of the speech produced is even poorer and more Dalek-like. Even after a good deal of experimentation, Votrax-produced words are often barely comprehensible, even to a native speaker. The reason is that phonemes are, strictly speaking, abstract entities. The actual sounds we utter are closely conditioned by their context, so that the /k/ of *keep*, *cat*, *cool* and *look* are all different. The Votrax chip provides a certain number of these allophonic variants, but not nearly enough to begin to approach the reality of spoken English.

The 'ideal synthesiser'

The inadequacies of the Digitalker and the Votrax chip can lead us to consider what we might expect of an ideal system of speech synthesis for language learning. This would accept as input normal written text, and would use inbuilt programs incorporating the sound/spelling rules of English to convert it to phonetic form. Among the components of those programs would be a list of the thousands of words which are exceptions to those rules. They would have to include a component which would place stress correctly on the basis of the written form (for example pho*tograph, pho*tog*rapher, photo*graph*ic*) and carry out vowel reduction in accordance with stress (compare the pronunciation of the *o* in *photograph* and *photographer*). It would also have to carry out an analysis of the whole text in terms of its division into intonation units, the placing of nuclear stress, pitch level and pitch movement.

The magnitude of this task can be assessed by considering the variations possible on a simple utterance such as *Why did he do it?* in which the stress might fall on any of the first four words, and the pitch movement could be a high fall, a low fall, a rise, or a fall-rise. The problem for a speech synthesis program is not the number of variations but the way in which each variation is conditioned by the context in which it appears and by the intention of the speaker. From this it follows that our ideal speech synthesiser is not a practical proposition – or not until that hypothetical day when a machine can be taught to act, think and feel like a human.

Using available systems

That is not the end of the story, however. Recently at least one system of speech synthesis has appeared which, while not meeting all the requirements of the ideal system, represents a considerable advance on what has been available hitherto, and which is able, using written text as input, to speak single words and short utterances on a neutral intonation curve with a considerable degree of verisimilitude and accuracy. Further systems on these lines will probably appear, and the cost in time will fall to what is affordable in an educational context. We can at present only speculate how such a less-than-perfect but still usable facility could best be used in language learning. Three possibilities come to mind:

1 They might be used as a sort of 'talking dictionary' or 'talking phrasebook' as a model for the student. This use would be limited since, for the reasons already indicated, interactive features of intonation could not readily be supplied from within the program along with the written text.

2 In Chapter 3, we show programs which synthesise language for a highly restricted field of knowledge. Given such a restriction, it would

be possible to program a speech synthesiser to demonstrate how the language would be spoken with appropriate intonation.

3 They could form the basis of a tool to be used by the learner in experimenting with how the language can be spoken. The learner would, for example, be given the chance to observe the effects of speeding up speech or slowing it down, or of shifting the placement of nuclear stress.

While these possibilities for speech synthesis in the teaching of English must, for the time being, be matters of speculation, it is even more a matter of speculation whether speech synthesis of the sophistication necessary for use in language teaching will become available for languages other than English.

Speech decoding

Most of what has been said here about speech synthesis applies in even stronger measure to speech decoding (machine comprehension of spoken language). Speech decoders of a sort already exist. They are mainly used for record-keeping functions, where people have to enter information about quantities and locations, but cannot use their hands, perhaps because they are standing half way up a ladder inspecting a shelf. Experimental work has been done with decoding a stream of speech rather than isolated words, in an attempt to create an 'automatic typewriter' which will transcribe speech directly. The accuracy achieved, even with very slow and carefully enunciated speech, is low, and we are a long way from a machine which can be trusted to correct every feature of a student's pronunciation of idiomatic language. However, there are ways in which the analysis of the speech signal can provide a tool for the student to improve his or her own pronunciation, and in Chapter 3.3 we describe a way in which this can already be done with intonation.

2.5 Administrative problems

'Where shall we put the thing?' is usually the first question that a Director of Studies asks on hearing that a new piece of equipment is to be provided. Over the years computers have become astonishingly smaller, cheaper and more reliable. Even so, they are at the moment bulkier, more complex and more fragile than, say, a cassette recorder. Though cheap, they are expensive enough to be attractive to a thief, so cannot be left around with no supervision. Who is to take responsibility? The cheapest ones tend to come as separate components. The components, namely the screen, the computer itself and the disc drives or recorder, can be assembled on a trolley, but trolleys are awkward to get up and down stairs. Who is going to move it? They need to be plugged in to the mains electricity, and the mains socket may not be conveniently located, or there may not be enough adaptors. Every time the equipment is moved there is a risk that it will be dropped or plugged in to the wrong voltage or stolen, so should it be kept in one place?

Place

These are the questions which tend to loom very large at the beginning, and there are no obvious answers. The place of use is going to depend on many factors: the teaching approach and the type of software, the size of classes, the availability of a library or study area. In practice, two solutions are frequently adopted in British schools. One is to have a 'computer corner' with one or two machines in an open-plan classroom, with students able to use them either on their own initiative or under the control of a teacher. This has the advantage that it makes it easier to integrate work with the computer with other activities. The other is that the school's computers come under the control of the department of computing studies with other departments having access to the machines at certain times. This implies a pattern in which the 'computer hour' is scheduled on the timetable, which is suitable for certain modes of computer-assisted learning but not, we would suggest, for all. In many cases one can assume that some teachers will want to have the machine in their classrooms for some of the time, so, unless the institution is rich enough to afford to equip every room, there is a need for mobility. Teachers who are going to use the machine, perhaps to create material and certainly to assess it, will want easy access to it in their free periods. What we suggest is that an institution should start with the smallest, cheapest and lightest equipment that is usable for their purposes, and should use their experience with that to decide what other machines to buy and where and how to use them.

Screens

What we have said about the computer itself applies also to the ancillary equipment, namely the screen and cassette recorder. There are a few 'one-box' machines in which all these components are built in, but it is more likely that a school will start with a cheap micro which plays through a TV set and can be connected to a portable cassette recorder to load or 'save' programs. The advantage is that the school may already own one or more television sets and so can avoid this expense. But there may be a danger. A school's existing television sets were probably bought in order to show broadcast programmes or play back video recordings to a whole class. It will have a large screen, and may be mounted on a high trolley. When used with a computer to show text, it may be a bit oppressive for a small group, and the keyboard operator may have to crane upwards at an awkward angle if the set is mounted on something high. In the long run it may be necessary to buy some smaller screens which can be used on low tables by two to four students working in a group.

Maintenance

When one spends thousands of pounds on a computer, it is customary to buy a maintenance contract which, usually for 15 per cent of the equipment cost, buys one year of free service. There is no equivalent deal available in most cases for a cheap microcomputer. If it breaks down within the guarantee period, you can send it back for a free repair. Beyond that limit, there is probably nothing to be done but throw it away.

To balance this depressing message, it has to be said that micros which survive the first few weeks of use have tended to be very reliable and durable. They contain no moving parts other than the keyboard, and one is far more likely to encounter problems with the cassette player or disc drive than with the computer itself. Of course they are likely to be damaged if dropped on the floor or if cups of coffee are spilt over them. It makes sense to have a 'no eating or drinking' rule in the immediate vicinity of the computer.

3 The computer in the classroom

3.1 Using the computer

There are three obvious ways in which a computer can be exploited: whole class activity ('the electronic blackboard'), group activity, or individual resource. No special teaching approach is implied with any of them, although some types of material will lend themselves to one form of exploitation rather than another.

Electronic blackboard

This use of a computer is the one which is most severely constrained by physical factors: the number of students, the shape of the room, and the size of the screen. The more unfavourable these factors are, the shorter must be the periods that students are asked to concentrate on what is on the screen.

The machine serves as a teacher's aid, and will mainly be operated by the teacher, although students can be called up to operate the keyboard, just as they can be called up to write or draw on the blackboard. The main value of the computer in this mode is its immediacy of response, the speed with which it can change a display or report the consequences of a decision. This can create a sense of excitement and participation in a class, particularly when the computer sets a task or plays a game. One primary teacher reported at a recent conference how this had affected her pupils attitude to her. 'What can we do to beat it today, Miss?' She had become an ally rather than an authority figure.

Group focus

Computers can be used for group work, either with or without immediate teacher supervision. The group will probably have a leader, possibly appointed by the teacher but more usually emerging in the natural give-and-take of group work. There will also be a keyboard operator, and this role should be switched around fairly frequently since it is the most active. There is no absolute upper limit on the size of a group, but common sense suggests no more than five. There is no need for all groups in a class to have access to a computer simultaneously. If there is only one machine, the computer assignment can rotate while other groups carry out different activities. One advantage that the computer has is that it is (or can be) silent. A computer, even if there is a conversational buzz round it, is far less distracting to other groups in the same room than a tape-recorder or video playback would be.

Individual resource

This mode of use conjures up visions of a computer lab with rows of machines in simultaneous use. In practice this is rather rare outside universities. Far commoner nowadays is the inclusion of one or two computer work-stations in a school library or resource room, to which students can go in their free periods. A supervisor or librarian will give initial training in how to operate the machine, but students are otherwise on their own. What is also becoming common is for students to have their own home computers and be keen to borrow or adapt software, but it will be some time yet before teachers can assume that the majority of their students will have their own machines and be willing to do computer homework.

Activity types

Some of the activities described in this book, programmed learning for example, are specifically designed for use by a single student. Some are for students working in pairs, i.e. competitive games displaying two scores. Some, such as the exploratory programs and some of the BOOH programs, are intended for group use, often with the presence of a teacher assumed. The vast majority are capable of being used in any of these modes. Quizzes, simulations and text reconstruction programs can all hold the attention of a learner on his own, and can be used in the library or at home. They tend to be even more effective when tackled by a group or even by a small class.

The mode of use will be affected to some extent by the students' previous learning experiences and expectations. To work well with a piece of programmed learning, one has to have acquired a habit of private study. Group work around a computer may not succeed if the class has no other experience of working in groups or pairs. However, experience suggests that if twenty students are sent into a room containing twenty machines, they will not by choice go one to a machine, but will tend to cluster into pairs or groups. The computer seems to bring out a latent gregariousness, part of which may be due to the need to co-operate with others in overcoming nervousness in using the machine.

Spoken language

In the group the machine becomes something to talk about as well as to 'talk' to. The instinct to form groups is a one that the language teacher can be glad of, since it provides contexts for spoken language. It will be a long time before speech decoders and synthesisers become commonplace in classrooms, and an even longer time before they can cope with the kind of divergent discourse that humans use. Meanwhile there is no need to worry that using computers will impoverish the learning of spoken language. Though most computers do not talk and listen, they are very good at stimulating people to talk and listen. When screen instructions are displayed, somebody in the group often reads them aloud quite unprompted and the reading usually sounds a good deal more animated than 'reading round the class'. As the group discuss their moves, they tend to introduce more and more of the language which has been used in the program. One notices this particularly when a monolingual group carries out an exercise, a simulation for instance, several times. On the first run much of the conversation will be in the students' native language, with just the odd word of the target language. On each subsequent run the students tend to use longer and longer segments of the target language as they become more confident of what to say. A lot of the language arises out of practical necessity, since only one member of the group can comfortably operate the keyboard. The others will want to play their part in the task, but can only do it by ordering, suggesting, reminding or persuading, all language functions for which natural contexts may be awkward to create in the classroom. They are learning to use language to 'operate' the operator.

3.2 Drills

This section and the next look at two aspects of 'training' in language learning, and the use of the computer as a trainer.

Training is the development of skills which must become habitual and automatic, such as the skills of controlling a car, serving a tennis ball or operating a keyboard. The objective of training is to reach a certain standard, and the measurement of training is usually carried out with performance tests which are criterion-referenced, measured against an absolute standard, rather than the norm-referenced tests used for many educational applications in which the learner is measured against other learners. Training is necessarily repetitive, but it also needs careful monitoring and feedback. Since the aim is to develop habits, it is vital that only the right habits should be developed. The requirement for patient and accurate monitoring makes the computer, and its big brother, the simulator, excellent means of training. The software catalogue for any popular computer is likely to include a typing trainer, a morse-code trainer and a sight-reading trainer for music, among other things.

Drill-and-practice

The usual application of a training approach in language learning involves drill-and-practice, where the assumption is that repetition and near-repetition is needed to 'internalise' a piece of behaviour and add it to the stock of language behaviours that can be used spontaneously. The strength of the learning is related to the number of repetitions.

Most teachers accept this assumption at the level of the motor-perceptual skills; recognising and making sounds and stress patterns, recognising letter and word shapes, forming letters and, nowadays, using a keyboard. Only a convinced behaviourist or structuralist teacher would carry the assumption further and try to teach the whole of language by 'training', hoping to provide the student with a large enough repertory of behaviours to cover all the situations in which the target language is used. However, an approach which uses a good deal of training has the merit of being reassuring for students, who know exactly what is expected of them and do not feel threatened, as they may be by a more open-ended task.

A computer 'drill-and-practice' program takes over the human trainer's role, and can provide the kind of endlessly patient and flexible supervision which the class teacher often cannot spare the time for. Certain grammatical and lexical skills lend themselves to a training approach, in particular those which operate on closed systems in a predictable way, where the application of a rule is automatic and bears little relation to choices dictated by meaning. These include regular morphological change, such as spelling rules for regular plurals, or syntactic features like word order and *do*-insertion in questions. In the area of lexis there are certain closed sets which present little conceptual difficulty to a foreign learner but which need to be memorised, such as the number system or the names of the months. A training approach can be appropriate for them.

Meaningful drills

Any grammatical pattern can be drilled by some variant of the substitution process, by replacing elements in a fixed or syntactically conditioned frame, for example:

tea	Is there any tea?
matches	Are there any matches?
money	Is there any money?
apples	Are there any apples? etc.

It is debatable whether training methods like these should be applied to features of language, such as tense selection or article usage, which are highly conditioned by meaning or appropriacy. At the beginning of the seventies the late Julian Dakin put forward the notion of the 'meaningful drill', a drill which could not be carried out successfully on a purely mechanical basis. Students would have to pay attention to the meaning of what they were saying. The example just given, for instance, could be made 'meaningful' by asking the learner to add an appropriate prepositional phrase:

tea	Is there any tea in the pot?
matches	Are there any matches in the box?

money	Is there any money in the bank?
apples	Are there any apples on the tree?

As soon as you make a drill 'meaningful' in this way, however, you remove one of the characteristics of the conventional laboratory drill, namely the unique right answer which is used to provide feedback. Students using this drill would have to be alert to the fact that, if they have answered 'Is there any tea in the cup?', they are not wrong, and this would require sensitive preparation. In the ten years since the publication of Dakin's *'The Language Laboratory and Language Learning'* such drills have been widely used in general purpose and specialist courses in English as a foreign language. Despite the influence of Dakin's work, some language teachers have remained uneasy about the concept because the association of language with meaning may be cramped by the format of the drill. We show in later sections that, when the computer itself generates the practice material, the resulting exercise may be in essence a meaningful drill, but one which is not confined by the rigid Cue-Response-Correction format of the typical language laboratory exercise.

Drill structure

The most commonly used structure for a training or 'drill-and-practice' program is that of a quiz, and can be described as follows:
1. Select task or question
2. Display question
3. Accept student's answer
4. Match answer against acceptable answer(s)
5. Report success or failure
6. Adjust student's running score
7. Return to (1)

To use this as the specification for a computer program, we would need to specify how many times the procedure was to be executed, since a computer, unlike a human teacher, is incapable of taking spur-of-the-moment or 'common sense' decisions. (Faced with the instructions on a shampoo bottle, 'Wet hair, apply shampoo, rinse, repeat', a computer would go on washing its hair until the bottle was empty.) We would need to specify a target score, for instance, and the appropriate action to cover the case of the student who never reaches the target standard or the one who interrupts the session. Each of the components of the quiz procedure itself can be elaborated as the following notes show.

1   Select task or question

The order in which one presents the questions may be fixed, possibly graded from easy to difficult, or questions may be selected at random, so that students get no clues from the ordering when they repeat a quiz. The selection may be made sensitive to the student's score, so that after, say, three consecutive right answers, subsequent questions are drawn from a more difficult block. Some of these decisions can be offered to the students themselves. They can be asked if they want the exercise to be easy or difficult, revision or new material, long or short.

2 Display question

It is possible to take advantage of the screen's versatility by blending text, graphics and simple animation. One can highlight parts of the text by using inverse video or, on some machines only, variable brightness and colour. One can use a split screen, with part of the screen scrolling and another part, containing reference information, static. A concept used in Programmed Learning is that of the 'panel', a sheet of information to which the student can refer at any time. A panel can be called up whenever the student types HELP, or the student can use a book or paper handout. One might also use a combination of screen with voice input from recorded tape. Some computers can govern the Start/Stop controls of a cassette recorder. Even without this facility, one can display the message 'Press Play and listen to Question One', and then have the recording terminate with the spoken message 'Stop the tape'.

3 Accept student's answer

The response the student makes can take the form of touching an indicated key, a letter or a number key in the case of a multiple-choice format or the Y or N keys for Yes/No answers. It can also consist of moving the cursor to the correct part of the screen by using the arrow keys or a joystick control, or of touching a key at a particular time to correspond to a state of the display. When the response consists of a word or sentence, it has to be typed in and usually needs to be terminated by a CARRIAGE RETURN. If so, it may be necessary to remind students when they have to press CARRIAGE RETURN, especially if there are mixed forms of response within one quiz.

Whatever the form of input, it is important that the program should be 'user-friendly'. One element that will make a program friendly is that whatever the student is asked to do should be as simple and natural as possible. For instance, where a blank has to be filled in a sentence, the missing word should be typed in to fill the blank rather than appearing in another part of the screen. Where the student has to press one key to identify a statement as 'True' and another to identify it as 'False', the two keys should be as widely separated as possible. Most people seem to find it more natural to use a right-hand key for 'True' and a left-hand key for 'False', but this is not universal, and it may be desirable to offer a choice. A further element in 'user-friendliness' is that the program should, other things being equal, allow students to change their minds and/or correct slips of the finger in typing.

4 Match answer against acceptable answers

With Yes/No and multiple choice quizzes there is usually little doubt about the rightness of an answer, which is one reason for their popularity. (Not, of course, that question-setters need to limit themselves to one right answer. There is no reason why a multiple choice task should not consist of eliminating the wrong cuckoo from the nest of acceptable alternatives.) It is also very easy to incorporate a timing element and measure speed of response. With word or sentence answers the program can look for an exact match and judge all other answers wrong. If so, it will be inferior to a human assessor who will usually distinguish serious errors from trivial ones. Suppose, for example, that the correct answer to a question is *Tuesday*. The student might embed this in a sentence frame:

> It is Tuesday.
> It's Tuesday.
> Tuesday I think.
> Is it Tuesday?
> Not Tuesday.

It is easy enough to write a program which will detect the expected answer within the student's response, thus dealing with the first two, but much harder to respond appropriately to the other three. Unless one is ready to use some form of parsing of the input, it is wiser to constrain the answer, for example in this case by asking for a single word.

Alternatively the student may give any of the following versions:

> tuesday
> Teusday
> Tuesdy
> Tursday

A human teacher will know exactly what to do about each of these. It is possible to program the machine to handle all these errors, but one must be careful about the procedure. If the machine makes a simple letter by letter comparison, it will judge 'Tursday' (one letter wrong) as more nearly correct than 'Teusday' (two letters wrong), although a human, alert to the possible confusion with Thursday, is likely to reverse this judgement. We shall see in Chapter 5.2 that it is possible to write programs in such a way that they check for the commoner kinds of typing and spelling mistakes, such as metathesis (the reversal of letters in 'Teusday'), doubling of letters (for example 'Tuessday') or omission of a letter (for example 'Tusday').

One of the most common problems is that the machine is

expecting lower case and the student types in upper case, or vice versa. This can be circumvented by setting the machine so that all input is automatically made in upper case, or – where the distinction between upper and lower case is linguistically signific- ant (for example with German nouns) – writing the program to check input for upper versus lower case mistakes. In addition, the program may check for feasible alternative answers and for wrong answers based on common learner errors, and again respond appropriately. Experienced teachers will usually have a good idea of their students' recurrent errors and know which are worth paying attention to.

Despite all such precautions, however, there will inevitably be occasions when a student comes up with an alternative answer, or makes a significant mistake, which the programmer has not anticipated. In both cases all the computer can do is label the answer as wrong. One strategy which has been adopted to overcome this problem – for example in Farrington's English/ French translation programs – is to have the computer store all unanticipated answers. The programmer can then inspect them at regular intervals and decide which ones need to be taken into consideration in updating the program.

5 Report success or failure

In the case of success one can give overt feedback – 'Right', or covert feedback – no message but continue to next question. It is as well to avoid effusive congratulations, 'Well done Fred!', 'You're a genius!', etc. which may quickly become condescending and tedious. One can also give purely visual rewards, such as a large tick or a smiling face or a screen firework display. Again there is a danger in over-elaboration. What gives pleasure on first viewing may become irritating after a few repetitions, and displays which take up time quickly become resented.

The case of failure is more complex. In Chapter 3.5 we discuss remedial instruction introduced after a mistake. However, assum- ing that a quiz does not incorporate remedial teaching, one still has several possible ways of continuing after a wrong answer. One can simply indicate that the answer was wrong and move on. One can show the correct answer and move on. One can give the student the option of repeating the question, 'No. Would you like to try again?', or one can repeat the question as a matter of course, subject to the condition that, after a certain number of attempts, the student will be helped out of his or her misery. When a question is repeated it may be desirable to give some indication of why the first answer was wrong, for example by highlighting parts of the answer. Otherwise there is a danger that the student, having had a near miss (perhaps a trivial spelling mistake) with the first attempt, will make wilder and wilder guesses at each repeat. One can report that the answer was wrong and return the question to stock so that it will turn up again during the session, or one can pass on to new material.

It is impossible to lay down rules as to which strategy is most appropriate. In the classroom a teacher may have a style which favours one of these strategies over the others, but will usually vary the response to error according to the nature and purpose of the activity and the expectations (both culturally determined and individual) of the students. It is to be expected that computer programs will exhibit as much variation as that shown by human teachers. There is one potential advantage that a computer has over a class teacher, however, in that it can offer the individual student a choice over which strategy will be adopted on a particular occasion. In this respect, as in many others, it may be that the crucial advantage of the computer as a medium for training is the opportunity to involve the trainee in the important decisions as to how the training will be carried out.

6 **Adjust student's running score**
Most scoring systems take advantage of the computer's ability to offer the learner a second chance to answer. A clean first attempt is awarded, say, ten points, with five points for a correct answer at the second attempt and two for a third attempt. There may be an additional score for speed of response, say a potential ten points from which one point is deducted for every two seconds delay. The score may be displayed continuously or only when a batch of items has been finished. As with other features, there is no reason why one should not consult the student about this, and ask whether he or she wants the time element assessed or the score displayed.

3.3 Demonstration

In the last section we were concerned only with the quiz or drill-and-practice aspect of training. The bulk of published CALL materials consists of such activities, and there will no doubt be many more produced. However, it may be that this dominance is obscuring possibilities of using the computer for language teaching in ways which come closer to what is usually thought of as training. To return to the analogy of learning to drive a car or serve a tennis ball, the first step will typically involve the trainer in demonstrating the skill: the learner must first of all grasp what the skill is 'as a whole' – what it involves and how it is put together. The learning may then proceed in one of two ways. The first is the method of gradual approximation. The learner's early clumsy efforts are little by little brought closer to the target behaviour with the aid of visual or tactile feedback. The second is by the gradual withdrawal of support to the point at which the skill can be performed without assistance.

Demonstration mode

In the case of language learning we believe that using the computer to demonstrate how a language operates is one of its most valuable functions, and extends far beyond the training context. A program may include a 'demonstration mode' as one of its options, as with the GRAMMARLAND programs described in Chapter 3.9, or be built entirely around the idea of demonstration, as with TIME (see 3.6).

The computer has a number of advantages as a medium of demonstration. Visual presentation in the form of pictures, graphs or tables can help to make clear the relationship between form and meaning. Simple animations can be used to tell a story or to show grammatical processes, such as *do*-insertion in English negation and question forms, or word order in subordinate clauses in German. Animation can also model specific skills, for example the order and direction of brush strokes in writing Chinese characters.

The computer is able to control the operation of different peripheral devices. Thus, using current technology, it is not difficult to link a computer to a two-track tape-recorder which carries a sound signal on one track and synchronising bleeps on the other, the computer stopping and starting the recorder as the screen display changes. There are many uses of such a facility in demonstration. For example, it would be possible to present the student who needed to develop note-taking skills in a foreign language (or, indeed, in his or her own language) with a 'dynamic' model of good note-taking practice synchronised with a recording of a lecture. The potential of the computer in this area is likely to be extended by technological advances. The possibility of linking the computer to videodisc, for example, will allow the flexible presentation of still and moving pictures, sound and text, under program control, and it is for its ability to show the language in action in a variety of modes that videodisc technology is likely to be of most use to language learners. The most important advantage of all for the computer as demonstrator is that the demonstration, whether simple or complex, can be placed under the control of the student, to be repeated, interrupted, slowed down, or even reversed at will.

Gradual approximation

The possibility of computer-controlled demonstration accompanied by gradual approximation was first shown by the work of Leon and Martin for the teaching of intonation in the 1960s. Intonation represents a particularly thorny problem for language teachers. They are aware of its central importance in communication, yet find it extremely difficult to teach. When given sufficient exposure to a foreign language, some students acquire appropriate intonation. Others notably fail to do so, and whatever the teacher does by way of explanation or drilling seems to have little effect. In terms of the Krashen theory of language learning (see 1.2), the basic patterns of intonation, having been acquired very early in the acquisition of the mother tongue, are too deeply ingrained to be accessible to the action of the monitor, or are perhaps protected by an 'affective filter' which resists tampering with what is felt to be a part of the self.

Leon and Martin employed visual feedback to solve the problem. The computer extracted an accurate trace of the fundamental frequency of an utterance from the total waveform. The trace of the target utterance was shown at the top of the VDU screen and the trace of the student's imitation underneath it. The student could repeat his or her attempt as often as he or she wanted until there was a match between the two traces. Similar work has since been done in the training of the deaf, and it is to be hoped that simple add-ons for fundamental frequency analysis will be developed for the available educational microcomputers, for use with the deaf and with foreign language learners.

A training sequence

The contrast between conventional drill and alternative training methods using gradual withdrawal of assistance may be shown by two different approaches to the teaching of spelling. In many drill-and-practice CAL programs in this area the word is flashed onto the screen or is presented from a tape-recording or (as in the *Speak 'n' Spell* machine marketed by Texas Instruments) in synthetic speech. The student then has to type in the correct spelling. There is no training in this except what comes from repeated attempts at the same task. In WORDSPIN, on the other hand, there is a planned training sequence for each word. The program is a game with three phases. In the first the word appears 'spinning' in an endless loop in the middle of the screen. The player has to recognise the word and 'trap' it by pressing a key. When the word has been trapped, a 'blot' (an inverse question mark) appears and traverses the word from side to side, eventually stopping to conceal one letter. The player then has to 'bomb' the hidden letter into the blot; if he or she chooses the wrong letter, the letter bounces back to the top of the screen. When the first letter has been accepted, the blot enlarges itself to a block of two or three question marks (depending on the length of the word) and, having traversed the word several more times, comes to rest obscuring more of it. The missing letters again have to be bombed into place. Now the process may be repeated with the blot extended to four or five question marks. In the final phases the complete word is obscured and all the letters have to be bombed in. Thus the activity progresses from simple recognition through stages of restoration in which support is withdrawn gradually to zero. The final task is the same as that demanded in the drill and practice form of exercise. (The program listing for WORDSPIN is given in Chapter 5.5).

3.4 Games

The essence of drill-and-practice is controlled repetition with monitoring and feedback. Although it can provide the student with security, it can also be very boring in the long run. Students have their own way of avoiding this boredom, which is to turn the computer drill into a game. The impulse to win, to beat the machine, can be very strong in both children and adults. It is unlikely that a language laboratory drill has ever been used in the same way, since the language laboratory can never provide immediate, objective feedback on success or failure as a computer can with its accompanying scoring on screen. It is natural that computer-assisted learning should attempt to exploit and develop the game element in practice materials: to replace 'You're wrong' with 'I win'.

Scoring

Essentially there are two types of games, the **competitive** which has points scoring and a win or lose outcome, and the **collaborative** in which there is a task to be achieved and in which all participants, including perhaps the computer, work together to achieve it. The second type will be covered in Chapter 3.7 where we discuss simulations; in this section we will look at competition. At its simplest level this means nothing more than adding competitive scoring to a drill-and-practice activity. When two students work on an activity at the same time and compete against each other, the machine can display both of their running scores, possibly using default scoring ('You have three lives left'). With one student it involves displaying the current score and a target score, for example the day's best score. One lesson learned from the arcade-type games is that large numbers motivate more than small ones. When the target score is in the thousands and even a modest performance scores in the hundreds, the effect is less discouraging than a report of 'nine out of twenty'. Timing a response, even if it is not central to the point of the program, has the incidental benefit of introducing non-rounded numbers into the scoring display. Motivation is not increased by scoring in thousands if every score ends in three zeros.

Gambling

A further possibility is to use a gambling format: the student is given a stock of points and has to stake a certain number on the chance of getting the right answer. Odds may be offered based on the computer's estimate of the difficulty of the task. This exploitation of human acquisitiveness can be a powerful incentive, but also has a serious point. Particularly with the more difficult tasks involved in language learning at intermediate and advanced levels, the act of making a wager shifts the attention of the player away from the question 'Is this the right answer?' towards the question 'How sure am I that this is the right answer?' To bet successfully one has to make an objective assessment of the nature of the task set (is it in fact clear-cut or might there be an alternative answer?) and one's linguistic resources for tackling it. A number of the programs we describe in Chapter 3.6 incorporate gambling routines of this kind.

Fruit machine

One can exploit a games-playing motivation directly by using the rules and procedures of an established game, one which the students will probably be familiar with as a recreational activity. To take an obvious example, teachers often use a form of WORD BINGO in the classroom to develop pronunciation and attentive listening. This principle has been used by Chris Jones in his excellent JACKPOT program for the ZX81. The computer functions as a fruit machine, but the contents of each window are phrases or words rather than pictures. One wins when the words on the centre line in the three windows form a set, for example adjective, comparative and superlative, or the root, past tense and past participle of a verb, or three words making up a coherent sentence. Teachers can modify the subject matter to fit in with the syllabus. What makes the game attractive is the way in which it reproduces the features of a 'real-life' fruit machine, with HOLD and NUDGE facilities. These are highly relevant, since the reasons for holding or nudging would be that one has spotted that two of the three windows relate, or that a word on an adjacent line will complete a meaningful sentence.

Quizzes within games

Another approach is to put quiz questions into a familiar game framework, so that a successful answer is needed before the student can make the next move in the game. Chris Harrison has devised two activities of this kind, NOUGHTS AND CROSSES and SNAKES AND LADDERS. To illustrate this, overleaf is the screen layout for Noughts and Crosses.

The first player chooses the number of the kind of question he or she wants to answer. If he or she succeeds, that number is turned into a nought. The second player chooses, and on answering correctly, gets a cross in the relevant square. As the game proceeds, so the choice of question is progressively constrained by the need to prevent

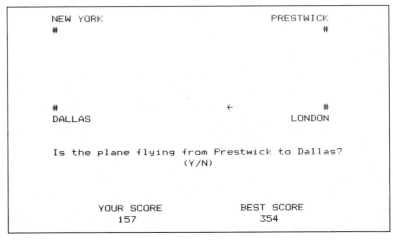

```
        GAME NO. 1
.............................  CHRIS'S TURN
.       .       .       .
.  1    .   4   .   7   . 1.  NAME THE BABY
.       .       .       . 2.  MAKE AN ADJECTIVE
.....................................  3.  UNSCRAMBLE A WORD
.       .       .       . 4.  GIVE THE COMPARATIVE
.  2    .   5   .   8   . 5.  GIVE A PAST TENSE
.       .       .       . 6.  FILL THE SPACE
.............................  7.  WHAT'S THE PLURAL?
.       .       .       . 8.  COMPLETE THE PHRASE
.  3    .   6   .   9   . 9.  REARRANGE THE SENTENCE
.       .       .       .
.............................  WHICH LOCATION, CHRIS
```

one's opponent from getting three in a line. For each kind of question there is a stock of twenty items which is drawn on at random, so that one can play the game several times without too much duplication.

The SNAKES AND LADDERS game works similarly. The board displayed on the screen contains a hundred numbered squares, but the actual snakes and ladders are not shown. Each player enters a move: a number between one and six. If the square the player reaches contains a ladder, he or she must answer a quiz question in order to climb it; if it contains a snake, he or she must answer correctly to avoid sliding down it.

Dynamic games

Yet another approach is to focus the learner's attention on a game-like task, but to introduce repetitive training activity incidentally. One program that does this is a game for language beginners called FLYING, for which the screen layout is as follows:

```
     NEW YORK                    PRESTWICK
     #                                #




     #                     ←          #
     DALLAS                           LONDON


     Is the plane flying from Prestwick to Dallas?
                         (Y/N)



            YOUR SCORE          BEST SCORE
               157                 354
```

The question is displayed and the little animated aeroplane appears and starts its journey. The learner has to press Y or N as quickly as possible, getting between twenty and forty points for a right answer, losing ten for a wrong one and getting nothing if the plane reaches its destination before a key is pressed. The questions are randomly compiled. Ten items constitute one run of the game, and each run will last about two minutes. The game can become addictive! A ten minute spell of play means that one has read and tried to understand fifty questions of the form 'Is the plane flying from X to Y?' or 'Is the plane flying to X from Y?', something one is unlikely to do with a printed book.

In this case the sentence to be read is static and the display is animated. One can achieve something similar with a static display, for example a grid of facts, and a sentence which slowly ribbons past underneath and which has to be check against the facts in the grid. This amounts to a simple True/False quiz, but the timing element makes it into a game. The learner's task is to check for the truth of each item, but there is incidental exposure to a large number of sentences of the same pattern, which may also have some value, particularly since the sentence patterning is not at the forefront of attention.

Strategy games

In all these games the role of the computer is 'game-setter' and the role of the student is 'game-player'. There is, however, a class of strategy games, of which chess is the best known example, in which human and machine compete on equal terms.

When a strategy game involves language, there is a possibility of valuable incidental practice. One of the best of such games is Feldmann and Rugg's JOT which is a simplified form of WORD MASTERMIND. Human and computer choose secret three-letter English words and score each other's guesses on the basis of the number of letters in common between the secret word and the guess. The computer plays a mean and intelligent game: the human has to play with the same rigorous logic as the machine to have any chance of winning.

ZX-HIT is an adaptation of the original game for use in language learning, the main difference being that it allows words with repeated letters (for example 'did'), so expanding the vocabulary to include all three-letter words in English. The vocabulary is graded into three levels, and the machine's logic routines are written in machine code and are very fast.

Arcade games

Many people nowadays equate computer games with the familiar arcade-type games, such as Space Invaders and various forms of 'blob-chasing'. There have been some attempts to harness this approach to language learning. There is a game called WORM for instance, in which an ever lengthening worm has to be manipulated round the screen so that it can gobble up the letters of a word in the right order. In general, arcade-type games have taught us a great deal about motivation, but, being 'real-time' activities, may have less value for the language teacher than move-based strategy games and the closely related activity of simulations. These are dealt with more fully in Chapter 3.7.

3.5 Programmed learning

One model of the teaching process is tutorial dialogue, in which one learner faces one teacher. The lesson consists of exposition, questioning, evaluating the answers, correcting and explaining errors, and answering the learner's questions. One-to-one teaching is far too expensive to implement on a mass scale, and the computer has been seen as a means of providing a cheaper substitute. The search for an automated means of teaching is by no means new, nor is there any need for it to be done by electronic means. The computer is, however, a very convenient way of delivering the teaching system known generally as **Programmed Learning (PL)**, in which the subject is divided into a sequence of small steps and learning proceeds by question-and-answer dialogue.

Divergent language

The drawback to using a basically unintelligent machine for tutorial dialogue (in any subject) is that conversation in natural language is highly divergent. You cannot make a unique prediction about how a dialogue will proceed. If you could, there would be little point in holding the conversation. Human beings, however, can call on their command of language systems and knowledge of the world to interpret divergent inputs, which makes it possible for them to sustain a form of tutorial dialogue which is very sensitive to the needs of the learner. No present machine can come close to this ability.

Metalanguage

A further drawback, one which applies principally to language learning, is that it is necessary to use a metalanguage, an open channel for communication between teacher and learner which conveys explanations, instructions, requests for help, corrections and reassurance. Trained classroom teachers can use a simple form of the target language as a metalanguage, since they have a variety of strategies to use whenever they become aware that the channel is blocked. They can repeat or paraphrase, use gestures or point to things. If a teacher does not speak the learner's first language or if the class does not share the same first language, these strategies are in any case forced. The machine, however, lacking this flexibility, is bound to use the learner's first language as its metalanguage at beginner and elementary levels. This is not necessarily harmful, although it entails code-switching which may encourage mental translation and thereby delay fluency. It does mean, though, that tutorial programs have to be prepared in multiple versions.

A much advertised set of home study computer programs offer French, German, Italian and Spanish courses for English-speaking learners. There are currently no equivalent programs for the EFL learner. We shall have to wait for a continental publisher to launch them and go to France, Germany, Italy or Spain to buy them.

Yet another drawback is that there is a temptation to over-use the metalanguage, to talk about the target language to the exclusion of talking with it. In Christopher Evans's best-seller '*The Mighty Micro*', the author speculates on what a computer tutorial with an 'intelligent' computer will be like, and offers a one-page sample French lesson, representing three or four minutes out of a half-hour session. The computer uses 174 words of English and ten of French. The student produces sixteen words of English and five of French.

Structure of programmed lessons

The solution offered by Programmed Learning to the first of these problems, the unpredictability of natural discourse, is to narrow the focus of tutorial dialogue to the point at which the student's responses become highly convergent and predictable. The process of constructing a PL lesson is roughly as follows:

1 Identify the skill or block of subject matter to be taught.
2 Identify a criterion, a piece of behaviour which will show that the student has mastered the skill or subject matter.
3 Divide the subject into a series of very small steps, each of which requires at most one new concept or decision.
4 Present each step in the form of a 'frame' containing any necessary exposition and a question. The question in the last frame or frames will embody the criterion behaviour.
5 Make the student give an overt answer to each question, usually by writing down a letter or word.
6 Then let the student check that answer against the right answer before continuing.

In a 'linear' or 'Skinnerian' PL lesson it is assumed that learners, even if they have made a mistake, will be able to correct themselves when they see the right answer, since the steps are so small. In a 'branching' or 'Crowderian' program the steps may be a little larger and the questions are normally multiple choice. This allows for a 'remedial loop' to be provided when a student makes a mistake, providing additional explanations and a follow-up question. One can blend both approaches within a single program. Both kinds of program can be presented on paper, the Skinnerian in the shape of a book which one reads with a mask to cover up the correct answers, and the Crowderian in a 'scrambled book', in which each multiple choice answer directs you to a different page, on which you will find either congratulations and a new frame or correction and a remedial loop (sometimes in the form 'Go back to page nnn and choose a better answer'). In the case of a linear program all students must complete all the steps, and the only variable allowed for is pace. A branching program allows for a range of student abilities but not for a range of learning styles. The subject matter determines the order of presentation.

Experience suggests that PL works well when the topic is finite and the objectives are clear, when the learner is reasonably well-motivated, and when there is an element of urgency, for example when a student is making up for missed work. PL is designed to be used independently of a teacher, and so, with elementary level students, it requires a great deal of ingenuity to avoid over-use of the meta-language. A good deal of PL's bad reputation in language work is due to programs which concentrate on translation tasks, often at word or sentence level, using contrived or inauthentic language samples, and adopting a chatty or verbose style of meta-language which patronises the student.

Advantages of the computer

The computer has obvious advantages over paper in the presentation of PL. With a linear program it is an effective mask, not allowing learners to peek at the right answer before attempting their own. With a branching program it can allow more than one attempt at the answer before introducing the remedial loop, and can accommodate far more elaborate branches than are practicable in print form. (A noticeable drawback of scrambled books is their bulk.) The form of a PL lesson is similar to the quiz structure shown in Chapter 3.2, with the addition of expository material at Stage 1 and/or of remedial branching at Stage 5. From a programming point of view they are no harder to write than quizzes, but in terms of content it is very difficult to write a good one, since the size and order of steps is critical. A training program or quiz is iterative, but a PL lesson is progressive.

Subject matter

It is doubtful whether even the most enthusiastic advocate of PL could claim that it is possible to learn the whole of a language by means of programmed lessons. The need to make the student's responses convergent inevitably impoverishes the range of what can be taught. The subjects in language which can be well taught in PL form tend to be the same ones that can be well practised by trainer programs, for example spelling and morphological change, and such closed systems as numbers or telling the time. However, it is also possible to learn, or practise, a certain amount of language incidentally in the course of following a PL lesson on any subject. If foreign-language learners are also interested in electrical circuits, the history of the theatre or the rules of chess, they can gain quite a lot from using a computer-based program which deals with one of these subjects. The language in which such programs are presented tends to have a lot in common with what Krashen calls 'caretaker speech'; it is simpler and more regular than face-to-face speech, and is often closely related to what is visible in the form of illustrations and diagrams, making it very suitable for foreign learners.

3.6 Computer-created material

Traditionally CAL materials have been prepared in advance by the teacher, and the computer's task has been limited to acting as a delivery medium. A generative approach to computer-assisted learning, by contrast, entails that no tasks are written in advance. What the computer program consists of is a series of instructions allowing the machine to create such tasks on the basis of its moment-by-moment interaction with the student. In giving the computer this more active role, we may also find that we can help to release the creative, investigative abilities of our students.

Value of the generative approach

The generative approach to CAL has, of course, an immediate and obvious appeal to the teacher. The writing of drills and exercises can become a chore in which imagination all too easily flags. That chore becomes even more time-consuming when any exercise has to be presented through the medium of the computer. It has been suggested that one hour of computer teaching requires from fifty to 500 hours of programming time. Programming time can be reduced, though, by the use of one of the 'authoring languages' such as PILOT, which provide a simple format for the input of questions and answers, and ready-made routines for answer-checking. Even with such assistance, the provision of an adequate supply of learning materials can be a daunting task. If, on the other hand, the machine can be programmed to generate the materials, and to do so in such a way that it creates a different exercise every time the program is used, the whole basis of the equation (the assumption of a teaching output fixed in advance and therefore measurable in 'teaching time') is overturned.

A further benefit can arise from the very nature of a computer program, which has to be completely explicit in instructing the obedient but stupid machine what to do. It is, therefore, an excellent test-bed for the teacher's linguistic and pedagogic insights. The job of writing a program and trying it out can lead to realisations that the assumptions we make about how language works, and how it is taught and learned, may need to be looked at afresh.

Flexibility

From the point of view of the students, there are more important advantages to the generative approach. It has the possibility of far greater variety in that every task is a new task created on the spot for the students. It allows far greater flexibility in catering for individual needs, interests and progress. Moreover, the extended choice and flexibility implies greater scope for students to direct their own learning. In future developments we should be able to add the benefit of adaptivity: that is to say, the program will be written in such a way that it 'learns' from the way in which students interact with it and, on the basis of that learning, prepares its tasks more effectively. An obvious example is in the grading of tasks or texts. A teacher may use experience to assess whether a task is likely to be easy or difficult but the machine, recording what students actually do, may modify the teacher's original assessment, bringing to light unforeseen difficulties or discovering that certain complex tasks are easier than they appear. The techniques necessary to achieve this 'autograding' approach are illustrated in Chapter 5.2.

Analysis and synthesis

The machine can create teaching material in two ways: either by analysing language held in memory or input by the teacher or the student; or by synthesising language using a stored vocabulary and a set of grammar rules. Each of these approaches, in turn, may employ two basic strategies which, for lack of better terms, we call 'unintelligent' and 'intelligent'. In the first of these, the machine operates in an automatic or random way on the forms of language, and has no sensitivity to meaning. In the second, the machine relates the language to some form of (possibly primitive) knowledge structure.

Unintelligent analysis

The basic idea behind unintelligent analysis is that the computer program undertakes a systematic and controlled manipulation of language held in memory in order to create a language learning task. The language may be single words, isolated sentences, or continuous text. The program performs a 'mechanical' analysis of the language in terms of its constituents – that is to say, where and what the letters, word boundaries, sentence boundaries, etc, are. The nature of the analysis depends on the type of manipulation or degradation to be carried out. Four such manipulations are possible:

Re-ordering
Deletion
Substitution
Insertion.

Some games using these techniques are already familiar, HANGMAN, used in EFL classrooms throughout the world, and now available in a number of computer versions, employs deletion, while an anagram generating program such as WORM is based on the idea of re-ordering. Both of these games, however, operate at word level only.

JUMBLER

The JUMBLER program, written in 1980 for a DEC20 mainframe, was the first of our programs to use the analytic principle on text as opposed to words. It is a suite of games based on the idea of re-ordering. In JUMBLEPARAGRAPH the sentences of the text are randomly re-ordered, the student having to reconstitute the text in the original order. In JUMBLECHUNK the words in a section of text between punctuation marks are re-ordered, and the student has both to identify the relevant section and to restore the original order. In JUMBLEWORD the student has to find and reconstitute an anagrammed word in the text, using contextual clues to help find the answer. All the games have a gambling format: the student is given an initial stock of points, and the computer offers odds based on the difficulty of the task (calculated from the number of sentences in the text, words in the chunk or letters in the word). The student in making a wager has, in order to play the game effectively, to estimate the likelihood that she or he has found the right answer, and can bet modestly when it is clear that there might be some ambiguity about the ordering.

It was realised, from experience of watching students playing the mainframe version, that in JUMBLEPARAGRAPH especially, students needed an opportunity of trying out the effect of different sentence orders on the screen. There is now a microcomputer version which provides a 'scratchpad' allowing rapid and easy manipulation of the text on the screen.

Deletion

TEXTBAG

This is a game which uses deletion, extending to its logical limits the Cloze principle. In a Cloze test every nth word is deleted from a text (the most usual interval being seven), and the student has to restore the missing words. Cloze is, of course, readily implemented on a computer, the advantage of a computer-generated Cloze being that students can choose the interval with which they wish to work. In contrast with the partial deletion of Cloze, TEXTBAG is based on the idea of total deletion: each letter in the text is replaced by a '~', leaving only information about word length and punctuation. The hidden text is accompanied by a simple information question to be answered or a statement to be completed on the basis of the text content. The player controls a cursor to identify any hidden word in the text. The word may then be 'bought' from the player's stock of points, or guessed to gain points. In the instructions at the start of the game the player is advised that it is a good strategy to buy the longer words and guess the shorter words between them. The player's goal in rebuilding the text is to find the answer to a short information question at the foot of the screen. The sooner the answer is found, the higher the player's reward. From the start the player has to guess the overall structure of the text as it emerges, and to use intelligent guesswork and trial and error to rebuild that part of the text where the answer is most likely to be concealed. When one question is successfully answered, it is replaced by another. A listing of the program is given in Chapter 5. It has the following additional features:

1   Players are free to 'change their minds', for example not to guess a word after all, or to leave one text and start work on another.

2   Many questions on a text may have more than one feasible answer; the program checks for alternatives and is not restricted to one right answer.

3   The program includes a routine for 'intelligent input checking' which, like a human teacher, is able to recognise that the player has attempted to give the right answer but has been let down by a spelling or typing mistake.

4   Colour-coding is used (red for a bought word, green for a correct guess or answer, purple for a guess or an answer which the computer has had to reconstruct from an incorrectly spelled input).

5   The method of storing texts, questions, and answers is relatively simple, and enables the teacher to build up a stock of material appropriate to a particular group of students.

```
2 TEXTS LEFT                        178
Once  ~~~~  ~  ~~~~  there  ~~~  ~
~  ~~~~~~  ~~~~~~  ~~~~~  ~~  ~~~~
~  ~~~~~~ .  He  lived  in  ~  foxhole
which  ~~~  previous  ~~~~~~  ~~~
deserted  ~~~  earned  ~~~  ~~~~~~
~~  ~~~~~~~~~~  ~~  ~~~~  ~~~~~  ~~~~
neighbouring  ~~~~  and  turning  ~~
~~~~  ~~~~~~~ ,  ~~~~~~  ~~  ~~~~~  ~~
~~~  ~~~~~~  ~~  ~~~~  ~~~~~  ~~~~~ .  ~~~
~~~  ~~~  farmer  ~~~~~~  sight  ~~
~~~  ~~~  chased  ~~~  ~~~~[~]~  ~
large  ~~~~~~ .  " ~~~~~ ! "  ~~
shouted.  " ~~  ~  catch  ~~~  ~ ' ~~
~~~~  ~~~  ~~~~~~  ~~~~  ~~~  ~~~  ~~~
breakfast! "  ~~~  Gabble  ~~~~~~~
~~~~  ~~~~~~  ~~~~ ,  ~~~~~  ~~  ~~~~~
farmer  got  ~~~~~  ~~  looking  ~~~
~~  ~~~~  ~~~~  ~~~  ~~~  ~~~
~~~~~ .

B=buy    A=answer   G=guess   Q=quit
The  farmer  liked           gnomes
```

TEXTBAG

STORYBOARD

Another program which uses the principle of total deletion is
STORYBOARD. In this, the HANGMAN principle is applied at word level
to a complete text which is displayed only in the form of dashes and
punctuation, with a helpful title to suggest a starting point. The
student is prompted 'Guess a word', and all occurrences of a correctly
guessed word are inserted, so that the text is built up in jigsaw
fashion. STORYBOARD contains no scoring routine, and there is a very
accessible 'Help' facility which will supply the first missing word
(together with other occurrences of the same word) whenever the
learner asks for it. An alternative form of 'Help', available in some
versions of the program, is to supply all occurrences of a specified
prefix or suffix, for example all the -*ing* endings, or to allow the
student to see the full text flashed up for ten seconds.

It has been interesting to see the variety of strategies that learners
apply to the task. Some use the 'Help' facility frequently, more or less
getting the machine to build up the text piecemeal for them and only
entering a few obvious words themselves. Others reject it except in
the very last resort, and will struggle for half an hour or longer in an
effort to reconstruct the text unaided.

CLOSE-UP

A different approach to deletion is used in CLOSE-UP, a program
which presents on the top half of the screen a list of eight titles, and
on the bottom half a single word taken from one of the eight short
passages to which the titles refer. The student can either wager the
stock of points on a guess as to where the word belongs, or can 'buy'
more context in the form of the preceding and following words. The
student can go on doing this until he or she has enough evidence on
which to base a guess. As soon as a passage has been identified, it is
withdrawn and replaced by another.

There is a large element of luck, in that the first word might be
something revealing like 'reactor' (pointing to 'Atomic Energy'

57

among the titles) or something quite unrevealing such as 'of'. The student sets his or her own target score, between 500 points which gives a short and relatively easy game, or 2000 for a much longer game. Each successful guess wins 200 points, but the penalty for a wrong guess is the loss of a third of the stock of points. Each extra piece of context 'bought' costs ten points. It is interesting to observe students finding their way towards a winning strategy, after an initial veering between over-caution and wild guessing. One of the effects of the game is that students seem highly motivated to read each passage attentively after a successful guess, to see where the fragment they have identified fits into the whole. This the program permits them to do without penalty.

Insertion and substitution
A form of reading test has been developed by Alan Davies in which words, which may be foreign or nonsense words or else plausible words of the target language, are introduced into a text and have to be struck out by the reader. This is most often used to measure reading speed, but seems, like Cloze, to have some value as a form of practice as well as a test.

When an exercise involves adding or replacing material, the new material obviously has to come from somewhere: a computer, as long as it is limited to unintelligent analysis, cannot make it up. This immediately suggests activities which are based not on one text but on two or more. There are many ways in which the material from two texts can be combined. For example, we are developing a suite of activities which we call SHUFFLER, in which the student selects one text and the computer selects a second one randomly. In SHUFFLER 1 the sentences of the two texts are shuffled together, retaining their internal order. Both titles or headlines are displayed. The student has to assign each successive sentence to one or the other, and watches the two texts as they separate and grow. In SHUFFLER 2 the sentences of one of the texts are also jumbled so that the student must re-order them, and in SHUFFLER 3, the most difficult, both texts are jumbled. Numerous variants of this technique are possible.

Sources of text
In all of these games the program is completely indifferent as to what text it uses, subject to restrictions on length of text imposed by the size and layout of the screen. STORYBOARD, for instance, exists in a polyglot version in which the user can opt for English, French or German texts. Texts are not normally stored within the program itself: instead the program contains an instruction to 'read' a text from an outside source, such as a cassette or disc file, or keyboard input. This provides for great flexibility in the combination of text and game. Students can select an activity and, on different occasions, carry it out with simplified stories, newspaper articles, scientific text,

poetry, or on compositions written by their classmates. This flexibility would hardly be possible without the computer. It would have particular value where the student has a specialist purpose in learning the language and where it might be impossible to find, or uneconomic to prepare, teacher-written materials to meet that student's need.

Text versus drill

The most obvious difference between the traditional CAL drill on the one hand and games such as JUMBLER, TEXTBAG, STORYBOARD and CLOSE-UP on the other is that the former is usually based on isolated sentences, while the latter employ continuous (usually paragraph length) text. There are some further differences which may be worth summarising briefly. The drill emphasises language as code: the text game emphasises language as information and the way that information hangs together. The aim of a drill is in general to reinforce appropriate linguistic habits: does the student respond with the right answer? The aim of the text game is to develop the student's ability to form appropriate hypotheses and to guess intelligently: can the student discover the correct answer? The drill is essentially authoritarian and the student's role in it is passive. The text game, on the other hand, emphasises student autonomy and student choice, both within the game itself and in the situation in which it is used.

Intelligent analysis

The possibility of intelligent analysis for language learning is still largely to be explored. One technique which has been used is pattern recognition. Both Jørgen Christiansen in Denmark and Helen Pain in Edinburgh have worked on spelling analysers, programs which will not only detect that a word has been misspelt but can also classify the errors involved. The sub-routine SPELL in Chapter 5.2 is a simple spelling corrector based on the same idea. The programs S-ENDING and A/AN, described in Chapter 3.8, use simple pattern recognition techniques of the same type for the practice of English morphology. Similar work has been done by Hanno Martin for German, although there the focus has been on syntax, using automatic parsing techniques. This is one of the many areas in which computer-assisted learning may expect to borrow in future from theoretical work in artificial intelligence.

Unintelligent synthesis

The idea of unintelligent synthesis is based on the ability of the computer to take decisions randomly. Using the computer equivalent of the familiar substitution table, we can program the computer to synthesise samples of language, whether for practice or – as with programs which offer to 'write poetry' or 'tell fortunes' – for fun. There is nothing new in our readiness to be entertained by such random processes of creation: it can be found throughout the seventeenth and eighteenth centuries, from John Peters's machine for the automatic writing of Latin hexameters, to Mozart's Werfelspiel (literally 'dice game'), which was in effect a program (recently implemented on microcomputer) for the random generation of minuets. It was over two hundred and fifty years ago that Joshua Steele in '*The Spectator*' and Jonathan Swift, in '*Gulliver's Travels*', satirised such endeavours, mocking the absurdity of the unintelligent machine producing language and the absurdity of the language that the unintelligent machine produced. The satire remains valid. Nevertheless, we may for teaching purposes exploit that very absurdity. In Burckhardt Leuschner's DIALOG-CRIT, for example, the computer suggests to the student that they should both try to write dialogues. The computer, however, confesses that its own efforts are not very good, as becomes apparent from the examples it begins to produce:

```
                 AT THE DOCTOR'S

A      Good morning, Madam.    What can I do for you?

B      Hi, my lord.   Mum sent me for a bowl of

       soap.                              ... etc
```

The program asks the student to correct and edit the dialogue on screen, and then prints out the revised version to show to the teacher.

Leuschner's program exploits randomness by requiring the student to reduce it – to change what the computer produces into something closer to natural communication. Daniel Chandler, in a program for first-language learners, has taken a different approach. His program STORYMAKER is designed to trigger off free writing. Here the computer creates 'situations' compiled from a store of nouns, actions and places. It might produce, for instance, 'An old man lighting a bonfire in a telephone kiosk', or 'Two nuns shouting in a railway station'. The student can go on asking for these prompts until one he or she likes comes up, and then the student writes the story that explains the situation. In STORYMAKER, then, the learner's task is not to reduce absurdity but to justify it.

Learning through modifying programs
We may, however, want our programs to avoid such absurdities in advance. There are two ways in which this can be done. One is by careful pre-selection of the elements to be synthesised and of the

frame or frames in which they are placed. This was the method adopted by Mozart and a careful teacher constructing a substitution table for classroom use will try to ensure that, while it generates a large number of examples, none of them are too wildly improbable. This requires considerable linguistic sensitivity to such matters as syntactic restrictions, naturalness of collocation, the structure of lexical sets, and the potential use of language. Since these are all essential elements in language learning, it is natural to consider how far it may be possible to develop such sensitivity by giving the learner an opportunity to develop or modify simple language generators. Work on these lines with poetry generators and with story generators using the ADVENTURE format (see 3.7) for first-language teaching has been reported by Papert, Chandler, Sharples and others. There is no reason why the same principle should not be applied in foreign language teaching, although there the emphasis might be more on non-literary texts, for example dialogues, letters and reports.

Limitations of intelligent synthesis
The second way of controlling the output of a language generator is to write the program in such a way that the computer 'understands' the language it produces. Our own understanding of language rests on and mediates our overall understanding of the real world to which language refers. As we pointed out in Chapter 1.2, neither now nor for the immediate future is there any way in which we can give the computer that knowledge, despite the fact that such machines have long been the stock-in-trade of fantasy. However, work in artificial intelligence from the 1960s on has shown that computers can be programmed to generate and respond to language appropriately, provided that the language relates to knowledge of a restricted world. The classic program in this field was Winograd's SHRDLU which 'knew' about a table-top world of three-dimensional objects, blocks, cones and pyramids of different colours. It could manipulate the objects in response to instructions in English, and answer questions about where the objects were and which manipulations were possible.

Holding a dialogue with a computer in natural language is now fairly commonplace, but it is based on the assumption that the input questions, as well as being grammatical, will be relevant to the restricted field of discourse. There are, for instance, systems which allow one to interrogate a database to obtain geographical information. There is even one system that handles spoken language: you can telephone it to get information on airline timetables.

TWO STICKS and TIME
The SHRDLU principle can be applied to a variety of programs allowing the user to practise and explore language. In TWO STICKS the computer's world of knowledge is restricted to two 'sticks' labelled 'A' and 'B' which it draws in succession at the top of the VDU screen.

61

Stick A may be longer than B, or B longer than A, or they may be the same length. The computer randomly decides whether to tell the truth or to lie, and generates a statement accordingly, which the player has to identify as 'True' or 'False'. The linguistic complexity of the output depends on the player's current score. At the start of the game it will generate statements such as:

A is longer than B.

A and B are the same length.

B is not as long as A.

As the game progresses and the player's score mounts, the computer may generate:

A is marginally shorter than B.

B is almost as long as A.

A and B differ considerably in length.

B is half as long again as A.

At the end of twenty turns the player is given a score based on the accuracy and speed of his or her responses.

While TWO STICKS is designed to be played competitively, TIME is more contemplative. The program demonstrates the five ways in which the time may be told in English, the student being given the facility to halt the program to study the language at greater leisure, or to delay its appearance for self-testing. Several of these features are brought together in GRAMMARLAND, which is described in Chapter 3.9.

Sociolinguistic meaning
The two programs just mentioned are able to generate language with reference to meaning: that is to say, they know whether a statement is true or false, or (as in GRAMMARLAND) whether it may be true. A further dimension to language is that a statement may be appropriate in one context but inappropriate in another. So far only two of our programs, LOAN and APOLOGIES, take account of this pragmatic dimension, but there is no reason why the simple artificial intelligence techniques cannot be applied to social relationships just as they have been to positional ones. LOAN and APOLOGIES are described in Chapter 3.8 and the program listing of LOAN is given in Chapter 5.4.

3.7 Simulations

Technically a simulation is an 'intervention model', a representation of a process during which one can intervene and change some of the values which affect the process. We are using the word 'simulation' as a general term, covering a range of activities which involve decisions based on data from realistic situations. A simulation can represent a scientific experiment, a commercial management exercise, a problem-solving task, a road race or a role-play.

Although simulations have some of the attributes of games, they are not necessarily trivial. Many of them have a good deal in common with case studies. They do not need to involve any dramatic skills, although some of them gain from the role-play element. What they share with games includes the motivation and concentration that games arouse, but there is no need to use competitive scoring or to let competition blot out co-operation. Often the computer is the implicit 'enemy', and the learners co-operate with each other and with the teacher in an effort to 'beat the machine'.

Realism

The activity of sitting down at a computer console is not really 'like' running a race, fighting a battle, driving a car or hunting wild animals. The computer can, however, abstract from these real-life activities just enough to permit some suspension of disbelief, and can calculate the effects of chance and of material factors so quickly and efficiently that it presents outcomes which we can accept as likely. If a good deal of effort is put into imitating the real-life activity, as in a cockpit simulator where one sits in a real aircraft seat and handles real aircraft controls, then the simulation is an acceptable substitute for authentic, practical training. In the case of board games, most of which are originally simulations of a form of war, we do not think of the computer version as a simulation at all. A game of chess or backgammon played against a computer is, for most people, just as real as one played against a human opponent. It is not really a valid criticism of a simulation to say that it is not the real thing, any more than it is a criticism of reading fiction to say that it is not the same as experiencing life for oneself. There is room for both real and simulated or narrated experience. Both are food for learning and communication.

Real-time versus move-based

The common feature of all simulations is that the computer is representing some of the consequences of decisions or actions on its screen, so that the user can follow a process through to an uncertain outcome.

63

Simulations can be broken down into 'real-time' and 'move-based' simulations. In real-time simulations the action is continuous, and the user can fail by simply doing nothing or reacting too slowly. Both the trainer simulations, such as flight simulators, and arcade-type game simulations, such as space invaders, belong in this category. Their direct value for language practice may not be very great for an individual user. There are instructions to be read, but little other necessary language. However, when they are tackled by a group, the language involvement becomes much greater. The instructions on the screen are often quite spontaneously read aloud by a group member. One member of the group will operate the keyboard or joysticks, but the others will have to talk to him or her if they want to get their ideas into the machine. (At times of frustration, they may just lean over the operator's shoulder and press the keys.)

There is usually even richer use of language in move-based simulations, during which the machine will hold the display constant while waiting for a decision. The users have time to discuss possible moves and compare one with another, and there is a real need for the modals *must* and *may*, and for *if* clauses. This language is student-to-student, and the actual language input at the keyboard does not need to be elaborate. If the group share the same mother tongue, they will, naturally, use it at times of difficulty. Experience suggests, however, that this is nothing to worry about. The problem itself has been presented in the target language, and the group will, without prompting, try to use the target language whenever they feel confident in it. The mother tongue may predominate at the first attempt at the problem, but on each subsequent attempt there will be more use of the target language, quite without the teacher's prompting or policing.

Process versus problem, and random versus determinate

One can make a further classification of simulations into processes, such as making a journey, running a country's economy, or containing a forest fire, and problems, such as detecting a criminal, discovering treasure, or winning a battle. The problems have definite outcomes; one knows when one has finished, and there is a clear difference between success and failure. Processes on the other hand can continue indefinitely, or may be given an arbitrary cut-off point. In a trading simulation, for instance, one can incorporate an objective to make a million pounds, so that players can 'retire' when they have this sum or be 'sent to jail' when they are a similar amount in debt. There is plenty of room for both processes and problems in language courses.

One can also classify simulations into those which have fixed data and those which involve random elements. Nearly all simulations use a random element in setting up, so that they are different each time they are used. Many also use random effects during the run. It is with the latter that the computer's advantages over paper-and-pencil techniques can be seen most clearly, since the calculations of probabilities can be carried out virtually instantaneously by the machine, and elaborate dependent conditions can be incorporated into a scenario. To do the same thing manually would involve dice throwing and complex look-up tables.

Role-play

The other important difference between simulations is the extent to which role-play is involved. Normally we do not ask users to modify their personalities. If they are to explore a desert island, they must imagine some way in which they might have reached that desert island in the first place, but we do not ask them to take on the characteristics of intrepid pioneers. (They may, of course, decide to do so anyway.) If the task is to interrogate witnesses and identify a murderer, then they must take on the instrumental role of detective, but they do not not need to adopt that role emotionally. However, there is a class of simulations called role-plays in which the activity depends on resolving a clash of interests or attitudes, and we must therefore ask users to adopt opinions or roles which are not their own. We brief them with a description of the role which may simply indicate which point of view they are to put forward, but which may also include an account of the characteristics they are to act out. With some learners and on some occasions this can lead to gains in confidence, particularly with pronunciation. Mimicry is far easier to undertake when one knows what one is supposed to be mimicking, and an instruction to play a part releases us from the social inhibition against mimicry.

Role-plays normally demand that some information is given privately to participants and not shared, so it is not suitable for exclusive presentation on a single microcomputer. The computer is still of enormous value in presenting the shared information, but one usually also needs briefing sheets, in order to keep the individual briefings private. This is not always the case, and there may be negotiation tasks in which it is perfectly natural and legitimate to know all the time what the opposing interests are with which you have to find a compromise.

Branching stories

One very simple form of simulation is the branching story, which has become familiar to EFL learners through Mario Rinvolucri's *Action Mazes*. The students, usually working in small groups, have a short piece of text to read which presents a problem. At the bottom of the page or screen are several possible courses of action. The group choose one and immediately learn the consequences. Then they are given further choices to make, eventually, one hopes, reaching a successful outcome.

The best known computer simulation of this type is DRAKE, which was written for English children studying history. This describes the round-the-world voyages of Sir Francis Drake from 1577 to 1580. From time to time students are asked to take the decisions that Drake himself was faced with at moments of crisis. They then learn whether their decision matched that of Drake, and whether the voyage can continue.

Exactly the same procedure can be applied to a wide range of subject matter, past or present, familiar or exotic. The programming technique is relatively simple, since it is almost the same as that of the multiple choice quiz, except that one learns that consequences of a decision rather than just being told an answer is Right or Wrong.

ADVENTURE

There is a particular form of simulation known as ADVENTURE which is familiar to computer users, both micro and mainframe. The under-lying scenario is that of exploring a maze. The settings are decorated with fantasy, captive princesses, hoards of gold guarded by goblins or dragons, spells to be cast, monsters to be slain. Alternatively one can find ADVENTURE scenarios set in the Wild West or in a Star Wars future.

A feature of the original version of ADVENTURE was that all information was given verbally. The player had to read the text with great attention in order to pick up clues, and to integrate the new information with what had been learned earlier. In other words, the ADVENTURE program provided a context in which 'reading for meaning' had a very clear and definite purpose. One way in which text-based ADVENTURE programs could be enriched for language learning purposes would be to store alternative and equivalent texts for the same situation. There is already one version of the original ADVENTURE in which the player can, at will, switch from English to French. The potential of the program for the English learner of French or the French learner of English will be self-evident. Using the same principle, one might have an ADVENTURE in which the player could choose between 'simplified' and 'unsimplified' texts.

All moves by the player in a typical ADVENTURE are made by entering short commands, either simple directions for movement (for example 'Up', 'North' or 'N') or one or two word imperatives (for example 'Enter', 'Get knife' or 'Drop box'). Part of the interest in the game comes from trying out commands in order to discover what vocabulary the machine responds to and what commands are legal in given situations. Daniel Chandler suggests that there may be a benefit to the learner from the attempt to reduce communication to such simplified formulae. His work has been done mainly with native

66

speakers of English, and it might well worry foreign language teachers that an addiction to ADVENTURE in the target language could well encourage learners to use exactly that type of 'telegraphese' that teachers spend much time attempting to correct. However, some recent versions of ADVENTURE have incorporated an 'advanced language interpreter' that is able to interpret commands that come much closer to natural language in their structure, for example 'Take everything off the table except the keys'.

Structure of a simulation lesson

The conduct of a simulation should fall into three phases: **briefing, execution, de-briefing**. The briefing phase is often best handled by the teacher or by distributing paper handouts, since the computer's screen is limited in the amount of information it can display, and there may be problems about re-displaying the information when the learners ask for a reminder. (It is possible to store the current page and any 'Help' pages in the memory in such a way that the computer on demand shows one or the other. However, this makes appreciable demands on computer memory, and, where this is limited, one can make a virtue of necessity by announcing that the background information will be displayed only once and that the students should take notes.) At the execution phase the teacher's role should be minimal in any case, and the computer should carry out all the tasks required of the 'controller', i.e. displaying the current report and judging the legality of each proposed move.

The teacher's most important function occurs at the de-briefing or 'post-mortem' phase, when the participants review what they did and what they might have done. The computer can be used to recall a 'history' of the simulation, or to calculate the effects of other decisions, for example in commercial simulations, in which the participants have had to decide on the scale of investment or the price of a commodity.

Subject matter

The potential subject matter of simulations is unlimited, and the remainder of this section simply describes a few simulations which have been used successfully with EFL learners. All of them can be used by a student working alone in a lunch-hour or at home, but are more rewarding if tackled by a group under the loose supervision of a teacher, who can then exploit the de-briefing phase to develop particular language skills.

CHAIR FACTORY
This simulation, devised by Nick Bullard, presents a simplified commercial venture. Participants run a factory which makes a

reclining chair of unusual design and markets it by mail order. Each year they have to decide how many staff to employ, how much to spend on advertising, and at what price to sell the chair. They then see the annual balance sheet based on the orders received (which is affected by random factors), and go on to plan the next year. There are several random events which may intrude, such as government support, strikes or fires. The game ends with either bankruptcy or twenty years successful trading or profits of a million.

BLEEPER

This is simulation of the same type as CHAIR FACTORY. The product is an anti-theft device for cars. However, this version contains a summarised 'post-mortem' phase, reviewing what decisions the user made year by year in the form of verbal messages and graphs, and showing what he or she might have done instead. The value of the computer-generated review is that it can provide the data for a written project, which the student, reporting his or own performance, might undertake with more enthusiasm than if the data came from a textbook.

PHOTOFIT

The computer draws a face (by making random combinations of shapes for face, hair, eyes, nose, mouth, moustache and beard stored in its memory) and announces that this is 'Bill Bolt the burglar'. The learner must study the face and later re-draw it by typing in the word for the part of the face, for example 'hair' or 'nose', and then modifying it by typing in a comparative adjective, for example 'wider', 'longer', etc. When the student is satisfied that the face is the same, he or she types 'compare'. Now the original and the learner's faces are displayed alongside each other, and all the points of difference are enumerated in sentences. Here the computer is taking over part of the de-briefing function. (The listing of a French version of PHOTOFIT is given in Chapter 5.6.)

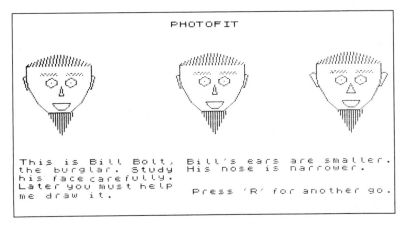

MURDER

The learner is cast as a police officer investigating a 'country house murder'. The police officer is summoned to a house where a murder has taken place, and given the names of the suspects and a plan of the house. He or she can call each suspect in turn and type in two questions, 'Where were you?' and 'Who was with you?' The 'rule' of the game is that there is only one murderer and that all the other suspects tell the truth. Sooner or later a discrepancy will show up. Two people will claim to have been alone in the same room at the same time, and the learner can now 'accuse' them in turn. (The player is not allowed to accuse more than two people.) The guilty one now 'confesses'. The facts in the game are generated randomly, so that each investigation is different. The logic of the problem is simple, but the program requires the learner to type in about ten past tense questions and read a good many sentences containing past tense forms.

WEIGHT

This is overtly a straightforward exercise in maths and logic. The screen shows a seesaw and six children. Under two of the children are printed their weights. The user has to 'place' children on the seesaw using cursor keys, in order to find out the weights of the other four children. This is a prime example of a program which does not 'teach' any language, but which provides a powerful context for the use of comparative forms *heavier than*, *the same weight as*, etc) whenever a group tackles the task consultatively.

CASTAWAY

This is an example of a survival simulation, in which the task is to explore a hostile terrain and reach safety. The students (this is ideally a group task) have been shipwrecked on a desert island, and must find food, water and building supplies for a raft. They must also discover (by climbing a hill) which way the mainland lies, so that they can sail the raft there. The computer alternates two displays, a diary page showing how much food and water is left and how far raft-building has progressed, and a map page indicating what lies one day's march in each direction. There are enough constraints to make each day's decision a matter for argument and, assuming a group working together, negotiation. The simulation is a simplified form of, Ken Jones's SHIPWRECKED, from '*Nine Graded Simulations*'.

TOWN PLAN

This simulation by Chris Harrison makes great use of role-play. Participants are assigned roles as various members of a town council. A new factory is to be built, and each councillor has reasons for wanting the factory to be built in a different place, and for making different decisions about traffic routes. A map of the town is displayed, and, by moving a cursor around, one can erect bridges, designate roads as one-way, or build and knock down buildings. The computer keeps score of the costs and other consequences of each decision.

FOREST FIRE

This is a group task which involves separate briefings of participants. Students work in groups of three to five, each group consisting of a captain, one or two helicopter pilots and one or two bulldozer drivers, together constituting a fire-fighting team responsible for a sixty-four square mile area of forest in which a fire has broken out. The team must use their resources to contain the fire. The captain has the information about the weather and the likelihood of the fire spreading to any adjoining sector. The pilots know what the effect of dropping chemicals will be and what the chances are of keeping the helicopters airborne. The drivers know how fast their bulldozers move when cutting firebreaks or when moving to a new location. The team has to share its information to work out tactics. The computer simply displays the map, day by day, to show which sectors are on fire, which direction the wind is blowing and where the equipment is. Several groups can fight different fires, with the relevant map being called up for each.

Other sources

Simulations belong in all disciplines, and should be freely exchangeable. One of the authors recently visited the offices of the Control Data Corporation for a demonstration of the PLATO system and its vast bank of software. Almost as an afterthought he was shown some science simulations, beginning with a fractional distillation experiment which involved building apparatus by manipulating screen silhouettes, and then controlling the temperature during the distilling process. Then he was shown a medical simulation in which the user plays the part of an ambulance driver, giving treatment to a road accident victim. (For the latter there were versions in English and French.) Both of these would be excellent language teaching material, but they were not catalogued as such. The language teacher should consult colleagues in science, geography and economics. If they use computers at all, the chances are that they have material which can be used as it stands or which requires only non-structural modifications for language practice, for example translation or simplification of instructions and texts.

3.8 Using the computer as an informant

In drill-and-practice and many other forms of computer learning activity, the computer assumes some of the roles traditionally associated with the teacher, particularly that of controller and source of knowledge. The rightness of the computer's answers or its judgements are hard to challenge, which is unfortunate if, through faulty programming, wrong answers are embodied in a quiz or drill. When the computer acts solely as quizmaster, it can acquire a mystique of authority which conceals its basic slave status.

Role reversal

There is a way of reversing the conventional roles of computer and student and letting the student act as 'quizmaster', trying to catch the machine and expose its limitations. The first programs we describe here were written for the smallest and cheapest of the 'hobby' microcomputers, the unexpanded Sinclair ZX81 with only 1K of memory. The very limitations of this model become an advantage since the centre of interest is now what the computer can or cannot do, and in particular its limitations in mirroring the target language. It is the student who poses the problems and assesses the answers.

Since the role of the student is now active rather than passive, the question of grading assumes less importance than it does in traditional CAL; different students can work on the program at different levels, and it will reveal as much or as little as they are prepared to get out of it. This in turn implies that the program is likely to be more effective if a group of students can work together on the materials and learn from each other, and more effective still if a teacher is present to explain what has to be done (there is little room for explanations in 1K of memory) and provide hints, clues, and even the occasional red herring.

Exploratory programs

The model of learning underlying these materials is cognitive: that is to say, the aim is not the establishment of language habits, but the development of strategies for use inside and outside the classroom, for the exploration and 'puzzling out' of the target language and its underlying regularities. This is why we have labelled such programs 'exploratory'.

The computer program itself has a different role. In place of the long and complex programs required for traditional CAL, we have short and apparently trivial programs which may take no more than an hour or two to write. The focus of the difficulty is linguistic rather than computational: that is, in establishing the linguistic rules that are involved and in finding an algorithm which expresses them as economically as possible.

The relationship of the student to the computer program is also different. In traditional CAL, the program that controls the teaching is normally a matter of indifference to the learner. The computer enthusiast may be interested to see some of the technical details of file handling and so forth, but inspecting the program could hardly be of much use in language learning. With exploratory CAL, however, it is a test of the effectiveness of a program that at some stage the students should demand to see it, to find out 'how the trick is done'. The program becomes part of the language learning process as a (partial) explanation of how the target language operates.

S-ENDING

S-ENDING offers to accept any 'English' word, whether real or invented, and to add an -s to form the third person of a verb or the plural of a noun.

One way of using it is to give a group of students five to ten minutes to test out as many words as they want on the program, keeping a record of its 'hits' and 'misses'. The group can then discuss with the teacher the rules that the computer has applied. The session will usually start with the class suggesting a large number of words (*cat/ cats, house/houses*) which hardly tax the program. Students will often then suggest some irregular plurals which seem to produce 'misses' for the computer (*sheep/sheeps, knife/knifes*). These can, however, form the basis for some valuable later discussion: for example, by the terms of the computer's offer, *knife* could be a verb and *knifes* a correct third-person form. At some stage a student will suggest an uncountable noun, which again produces a 'miss' for the computer which will innocently produce *informations* from *information*. This can again be a springboard for discussion as to how the rule which blocks *informations* differs from the rules which the computer does know, or indeed from the rule which blocks *sheeps*. Eventually, with examples such as *marry/marries* and *wash/washes*, the program will start to come into its own. In a good group of students at least one will realise that one of the plausible hypotheses for the computer's ability to handle *marry/marries* will have to be tested with a word like *valley/valleys* (a hit), and examples such as *wash/washes* and *coach/ coaches* need to be tested with *bath/baths* or *graph/graphs* (also hits). Only if prompted by the teacher or a preliminary search through a standard work of reference (one way of preparing for exploratory CAL, as exploratory CAL can be a way of introducing students to, and teaching them to use, reference books) will even a very good group of students uncover all the remaining secrets of the program, such as its ability to handle *hypothesis/hypotheses, quiz/quizzes* and *loch/lochs*.

A/AN

A second program of the same kind, called A/AN, offers to make the choice between *a* and *an* before noun phrases. This is slightly more elaborate but still just fits into an unexpanded ZX81. It is sophisticated enough to distinguish on the basis of pattern recognition between such 'minimal pairs' as *an unillustrated book* and *a unilateral decision*, between *a sob* and *an S.O.B.* and between *an* 11-*metre yacht* and *a* 110 *yard dash*. The same program can be used as a sub-routine within a larger program to check a noun input by the student and ensure that it appears in its correct environment. We use it this way in Chapter 5.3.

Other applications
As the above examples show, the exploratory approach lends itself particularly to morphology. Programs by Gianfranco Porcelli show that the approach is even more powerful when used with a language such as Italian, where grammatical inflexion plays a larger role that it does in English, and where the inflexions and the sound/spelling correspondences are more regular than they are in English. It is not restricted, however, to the 'nuts-and-bolts' end of language learning, and can be extended to such matters as appropriacy decisions and stylistic choice.

In the real world the language we use varies according to a number of situational factors, the most important being the participants (who is speaking to whom), the topic (what is being spoken about), the speech event (which distinguishes an invitation, say, from either a request or an order), and the setting. It is one of the most important tasks in learning a foreign language to discover how these factors interact, and to develop a feeling for what is appropriate and what the range of appropriacy is in a particular situation. It is also the task that is most difficult for the learner. What is needed is an opportunity to experiment with the factors and to develop a sense of how a language relates to the society from which it springs and which the language in turn helps to form. The traditional foreign language classroom offers little opportunity for such experimentation, with the result that we tend to assume that this aspect of the foreign language can only be learned by living in the country where it is spoken for a length of time. The computer, however, can come to the learner's help if we can model the sociolinguistic rules that link language to situation.

LOAN is an experimental program designed to let the learner explore what could or could not be said in one specific simplified scenario, and in doing so to begin to develop a feeling for how language depends on the context in which it is used. The computer offers to synthesise requests to borrow money. It first asks how much is to be borrowed (from 1p to £1,000) and then from whom the money is to be borrowed (offering a choice ranging from a brother or sister up to one's employer or bank manager). Deviant situations are rejected (the program will not, for instance, attempt to borrow £500 from a stranger), but providing the request is feasible it will suggest a range of request forms for that situation. These extend from, for example, 'Got 2p on you?' (to a brother or close friend) to 'I wonder if you could possibly see your way to letting me have an overdraft of £500?' (to one's bank manager). In investigating the range of requests that the computer generates for one situation, and also the way in which changing one or both variables affects what is suggested, learners are at one level getting a firmer grasp of a number of difficult structural points (for example direct or indirect questions, question tags, 'borrow' versus 'lend', etc.) but also, at a deeper level, being led to discuss and work out the principles that the program is using to relate language to situation.

For a program such as LOAN we have found it useful to prepare a handout with a number of questions which can be used as a springboard for the students' own exploration, for example:

What are the shortest and longest requests that the computer suggests, and in what situations?

What word is only used in asking to borrow money from a bank manager?

When does the program *not* suggest that you say 'Please'?

The same approach is used in APOLOGIES. The machine is now giving advice on how to apologise for lateness. The user selects an occasion, for example dinner at home, birthday party, business appointment, cinema show or job interview, and specifies the number of minutes of lateness. Once again his or her task is to discover how many different forms of apology the machine knows and to assess the aptness of its cut-offs.

Role of the learner
One point that needs to be borne in mind in using exploratory programs such as those described above, is that they make demands on the student, requiring an alert and intelligent attitude to the task of learning. This is an important point in the programs' favour but it would be expecting too much of the computer to imagine that it could effect single-handedly a total change in a student's approach to language learning. Learning from an informant entails a different set of techniques and expectations from the more familiar situation of learning from a teacher, and the learner needs to be trained in the approach if it is to succeed. With learners accustomed to a 'passive' role in language learning, such programs may mystify and confuse if they are not carefully prepared for, and integrated into, an overall programme which incorporates such a training element.

3.9 'Talking' to the computer

There is one group of programs, still experimental, which seems to have the potential of bringing together several features of other programs into a single, flexible resource. We have called this group GRAMMARLAND, by analogy with Seymour Papert's MATHLAND, the hypothetical country where maths is learned as a living language.

Artificial intelligence

One of the early demonstrations of artificial intelligence (AI) was Weizenbaum's ELIZA, written in the early sixties in response to the 'Turing Test'. Alan Turing had suggested in an article published in 1950 that the only test of whether a machine was intelligent should be an operational one. If somebody could communicate in natural language via a teletypewriter with two other terminals, one operated by a human being and the other controlled by a machine, and if, after a lengthy spell of interaction, he or she could not tell which was which, then the machine was, by his definition, intelligent.

ELIZA was an algorithm which could be supplied with different scenarios, of which the best known is DOCTOR (Weizenbaum). In DOCTOR the machine takes on the role of a 'non-directive' psychiatrist, and issues noncommittal responses to the user's input sentences. In Colby's PARRY, an extension of the same idea, the computer assumes the role of a psychopath responding to a psychiatrist and issues aggressive messages. It is fairly easy to make either of these programs talk nonsense, so they do not 'pass' the Turing Test. However, it is also possible to sustain a very plausible connected discourse over a lengthy set of exchanges. The effect is achieved by searching the user's input for a keyword, and then either manipulating the input in a fairly obvious way ('My mother hates me'/'Is it because your mother hates you that you came to see me?') or simply using it to select from a carefully compiled set of fixed responses (thus the word 'machine' will always elicit 'Are you afraid of computers?'). Weizenbaum himself has expressed worries about the ease with which people let themselves be taken in by this 'trickery' and attempt to use it for therapeutic purposes. A lot of people, however, have had a lot of innocent fun playing with it, and it has now been used in foreign language tuition simply as a practice framework or as an 'exploratory' program in the sense described in Chapter 3.8.

GRAMMARLAND

We have already described in Chapter 3.6 Winograd's SHRDLU, which took natural language understanding a step further by parsing and reacting to the whole of the input utterance rather than just scanning it for keywords. Winograd achieved this by limiting the field of discourse to a self-contained table-top world of blocks, cones and pyramids of different colours which could be manipulated in response to commands. GRAMMARLAND is an attempt to harness the SHRDLU principle to language learning objectives, to create a miniature universe of discourse and a program which will manipulate things in that universe, answer questions about it, ask questions, or do any of these things at random if the user merely wants a demonstration. The universe can take the form of a picture or set of pictures, tables of facts or figures, or graphs and diagrams.

One working example is called JOHN AND MARY, in honour of a

remarkable AI program by Richard Power. Power devised his program to model the use of discourse for collaborative ends. His John and Mary were two robots, represented by different sections of his program, who had to talk to each other in order to carry out a task. Their universe consisted of two rooms, a door and a bolt, and the task would involve moving from one room to the other, which might entail undoing the bolt or opening the door. The apparently trivial tasks revealed some fascinating insights into the structure of certain kinds of discourse. Our program has borrowed the mini-universe of John and Mary, but does not otherwise resemble Power's program, since the user communicates with the machine about the figures, rather than the figures communicating with each other. The screen shows a room with an open door. Inside the room is a male figure, John, and visible through the door (in the 'kitchen') is a female figure, Mary. An interaction with the program might run as follows. (The listing of the JOHN AND MARY program, in a relatively skeletal form, is in Chapter 5.7.)

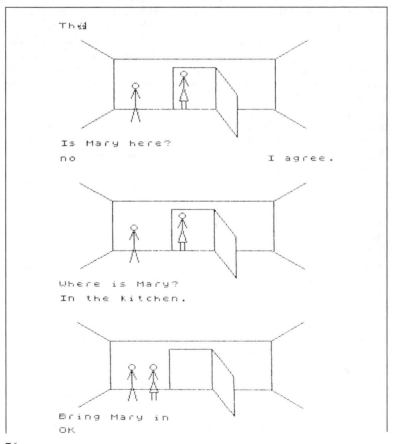

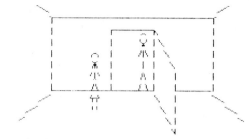

send John out

OK

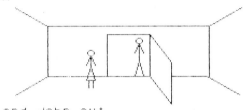

send John out
OK

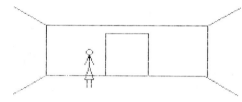

shut the door
OK

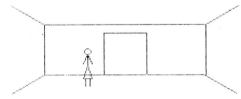

shut the door
OK

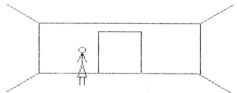

Are John and Mary together?
No.

The program shares with the exploratory programs the feature that most of the initiation is done by the student, who may well be wanting to try out a range of interactions in order to discover the program's limits, to catch it out in some way. It shares with demonstration programs like TIME the ability to present an endlessly varied set of 'true' exchanges, since an empty input (pressing ENTER before typing any letters) is always interpreted as ASK or ANSWER according to context and is obeyed. Thus, by repeatedly pressing the one key, the user can watch the machine holding a kind of conversation with itself. The discourse structure is rather limited, since each question and answer or command and acknowledgement pair is self-contained, but one cohesion marker has been built in: the noun subject is stored, so that the appropriate pronoun match can be made. It is a feature of the program that there is no scoring routine of any kind. Students can 'test' themselves by answering the computer's questions and seeing if their answers match, but the essence of GRAMMARLAND is that it is a 'place to be visited', perhaps on several occasions, not a structured activity.

TENSELAND

Another version of the program which is under development is called TENSELAND, and this one uses as its 'universe' a set of captioned drawings of named people whose jobs are specified but who are doing things unrelated to their work. The central grammatical distinction here is between simple and continuous aspects, 'She plays tennis' and 'She is playing the guitar' (both true of the tennis champion). The values for these statements or the corresponding answers are derived from a truth table, but the truth table admits other values than true or false, also accommodating *perhaps* (to answer 'Does the taxi-driver play tennis?') and *probably* (to answer 'Does the tennis champion own a TV?', for instance). It is worth pointing out how rare it is for a learner in a conventional language course to have the chance to give the answer 'I don't know' as the correct answer rather than as an admission of failure. In programs of this kind, 'I don't know' is often correct.

Types of interaction

In the programs written so far, the only interactions possible are:

1 **Student commands**/*Machine obeys and acknowledges*
2 **Student commands**/*Machine reports why command cannot be obeyed*
3 **Student enquires**/*Machine answers*
4 **Student enquires**/*Machine fails to understand*
5 **Machine asks**/*Student answers and machine agrees*
6 **Machine asks**/*Student answers and machine disagrees*
7 **Machine asks**/*Machine answers*

78

A further elaboration would be to provide the machine with a learning facility, so that it could be told new facts about its environment. Where the facts were consistent with the world knowledge that the machine has, they would be accepted. Suppose, for example, that we give the JOHN AND MARY program a database which classifies everything into *persons* which can move and *objects* which cannot. We might have an interaction on the following lines:

There is a table in the lounge.

IS A TABLE A PERSON?

No.

IS A TABLE AN OBJECT?

Yes.

OK. THERE IS A TABLE IN THE LOUNGE.

Put the table in the kitchen.

THE TABLE CANNOT MOVE.

Make John take the table into the kitchen.

I DON'T UNDERSTAND "TAKE THE TABLE INTO THE KITCHEN".

Make John put the table in the kitchen.

OK.

(Screen display changes).

What one can do within the memory confines of a small micro is limited, but any ability to manipulate and elaborate the miniature world of GRAMMARLAND should increase its value as an environment for learning through interaction.

Subject matter

There is room for a great diversity of subject matter in GRAMMAR-LAND: rainfall statistics to provide a focus for comparatives, the shelves of a shop to practise quantity and request formulae, a table of dates for work with the past tense, to name but a few ideas. One hopes, too, to be able to elaborate the forms of discourse into something more coherent than the two-part exchange. Ideally each GRAMMARLAND should contain a good deal more than just a single grammatical contrast. There has to be enough to encourage return visits, to allow for a range of abilities, and to permit flexible use. A library of GRAMMARLANDS can never replace an obliging native-speaker informant always on hand, but they can be at least a second best.

3.10 Having fun

It is possible to write a very simple program (one which fits the unexpanded ZX81) to play the game of TWENTY QUESTIONS. A session of play might go as follows:

```
     I AM THINKING OF AN OBJECT.   TRY TO GUESS IT.
     REMEMBER I CAN ONLY ANSWER YES OR NO.
     YOU HAVE 20 QUESTIONS LEFT.

     Does it fly?

     NO.   YOU HAVE 19 QUESTIONS LEFT.

     Can you eat it?

     YES.   YOU HAVE 18 QUESTIONS LEFT.

     Does it grow on a tree?

     YES.   YOU HAVE 17 QUESTIONS LEFT.

     Is it an apple?

     NO.   YOU HAVE 16 QUESTIONS LEFT.

     Does it grow in England?

     NO.   YOU HAVE 15 QUESTIONS LEFT.

     Is it a banana?

     NO.   YOU HAVE 14 QUESTIONS LEFT.

     Is it a pineapple?

     WELL DONE.   YOU GUESSED IT IN 7 QUESTIONS.
```

First-time users of the program are always highly impressed at the machine's 'vocabulary' and 'intelligence', until they realise, as they must eventually, that all the machine is doing is issuing 'Yes' and 'No' answers at random. The 'intelligence', i.e. the collection of information and narrowing of the guesses, is entirely supplied by the user. Whenever the machine selects YES, it will first scan the input to see if it has the form 'Is it a ...' or 'Is it an ...', so that it can finish the round if so, but that is the only form of input-parsing that it does.

Insulting the machine

As soon as one has cracked the program's secret, one's immediate instinct is to give it inconsequential input in order to 'get one's own back'.

```
YOU HAVE 20 QUESTIONS LEFT.
Does Mrs Thatcher have one?
YES.   YOU HAVE 19 QUESTIONS LEFT.
Are you stupid?
YES.   YOU HAVE 18 QUESTIONS LEFT.
Have you ever seen a whale?
NO.   YOU HAVE 17 QUESTIONS LEFT.
You don't understand a word, do you?
YES.   YOU HAVE 16 QUESTIONS LEFT.   and so on.
```

The impulse to insult the machine and to make it look stupid is very powerful, and the machine serves it by being basically stupid, by treating sensible and senseless input in the same fashion. One sees this particularly if a program prompts the user to type in his or her name. The world seems to divide into sheep who obediently enter their real names, and goats who miss no opportunity to call themselves 'Sherlock Holmes' or 'Raquel Welch' or 'Kiss-me-quick', but many of the sheep turn into goats with experience. Some programmers obviously find this worrying. We have heard of a mainframe bank of CAL materials which incorporates a special dictionary of common swearwords and obscenities, so that, whenever a student types in one of them, the supervisor can be alerted to come over and administer a rebuke. The effect of this has, however, been the opposite of what was intended. Students enthusiastically try out a range of rude words to try to make the buzzer sound: 'Let's see if it knows this one'.

The BOOH factor

Muriel Higgins has christened this instinct to use playful or insulting input the BOOH factor, and believes that it can be exploited in language learning. The name is an acronym for 'Bat Out Of Hell', which is how at least one user responded to the prompt 'Please tell me the animal you are thinking of' in the program ANIMALS.

ANIMALS itself is a rather BOOH program, similar in some ways to the TWENTY QUESTIONS program, but with a more serious educational purpose. In it the computer offers to guess an animal that the human user is thinking of, and asks a yes/no question, say 'Does it live on a farm?' Its first attempt at an answer is bound to be 'Cow' if the answer is 'Yes', or 'Elephant' if the answer is 'No'. In nearly every case this

81

answer is going to be wrong. The interesting part now begins. The computer prompts with 'Please tell me your animal' and the user types in the animal, for example 'crocodile'. Next, the computer asks 'Please give me a question to distinguish an elephant from a crocodile'. On subsequent runs it will incorporate what it has 'learned' and will offer a longer series of questions and a greater variety of guesses. The user's fascination comes from watching the machine apparently learning, and there is useful language practice in answering the prompt: 'Now give me a question to distinguish a crocodile from an elephant', since the students have to form questions and think how to express distinctions. The subject matter does not have to be restricted to animals. An elaboration of the original ANIMALS which we call JACKASS allows the user to choose between four topics: Animals, Objects, Cities and People. This version incorporates a report phase in which the machine puts the information it has learned into a piece of connected prose.

MADLIB and INVENT A MONSTER

BOOH phases can be incorporated into drill-and-practice programs, and Muriel Higgins illustrates this with a sequence of exercises practising the items *all*, *both*, *none* and *neither*. A demonstration phase leads into true/false and gap filling exercises which are scored. These are followed by freer forms of exercise, in which there is a recommended answer but other answers are possible, and a final phase in which the machine issues prompts of the form 'How is an apple like a mountain?' and the learner can respond, using the target grammatical pattern, we hope, in any way he or she pleases, for example 'Neither of them speak French'.

A purely BOOH activity is one which derives from the party game of Consequences, which was first suggested as a computer language practice activity by David Ahl under the name MADLIB. The user is invited to contribute words of particular grammatical classes, which are then incorporated into a story framework with grotesque effect.

A similar activity is exemplified by Muriel Higgins's INVENT A MONSTER, in which the user has to answer a succession of questions about an imagined creature. 'Size?', 'How many legs?', 'Eats ...?' etc. All this information is then combined into a screen layout which describes the 'monster'. This makes an excellent group activity, since one of the motivations one is exploiting is the instinct to show off. Having created a monster, the user needs an audience to admire it. (See also Chapter 5.3.)

```
        THE BLEEPER

A Bleeper is a minute white
creature with no legs which
lives in a dashboard.    Its
favourite food is burglars but
it also eats small boys.    When
it eats it sounds like a buzzer.
It sleeps in a garage, and when
it sleeps it looks like a geiger
counter.

Have YOU ever seen a Bleeper?
```

```
        THE HUGGERMUGGER

A Huggermugger is a long striped
creature with a thousand legs
which lives in a swamp.    Its
favourite food is piglets but it
also eats nuts.    When it eats
it sounds like a carpet being
dragged along a corridor.    It
sleeps in a coil, and when it
sleeps it looks like a nuclear
reactor.

Have YOU ever seen
a Huggermugger?
```

3.11 The computer as a mechanical aid

Word processing

Word processors are often thought of as devices to automate office work, to save the secretary from the drudgery of typing hundreds of similar letters. They have turned out to be rather more than this. They make on-screen editing so easy that they encourage the user to try out the effect of changing or adding words, changing the order of sentences or even paragraphs, and playing around with the aesthetic effect of different layouts. As a result, they seem to be affecting the quality as well as the quantity of what is written on them. Already there have been some experiments using them to teach composition skills to native speakers, one result being a change of attitude among learners who may previously have hated the writing class. The pleasure of seeing instant 'clean copy' of one's corrected text or second thoughts has created a powerful new motivation to write.

Word processing in composition teaching

If native speakers can benefit from this, so too can the foreign learner. Learners' attitudes to writing tasks are likely to be affected

83

by their difficulties with the writing system, obviously great if they have had to transfer from a different script, and by their educational experience with writing. It is still fairly rare for learners to be trained in the skill of re-drafting, or even to realise that it is relevant to what they do. If the teacher collects the written work and corrects all the errors, then it is the teacher who develops proof-reading skills while the students do not. Some teachers demand that students make a fair copy, but more often they only demand this of those below a certain standard, and the students so singled out perceive this as punishment. Implicitly the students are being trained to submit their first effort as the final version, and to take no responsibility for identifying and correcting their own errors. Those who do make some effort to edit and correct their own work often lack the time or the stamina to prepare a fair copy, and submit an ugly-looking page. If the teacher criticises this, he or she may be killing an instinct that should be encouraged.

Foreign language learners can benefit from the facilities a word processor provides, namely re-forming the text to accommodate any insertions, deletions or re-orderings, so that they always see the text in the form in which it will be printed. But this by itself will not teach them to write better. What one can do, though, is provide other kinds of aids which will gradually be withdrawn as the student gains proficiency.

Anthony Crispin has written an attractive LETTER-WRITER program for learners of German, which prompts students with questions about themselves and then inserts the information into a model composition, a letter to a penfriend. A similar program has been developed by Johannes Schumann for the Goethe Institut in Munich. The technique is very much the same as that of MADLIB, described in Chapter 3.10, but the output is designed as a model for a real-life activity rather than as amusement. The help could be progressively withdrawn, leaving the students to create more of the body of the text, until eventually they are left with a plain word processor, a mechanical rather than a cognitive aid. One can imagine similar programs focusing on other writing tasks, such as business letters or scientific reports.

VIDEO-VIEW

One of the pieces of advice that Bright and McGregor give in the chapter on writing from '*Teaching English as a Second Language*' is that all written work should be published. By this they do not only mean published in the school magazine or class newsletter, but displayed on a notice board, so that the writer always knows that the work will have an audience, and he or she is not writing just to have the work corrected and handed back. Many teachers do maintain some kind of wall newspaper or open file of written work, and have their students collaborate on writing projects so that their collected work covers a subject coherently.

84

The computer opens up some new possibilities for this form of work. For instance, a commercial program called VIDEO-VIEW allows the user to design a set of pages to create a personal bank of information presented in the style of such public access systems as TELETEXT. The program was intended in the first place for shopkeepers, who could fill the pages with advertising and special offers, and have them displayed in rotating style in their shop-windows, or else leave the computer accessible on a counter so that customers could browse through the pages or look up price lists. One could use this for a class composition activity by, for example, asking the students to design an information system for new pupils or visitors to the school. The pages might contain plans of the premises, a history of the school, names of staff, the school calendar, fixture lists for sports teams, local bus services, or anything else thought relevant. Information could be altered or updated very easily, and the class would feel genuine satisfaction whenever their system was put to practical use.

Databases

Yet another way in which the learner can make use of a computer is to retrieve the very same data that teachers and textbook writers draw on in order to create reference works and teaching material. In Chapter 4.1 we shall be looking at ways in which using a computer concordance can sharpen up the language perceptions of the teacher. At different levels the learner may be able to use authentic databases. This, of course, demands access to a mainframe computer, but it is increasingly likely that such access will spread to microcomputer users via such systems as PRESTEL GATEWAY. Until it does so there are other possibilities. If the school owns a word processing package, there will probably be long texts stored on disc, perhaps information handouts or teaching material. A student, rather than be given constructed examples of, say, *if*-clauses, can be asked to use the FIND command in the word processor in order to locate all the occurrences of the word *if* in a piece of text, and to try to state a rule which will account for the way the word is used.

Another use of databases might be simply to set information searches, so that students have to use their reading and classification skills in order to track down facts. Many television sets in Britain are now able to receive Teletext, the BBC and ITV public information services which transmit several hundred pages of information throughout the day. Students might be asked to find out the weather in Vienna or the price of tomatoes. To succeed they will have to read several directory pages and guess which general heading their information falls under, a skill which is just as useful in using a library catalogue as it is for computers.

3.12 Computers and the syllabus

In the heyday of the language laboratory, materials usually came in comprehensive packages, covering the whole syllabus of the course-book they accompanied, with advice on how much time to spend and how to relate laboratory work to classwork. Similar packages have been assembled for computers, and no doubt there will be many more, since they are strong selling points for the machines.

The place of CALL

In the preceding chapters we have not attempted to propose a 'CALL syllabus' or offer any kind of integrated package (often referred to as computer courseware). This is partly because the only use of computers in language teaching so far has been drill-and-practice treatments of grammatical contrasts and lexical inventories. We do not yet know whether the computer is a suitable supplement or aid to the vast bulk of the work done in classrooms or by learners on their own. We do not know whether all students should be urged to spend time on CALL activities, or whether it should remain as it largely is now, an occasional and mainly voluntary activity. We do not know whether CALL has equal value for students at all levels, or whether it favours one particular level. Until there is more material available and more experience within the language teaching profession, these questions cannot be answered with certainty.

CALL as a resource

Leaving that aside, it can be argued that packages, with their assumptions about the order in which tasks are to be undertaken and the time which should be spent, are taking decisions that should be made by the teacher and the student, particularly by the student. There needs to be bulk and variety, or else one arouses an appetite one cannot satisfy, but CALL programs should perhaps be treated as resources, like books in a library, rather than as elements of the curriculum. Like books, they can be worked through intensively or dipped into occasionally; used to introduce a topic or to follow it up; prescribed centrally or selected individually; approached with a serious learning purpose or indulged in for recreation with any learning being incidental to fun. Another characteristic they share with books is that they can provide shared experience which then becomes the fodder of discussion. In view of all this, we can offer no easy recommendation that there should be, say, half an hour of

CALL activity once a week to follow up the main grammar point introduced. Our only recommendation is to experiment with as many different modes of use and kinds of material as possible, and not to generalise too readily from what may be an untypical first experience with a particular kind of program. Valuable programs may fail because they are unfamiliar, just as meretricious ones may succeed in the short term thanks to the glamour of the machinery.

4 The computer outside the classroom

4.1 Computers and linguistic research

In the early part of the twentieth century, the Swiss linguist Ferdinand de Saussure drew a distinction between **parole** – the individual acts of speaking and writing by the members of a particular speech community – and **langue** – the underlying abstract scheme of connections that makes those individual acts of speaking and writing possible. More recently the American linguist Noam Chomsky re-defined de Saussure's distinction in terms of language **performance** and language **competence**. In both cases the dichotomy was put forward as a means of defining what the proper subject of linguistics should be (**langue/competence**), in contrast with the 'unmanageable' or 'irrelevant' evidence of **parole/performance**. More recently there has been renewed interest in **parole/performance** and in the data of actual language use. In the present context, the distinction between these two pairs of terms points to two alternative uses of the computer for research into language: data-based (or 'corpus-based') research dealing with language acts which have already occurred (**parole**); and artificial intelligence research, dealing with language acts which are potential, and with the underlying system (**langue**).

Data-based research

Here the computer is used as a means of storing, analysing and documenting data on a particular language or on a range of languages. This may be done as an end in itself or as a way of answering questions raised in other disciplines, ranging from interpretations of the Bible to the origin of plant species. The advantage of the computer is its ability to process large amounts of data rapidly and accurately: this in turn makes it possible to examine language data from a number of different points of view, and to investigate questions which could not feasibly be answered if the analysis was carried out manually.

Vocabulary

In examining vocabulary, those questions would include the following:

1 **What are the words that occur in a text or a corpus of texts?**
   Using the computer we can produce a word list of every word that occurs at least once in the corpus.

2 **How often does each word occur?**
The computer gives information on frequency, which can be presented in whatever format is most convenient: for example from most to least frequent.

3 **In how many of the different texts in the corpus does each of the different words occur?**
This will specify the range of each of the different words in the list: how far is a word in general usage, or restricted to a particular subject area (for example, science) or mode (for example, journalism) or medium (for example, spoken rather than written English).

4 **How many of the total number of words occurring in the corpus are accounted for by a particular subset of the word list?**
Or – asking the question another way – what subset of the word list is necessary to account for, say, 90 per cent of the corpus?
The answer to such questions will indicate the cover of a subset.

5 **What words tend to occur in the environment of a word?**
This will show what the collocations of a word are. Collocations may be interpreted in terms of a semantic field (for example three senses of the words *king* and *queen* would be shown up by their association with respectively *prince* and *duke*, *rook* and *pawn*, or *ace* and *jack*), or in terms of colligation – that is to say lexical or syntactic linking of words (so that *king* would be found as the object of, respectively, the verbs *crown*, *move* or *trump* in its three senses).

6 **What are the contexts in which a particular word occurs?**
This information is presented in the form of a concordance of the word, with the word centrally printed and the context (for example ten words or fifty characters) printed to the left and right of it.

The availability of such information is likely to increase greatly in the next few years. The problem of recovery of the information has largely been solved by the development of such text-processing packages as SNOBOL, CLOC (University of Birmingham), OCP (Oxford University), CASETEXT (University of London) and LEXSTAT (Jiaodung University, Shanghai).

The problem of entering large quantities of data has, for written material, been solved by the development of optical readers which can scan printed or typewritten text and automatically convert it to computer readable form. And access to data and to the means for analysing it – hitherto the preserve of universities and other research organisations – is likely to be made a great deal easier through the networking of data banks and text analysis packages, via telephone links or even communications satellites.

Applications

The potential value of this information in the teaching of languages should be apparent. At the level of syllabus planning and materials preparation, it gives the basis for the definition of core vocabularies for teaching purposes (combining information from questions 2 and 3); the evaluation of the lexical difficulty of a potential text (using information from question 4); tracing the first introduction and repetition of vocabulary in a sequence of teaching texts (comparing information from question 1 on different texts); deciding on the vocabulary to be taught in relation to a particular semantic field and on significant colligation (information from question 5).

Work on these lines is already in progress, ranging from the statistical investigation of large corpuses for the purpose of writing bilingual and monolingual dictionaries, to the establishment of a core vocabulary for the teaching of technical and scientific English in the People's Republic of China.

Dangers

There are dangers in the possibility of far stricter control over the systematic grading and presentation of language. While strict control can have a beneficial effect in the early stages of language learning by reducing the learning load on the student, it can have a debilitating effect if it is continued too long, since an important motivating factor in learning a language is the desire to tackle as early as possible unmodified, authentic texts in that language. If strict grading is continued too long, we may be depriving the student of opportunities to develop those strategies for puzzling out language – for guessing what is not known and for skipping what can be avoided – that are associated with successful language learning. In other words, re-search using computers gives us evidence that can be used in language teaching; whether that evidence ought to be used is a different matter.

Teacher access

If the problem of access can be overcome, the results of linguistic research could be used in two rather different ways from those outlined above. In the first place, it would be a resource which would help practising teachers to gain new perceptions and insights. Teachers can all too easily lose sight of the living reality of the language they teach; the stereotyped patterns of the textbook can become an end in themselves and the prescriptions of the textbook acquire the force of absolute truth. When the teacher is a native speaker, the danger may be even greater, since intuitions and ill-founded generalisations may be elevated to the same status. 'It's my language, so of course I know how it works.' The computer gives practising teachers the opportunity to do simple on-line research into how the language actually operates in the real world.

RMOUS WOULD'T IT . THE BACKING NET WOULD BE ABSOLUTE.Y ENORMOUS AND WOULD BE JUST ERM LIKE A
en to the first variation there, you see an absolutely equal partnership between both of us.
m, money, but also in terms of leave. It is absolutely essential for serious research purposes
((MB)) Yes, I mean the musical comparison is absolutely essential to this book, isn't it. I am
so my personal judgement is that it will be absolutely essential to meet the energy needs of t
it's like saying 'Here are chips, chips with absolutely everything ...and (er) he does need so
he brochure because were we to put in there absolutely everything that one might wish to cons
e're just going round, talking endlessly to absolutely everybody you can think of ard then at
a lot of people are going to find that in absolutely execrable taste. It was Mel Brooks of C
THAT MILE DOWN TO THE GARDENS I USED TO FEEL ABSOLUTELY EXHAUSTED I WAS JUST YES DRAGGING MY FE
we read, on tour in the United States. It's absolutely extraordinary to think that Mick Jagger
PPOPOTAMUS GODDESS MMMM IS THAT GOLD YES YES ABSOLUTELY FABULOUS WHERE DID THE GOLD COME FROM I
ces..people will apply, and the quality is absolutely fabulous. I tend to believe there is a
rted by a historical process. ((SW)) That's absolutely fair and (YES) (MM)) And we're asking
mer's adaption enormously. I thought it was absolutely faithful to the intention of the origi
out to be a lecture on illiteracy, which was absolutely fascinating but not quite what I expect
to say, but occasionally they come out with absolutely fascinating snippets of information. Wh
ngs to listen to in radio drama. I found it absolutely fascinating piece of work. And there ar
the unfinished I, CLAUDIUS. ((DP)) That's an absolutely fascinating. I did smile. and the ver
ed that. I found the early theatre chapters absolutely fascinating, when he was an ASM and one
uters under some circumstances. ((I)) Sounds absolutely fascinating. I suppose one advantage o
acting with patients. ((I)) Well that sounds absolutely fascinating. I believe there's one oth
ely and asked a number of questions and was absolutely fascinated and intrigued by the various
publishers and writers and if they write an absolutely filthy evaluation. they're going to be
AND SHE TOLD ME THE OTHER DAY YOUR FLAT WAS ABSOLUTELY FILTHY AND I HAD JUST FINISHED CLEANI
House of Commons. And they are most of them, absolutely first class. And we treat them with co
y of Vincennes and there it was for a while absolutely forbidden to think that some books were
ntil really I went to theatre, which was an absolutely fortuitous event. and I had this rather
the things - one of the things which I find absolutely frightening is Judith Hart's reply to
NG ROUND A TABLE HERE EATING AND IT WAS JUST ABSOLUTELY FULL OF INSANE LAUGHTER I MEAN IF IT WAS A
children about what you've just said? ((H)) Absolutely (G) That that is how you will approac
h as Ragtime. And Liza, the heroine, is also absolutely genuine creation. And the way you go th
AND THAT SORT OF THING. MMMM LOOK AT THAT DOG ABSOLUTELY GORGEOUS HEAD OF A FUNERAL COUCH IN THE
EEN IT NO DAVID GAVE ME FOR CHRISTMAS OH ITS ABSOLUTELY GORGEOUS AND MOST BEAUTIFULLY PRODUCED
SUICIDE GOSH IT DOES LOOK A LOVELY BOOK ITS ABSOLUTELY GORGEOUS THE MOST LOVELY ILLUSTRATIONS
E THIS IS MAGNIFICENT THE MOST LOVELY THINGS ABSOLUTELY GORGEOUS I SAW THE CONTENTS OF THIS TOM

An example

Computer-generated concordances are especially likely to provide useful insights. For example, one of the authors recently found his students having difficulty with adjective intensifiers in English – those awkward words such as *very*, *quite*, *highly*, *entirely*, *completely* and *absolutely*. They are awkward because it is difficult to pin down their precise meanings and the way in which those meanings interact with the meanings of the adjectives they occur with. In some contexts the use of an intensifier seems obligatory, while in other very similar ones it seems redundant. They seem to be unstable: words like *frightfully* and *awfully* pass in and out of use, and, even when in fashion, carry clear social overtones. We are fortunate enough to have access to a computer-generated concordance based on one and a half million words of spoken English. Part of the data for *absolutely* is shown here (page 91) in order to give the reader a flavour of a computer-generated concordance.

The author was glad to find that the data confirmed a number of his intuitions, for example that 'non-polar' adjectives such as *nice*, *difficult* and *interesting*, which occur frequently with intensifiers such as *very*, do not occur at all with intensifiers such as *absolutely* and *completely*; that, vice versa, those intensifiers are frequently found with 'polar' adjectives such as *vital*, *certain* and *right*, which are hardly ever intensified with *very*; and that there are a number of common adjectives such as *different* which seem to represent an overlap of the polar and non-polar sets. The concordance also revealed certain things he had overlooked – for example the very common use of *absolutely* as an intensifier of the negatives *no* ('There is absolutely no doubt . . .') and *nothing*; and certain things of which he had been unaware. In his own usage he accepted *absolutely* with adjectives which indicate a negative evaluation ('absolutely terrible') as readily as those which have a positive evaluation ('absolutely marvellous'). The concordance, however, showed that the tendency of the speakers in the corpus was overwhelmingly to use *absolutely* with adjectives indicating positive evaluation. The following table shows all collocations with a frequency of two or more:

right	11	brilliant	3
marvellous	7	crucial	2
sure	7	necessary	2
vital	7	specific	2
certain	5	splendid	2
clear	4	true	2
wonderful	4		

Unanswered questions

Two points need to be made about the possibility of simple on-line research like this. Firstly, it is necessarily not as secure in its conclusions as long-term investigation in depth. Our small investigation of *absolutely* raises several unanswered questions. Does the preponderance of favourable adjectives with *absolutely* reflect, in whole or in part, a preponderance of such adjectives in the corpus as a whole? Or – a subtler and more interesting question – does it reflect a general tendency of such adjectives to be accompanied by intensifiers? Other questions remain at best half-answered. Is the use of such intensifiers an indicator of social class in the United Kingdom? It may be significant that these fascinating snatches of overheard conversation seem to reflect a degree of class bias, but the objective evidence as to the social status or profession of the participants which might confirm this is missing. These shortcomings are not necessarily disadvantages. One of the most powerful assets of the concordance might be its suggestiveness and its way of opening up questions that might not otherwise be asked at all.

The second point is that there are many ways in which such material could influence or be incorporated into language teaching practice. In some cases, what is discovered from research could be incorporated into materials by way of explanations and generalisations. In the present case the author checked the examples in his handouts in order to make certain that they conformed to the authentic usage revealed in the concordance. Another and more interesting idea would be to incorporate sections of concordance directly into teaching materials: if examples of authentic usage, analysed and tabulated in this way, can be so powerful a way of connecting the teacher with the reality of language, could it not, as we suggested in Chapter 3.11, have even more value to the learner?

Syntax
So far we have concentrated on lexically-based research, which reflects a general emphasis in data-based research to date. Syntactic research presents more difficulties, since the syntax of natural language is not so accessible for the sort of mechanical examination used for lexis. If we are interested, for example, in the distribution of the articles in English, we can readily identify the presence of the definite article in: *There are many problems in* the *chemical industry* but we cannot, unless the sentence is already decomposed into its syntactic constituents, readily identify the equally significant absence of the article in: *There are many problems in British industry.*

There are three approaches to the analysis of syntactic data. The first is indirect – to use the tools provided by collocation and concordance programs already described to assist in examining the contexts in which words, in this case the word *industry*, appear. Secondly, data can be manually 'tagged' with syntactic markers as it is inserted – clearly a lengthy business. The third method foreshadows the next chapter, namely the automatic tagging of text through the use of a computer parser, leaving only those parts of the data that the machine is unable to process to be tagged manually. Considerable advances have been made in recent years with automatic parsing, with over 90 per cent of text being correctly parsed by the more advanced programs. Eventually we can hope that the benefits of this work will be felt both directly and indirectly in language teaching.

4.2 Artificial intelligence and language

We have already had occasion to describe two pieces of artificial intelligence research, Weizenbaum's ELIZA (see Chapter 3.9) and Winograd's SHRDLU (Chapter 3.6). These are the best known but by no means the only significant contributions to the attempt to model language competence and knowledge structures on machines.

Research into language competence focuses on the question of how knowledge is organised in the mind in order to produce and interpret linguistic messages.

The value of the computer in investigating this question is its initial total stupidity: before it can perform any task it is necessary to give it totally explicit and unambiguous instructions. If we can model linguistic behaviour plausibly and economically on a machine, then we can expect the nature and structuring of those instructions to throw light on what human beings do when they produce and understand language. The machine, thus, can give us a test bed for validating one model of language against another.

The theory behind the use of artificial intelligence (AI) techniques itself raises a number of unresolved issues, most notably how far the inherent architecture of the hardware is comparable – does the brain in fact function like a vastly more complex but in some ways less efficient microchip? For our purposes, two points should be noted about the relationship between work in AI and language learning:

1 There are large numbers of practical spin-offs from the work, many of which are of immediate relevance to language teaching and language learning, ranging from 'expert systems' which will answer questions on specialised topics such as the design of electrical circuits or airline timetables, to systems which offer to check and correct the grammar of text (such as IBM's EPISTLE). In our own work, described in Chapters 3.8 and 3.9, we have attempted to apply simple artificial intelligence techniques to various types of computer-assisted learning materials. The development of CAL (not only for language learning) in years to come will, we believe, require the application of more sophisticated techniques, as CAL moves away from the pattern of a pre-established tutorial dialogue, towards an 'intelligent' interaction between learner and machine.

2   The concerns of theoretical work in AI can be expected to throw light on questions of general interest in language teaching: in particular on the relationship between language form and language function, and, within language function, on the relationship between language meaning (semantics) and language use (pragmatics).

The influence of work in AI can already be felt, for example in the application of Minsky and Fillmore's theories of frame semantics to the classroom analysis of texts for developing reading skills.

Machine translation

Some of the very earliest AI projects, going back to the early fifties, had the objective of developing translation programs which would automate the process of scanning technical journals published in foreign languages. This turned out to be vastly more difficult than the first researchers had assumed, and their programs produced some comic mistranslations. In fact, the failure had a stimulating effect on the discipline of modern linguistics, many of whose insights relate to some of that experimental work.

We are still some way from a machine which will produce polished translations of any kind of text, but commercial programs exist, notably the Weidner program, which will produce 'first draft' rather than 'fair copy'. This, they claim, can increase the output of a professional translator up to tenfold, but it still requires a human being with some knowledge of the source language and excellent knowledge of the target language to undertake the editing and polishing. At a far more primitive level, we have recently begun to see hand-held translating machines which offer an electronic equivalent of a pocket dictionary or phrase book. Most of them store vocabularies of up to 2000 common words and a set of twenty or so 'frame' sentences into which the vocabulary can be inserted, such as 'Can you tell me the way to xxx?' or 'How much does xxx cost?' The performance of these machines has been disappointing. You cannot type in your question in English, press the French button, hand the machine over to a Frenchman to type in his answer and then see it translated, since the actual sequence of button pushes is too complex to permit this. The sentences generated are often situationally inappropriate, and none of the machines we have seen can cope even with gender or singular/plural concord, let alone with clause-level grammar. As language learning aids they are woefully inadequate, but a machine of this kind might provide a teacher with an interesting peg on which to hang a discussion of grammar, asking the students to spot the machine's howlers and account for them. Used this way, they are a counterpart to the kind of 'exploratory program' described in Chapter 3.8.

4.3 Storing teaching materials

Any computer which has a printer and the appropriate software can be used for word processing. The word processing program combines a screen editor with a set of printer-control commands. It allows you to set up a format (margin settings and, if a choice is available, print faces), to type in text which is displayed on the screen, to edit that text, either immediately or perhaps months later, by moving the cursor to the relevant part of the screen and then making deletions or insertions, and then to save the text on disc or tape. Nearly all word processors provide facilities like automatic word wrap (making sure that words are not broken at the end of a line) and automatic re-formatting of a paragraph after changes have been made. On most of them you can also justify the right hand margin, so that your text appears squared off like a printed page, but we do not recommend you to use this, since, without proportional print spacing, it may reduce legibility. Many word processors also provide such facilities as 'find and replace' all occurrences of one word with another. Once the text has been edited to the writer's satisfaction, it can be printed out, many times over if necessary (though this would be a very slow way of making multiple copies).

The advantages of using word processing in the preparation of teaching handouts are threefold:

1 Storage and Recovery   Any teacher who has prepared much in the way of his or her own teaching material will have experienced the frustration of storing copies so that they can be found at a later date; all too soon every spare corner is taken up with filing cabinets, the contents of which never exactly reflect the filing system. Storing teaching materials on floppy discs which can be printed out as required takes up much less space. To give an idea, the typescript of this book was produced with the WORDSTAR package and occupied four double-sided discs. Each disc is slightly smaller than a 45 rpm record.

2 Composition   The process of writing using a word processor is quite different from more traditional methods. Those involve drafting rough notes and then, through drafting, re-writing and scissors-and-paste editing, getting to the point at which a final version is ready to be typed up. The procedure is discontinuous and wasteful, and the temptation to cut corners is always present. With the word processor, on the other hand, the first draft can be typed in then worked over, polished and re-ordered as a continuous process until it reaches the point at which it is ready to be printed out.

3 Adaptation   The greatest advantage of the word processor in preparing teaching materials is that no version need ever be thought of as 'final': the continuous process of revision and adaptation begun with the first draft can continue in the light of second thoughts on the part of the teacher and reactions from students. There is an inevitable tendency to re-use old materials because the time and expense required to re-type an old handout hardly seems worth while, especially where only a few changes are needed. We could go further and envisage a new style of materials explicitly designed for experimentation and adaptation. This could be important in the teaching of languages for specific purposes, where each group has its own particular needs but where the time needed for the production of a completely new set of materials may be prohibitive. For this situation 'skeleton materials' could be prepared which, by the insertion of different texts and different examples, would be fleshed out for a group of accountants, say, on one occasion and a group of traffic engineers on another.

4.4 Computers and language testing

A test may serve one or more of three separate interests: society's, so that scarce educational places or responsible jobs may be allocated to the worthiest candidates; the teacher's, so that he or she can check whether teaching has been effective; and the students', so that they can measure their own progress.

For the first, and to some extent the second, security is important, since 'leaked' questions can badly distort the results. The normal way of ensuring security is to have supervised mass testing, using paper-and-pencil procedures. It is unlikely that the computer will, for the foreseeable future, replace paper and pencil as the direct medium for the student to use in a mass test. Apart from anything else, the expense of setting up a large number of machines simultaneously and the risk of a breakdown in one of them would make such use unattractive to the organisers. For the individual student the computer is, of course, an ideal medium for self-testing, providing diagnostic information that may be rough-and-ready or fairly sophisticated.

Test statistics
The computer can be of great use to the tester as a means of facilitating calculation. Any test involves assigning scores, either impression marks or objective scores, and adding these up to yield a total score for each testee. Unless there are vast numbers of candidates, this job can readily be done by hand. The next stage of calculation is usually to produce a ranked list of scores, showing who did best and worst, and to calculate a group average to show how far above or below the mean any individual is. The calculations are straightforward, and a pocket calculator is quite sufficient as an aid. However, for tests which need to be refined and developed, either

because they will be used for large numbers or because the results they give will affect important decisions, there are further calculations which are rather more tedious and demanding: reliability indices, rank correlations and significance tests, and item analysis to show how the separate parts of the test are contributing to the aggregated score. A computer can take on the calculation task, but must, of course, have all the relevant data read into it, itself a potentially tedious process.

Optical scanners

To overcome this drawback, there have for many years been systems which allow entry of data from multiple-choice tests directly into the computer. The best known of these involves the student marking with a graphite pencil on a card the 'cell' corresponding to the answer chosen. The card is then read by means of an optical scanner, and the information converted directly into digital form. In practice there are often problems. The student may not find it easy to identify and mark carefully the right cell on the card. The scanner may read random smudges or miss pencil marks which have been made too lightly. Moreover, the systems are usually expensive and are designed to be linked to expensive mainframe computers. We know of no system which is foolproof, inexpensive, and capable of being used with the sort of microcomputer currently appearing in schools.

Once the data are entered, though, the machine can carry out calculations so efficiently that it encourages us to ask questions which we might not bother to ask if the answers had to be calculated manually.

Material grading

We can use the computer not only to undertake calculations of the student's performance but also to calculate the difficulty of materials.

A teacher can usually inspect a set of questions or reading texts and grade them roughly from easiest to hardest, using as criteria the familiarity or obscurity of the lexical items and the complexity of the sentences. Item analysis of examination questions shows that these subjective gradings can sometimes be wildly wrong, as it is easy either to overlook a trap or to ignore associations which provide help. Some years ago one of the authors set a spelling test as part of an elementary examination, and included the word 'present', putting it late in the test and expecting it to cause difficulty, since it was not in the target vocabulary of the first two years of the school syllabus. It turned out to be the easiest item in the whole test, yielding fewer errors than 'girl' or 'apple'. What he had overlooked was that, in the context 'present tense', the word had been prominent in chapter headings and exercise rubrics from the beginning of the course. If such mistakes can be made with single words, they are even more likely with complex test items or with complete texts being graded for readability.

We include in Chapter 5.2 an example of an autograding procedure applied to a simple quiz, so that the machine calculates the difficulty of each question and then reorders the questions if necessary after each run. The real value of such procedures may eventually come in increasing the reliability of alternative forms of the same test. In an important test all candidates are presented with the same questions so that there is no 'unfairness' due to some candidates getting an easier set. If the computer contains a large store of questions and the records of how they have been answered by a large number of students, it may be able to generate parallel forms of a test whose results will be fully comparable. If enough questions are available, each candidate could have an individualised test paper which would be different from those of all the others, thus eliminating at least one kind of cheating and the need for mass testing.

Constraints

There are two important constraints affecting computers in testing, one legal and one psychological. Where a computer stores records of individual student performance in tests, then the institution owning the computer is subject to whatever laws may be in force regulating security and access. Educational records are no different in this respect from those of a credit agency or a hospital. In some countries it is a legal requirement that individuals must be given access to their computer records on demand. In most countries there is a requirement to maintain proper security and confidentiality, so that no unauthorised users can look at individual records.

Psychologically there can be strong hostility to the kind of computer facility which maintains and searches individual records over a period of time. Some people would hate to do a computer exercise and then get a message such as 'You scored 57 per cent. In June 1981 you did this exercise and scored 59 per cent.' Part of the appeal of the microcomputer is that it does not usually store the record of a session's work unless the user deliberately saves the current program on tape or disc. Otherwise, when the machine is switched off, the working memory is erased.

5 Programs for language teachers

5.1 Designing a program

Teachers can become involved with computers at three different levels. They may wish merely to evaluate computers and their programs as learning aids, and to make use of those programs which seem worth while, much as they might make use of a slide projector and a set of slides. At a slightly deeper level, they may wish to find out enough about the underlying technology in order to modify programs, to tailor them to local needs or embody some of their own ideas. At a third level, they may wish to master the medium sufficiently to become authors in it, to create their own programs from scratch.

This part of the book is aimed at the second and third levels. It makes no attempt to be a complete course in BASIC programming. What we try to do instead is to 'talk you through' a number of complete program listings by means of extended commentaries. We hope this will give prominence to some of the techniques that a language teacher needs to control but which are often overlooked in programming coures aimed at the general user.

Structured programming

Most people use the word **programming** to cover the whole process of creating computer programs, but think of it mainly as the process of typing in lines of computer code, either in a high-level language such as BASIC or in some other form. Experienced programmers prefer to distinguish three distinct stages: **analysis**, **design** and **coding**. There is also a fourth stage, **de-bugging**, which only arises through a failure in one of the first three, and they would regard it as a matter of some pride if a program ran perfectly first time and required no de-bugging.

In the very early days of computers, programming sometimes had to be done with a soldering iron, while de-bugging was done with a chisel. Even when this was not so, programming consisted of using punched paper tape to enter machine code – interminable sequences of ones and zeros which were quite incomprehensible to the outsider. As long as the actual coding process was so laborious (as it still is to some extent), it was clearly good sense to think the problems out thoroughly in advance, starting with the most general structure and elaborating the details later, and reducing as far as possible the effort of de-bugging. It also made sense to design the program in distinct sections, each section doing an identifiable job, so that one could track down a section with an error and not have to make changes throughout the program. These two ideas are known as the 'top-down approach' and 'modular construction', and are together referred to as 'structured programming'. They still make a great deal of sense, even though circumstances have changed. It is much easier in these days of interactive screen editors and interpreters to program by trial and error or by 'patch and mend'. In the process one learns a great deal about programming and has a chance to try out ideas. But programs which are to be used by other people or modified later by the programmer need to be properly structured and presented, and this requires planning.

Analysis

Analysis is the stage of thinking out the problem or the task. If, for instance, one of the program's operations will be to extract sentences from a continuous text, we will have to work out in advance, and explicitly, how humans identify sentences. It is no good saying to yourself, 'Anything which begins with a capital letter and ends with a full stop is a sentence'. Plenty of sentences end with question or exclamation marks. A sentence in inverted commas would neither begin with a capital letter nor end with a full stop as the computer sees it. All these cases have to be taken into account, even if we assume that all the input text is going to be punctuated normally.

The solution to a problem like this may well be a 'lateral' one. Rather than try to enumerate all the special cases, one might simply adopt a convention for text entry that every sentence is to be separated by two or more spaces, but words and weaker punctuation (commas, semi-colons and colons) are to be followed by single spaces. Now the computer merely has to search for two consecutive spaces.

Design

The design stage deals with two sets of questions, how the program does its work and how the user interacts with the program. In the first of these we work out the sequence of events that must occur as the program carries out the job we have assigned it, what is sometimes called the 'flow of control'. In the second we consider the screen layout, the way we convey instructions, the use of the keyboard and what should happen if the wrong keys are pressed, whether we are going to use sound or colour, and what style to use in screen messages.

Coding

When we reach the stage of coding, we begin to have to think very specifically about the machine we are using and the computer languages which are available on it. The programs in this book are written in the dialect of BASIC which is the standard programming language for the Spectrum. BASIC is what is known as a high-level language: the language is constructed so that it is relatively easy for the human user, but has to be translated by a program resident in the machine into the digital instructions which the micro-processor (in the case of the Spectrum, the Z80) can understand.

BASIC

Every high-level language has its advantages and disadvantages. The points in favour of BASIC are that it is widely available; it is relatively easy to learn, so that a beginner can write simple programs after only a short period; it is very flexible; and it is interactive so that programmers can try things out as they go along. When things don't work, a process of trial-and-error will usually show what has gone wrong. The dialect of BASIC used on the Sinclair machines has a particular advantage for CALL in that it offers powerful facilities for manipulating 'strings' of characters. The major disadvantages of BASIC are that, because it is so flexible, it allows a disorganised and unstructured style of programming which may make it difficult to understand or amend a program after it has been written, and it is relatively slow, especially when a large number of repetitive operations have to be carried out.

Other languages

For these reasons many people would regard languages such as PASCAL or FORTH, which require a structured approach to programming and which run faster, as more suitable for CALL. In defence of BASIC it must be said that it is possible to write BASIC programs in a relatively structured and coherent fashion. On the question of speed, it is often possible to identify one or two sections of the program which slow things down, and to rewrite them using an Assembler in the low-level language of the micro-processor. An example of such a rewrite, using a Z80 Assembler, is shown in Chapter 5.6.

Author languages

Another solution would be to make use of an even higher level language, what is known as an 'author language'. This is a language developed for a particular purpose. In education by far the best known is PILOT, a language which provides ready-made routines for matching a student's input answer with a model answer and for branching to different parts of the program according to the answer given. It is easier to learn than BASIC. It is also, inevitably, far less flexible.

Authoring systems

One can go up to an even higher level by using what are known as 'authoring systems'. These are programs which are designed to create exercises of a particular kind, but nothing else. The advantage is that the user does not need to have any programming skill. For instance, there are a number of such programs which will generate multiple choice quizzes and tests. The program gives all the instructions, and what the user does is limited to entering explanatory texts, questions, right answers, and distractors. The machine looks after screen presentation, branching and score-keeping. There are other authoring systems which will generate cloze exercises from typed-in texts. Indeed any program which makes it easy for a non-programmer to alter the textual content could be called an authoring system.

Variables

A crucial concept in programming is that of **variables**, which are, as the name suggests, values which can be altered during the run of the programs. Variables are identified by names, which can be thought of as storage locations. Whenever you ask the computer to print or otherwise make use of a variable, it retrieves whatever is currently being stored under that name.

In BASIC, variables are limited to two types, **numeric variables** where what is stored is a value, and **string variables** where what is stored is a set of characters. Obviously one can do arithmetic with numeric variables but not with string variables. The name of a variable must begin with a letter of the alphabet, and the name of a string variable must end with the dollar sign **$**; these restrictions are universal. Different dialects of BASIC have set other restrictions. In Sinclair BASIC for the Spectrum, the name of a numeric variable may be of any length. This usefully allows one to use long names to remind oneself what the variable means. A variable which holds the student's current score can be called **score** for instance. Unfortunately one cannot use long variable names for strings. Sinclair BASIC limits you to just one letter plus the dollar sign.

As part of the planning of a program, it is a good idea to list in advance all the variables which you are going to use, and to update this list if you change your mind while coding.

De-bugging

De-bugging is concerned with three different sets of problems. In the first place there are actual errors in the coding which have caused the program to 'crash', to come to a stop before finishing, perhaps displaying a 'syntax error' message. In the second there are errors in the logic or in the order of events which have caused the computer to do its job faultily, for example to label a right answer as wrong. In the third place, there are adjustments to the layout of the screen messages or to the scoring systems, improvements which arise from seeing the program in use. All three kinds of de-bugging are an inevitable part of programming for most people, and the third is probably an essential part of the process where educational programs are concerned, making creative use of feedback from users.

Documentation

Documentation can be as little as a few words scribbled on a cassette label or as much as several hundred pages in a binder. More is not automatically better than less. It all depends on the nature of the program and who it is for.

Documentation aimed at the user is the minimum needed to operate the program successfully, and in a straightforward game-like activity which has all relevant instructions given clearly on the screen, it need consist of no more than simple loading instructions. The most important element will be the program name, if that is needed as part of the loading procedure.

Documentation aimed at a teacher or supervisor should be more complete, consisting of a plain language description of the program, plus suggestions for exploitation and follow-up. A third kind of documentation is that aimed at another programmer who may need to modify the program or translate it into a different language to run on a particular machine. It is the practice of the authors to provide a sheet of suggested modifications that can be made to the program.

Another important element in documentation is a name and address to which the user can write with comments, questions and complaints. It is important for the originator of a program to know how a program is being used and what may go wrong with it. The feedback he or she gets this way can lead to improvements, perhaps in the coding or the documentation or even in the quality of tape used in the recording, any of which can be a source of trouble.

Time

We are often asked how long our programs take to write. This is often difficult to answer because the more ambitious of our programs are subject to continual trial and modification and are never 'finished' in our eyes. Also, a certain amount of the time spent developing one program can be designated as learning experience, and will lead to greater efficiency in developing other programs later.

In the case of one of our more recent programs, CLOSE-UP described in Chapter 3.6, the author logged the time spent. The first working version was created after about eight hours thinking and planning, and took four hours to key in. Since then the program has gone through several revisions. Altogether it has accounted for about twenty-five hours of work, of which thirteen were spent at the keyboard (including at least two spent on saving and verifying back-up copies of various intermediate versions and versions to be sent to colleagues). The length of time it has occupied any single student has been, on average, ninety minutes spread over several sessions. So far the users have been restricted to the twenty texts stored within the program. Once the program has been modified to read in texts from an outside source, the same students may wish to return to it.

5.2 QUIZ

There are two reasons for showing a quiz as the first program in this section of the book:

1. The quiz and its derivatives (tests, drills, exercises, programmed learning) have hitherto had a predominant role in CAL. Placing it first among our listings mirrors the historical development of the methodology. We anticipate that in future more attention will be paid to other uses of the computer. Nevertheless, quizzes and quiz-related programs will clearly continue to play a part in CAL.
2. A quiz program can illustrate a number of programming techniques which are required in less conventional forms of CAL and will, indeed, be necessary where a self-test option is provided.

The format chosen for the quiz is the familiar one of a four-way multiple-choice quiz on English prepositions. The basic form of the quiz as first presented differs from its traditional 'hard-copy' counterpart in that the multiple choices are generated on the spot by the computer, and immediate feedback is given on the student's response.

As with all the programs in this book, the listing is broken up into sections, with comments attached to each section. We suggest that readers with access to a Spectrum/TS2000 type in the program section by section, reading the comments as they do so. It is good practice to save the program after each section is typed in. This slows things down a little, but has the advantage that if the program is lost through a power failure or the computer overheating, one has only to go back to the start of the last section. Do not be too alarmed if the program does not run perfectly first time: no matter how careful one is, errors creep in as a result of mistyping. However, by the time you have typed in the program you should have a clear enough idea of its overall structure to be able to work out where a bug might have got into the program, and a careful check against the printed listing should reveal the error. After running the program a few times – and preferably letting some 'final users' try it out – you will then be in a position to decide which of the suggested alterations and extensions to the basic program you would like to try out. We hope that experimenting with the program in its various versions will also give readers ideas for further changes and improvements that we have not ourselves suggested.

As with some other programs in this book, QUIZ consists of a series of subroutines which are called in turn by the **controller** routine. Writing the program in this way makes its structure more 'transparent' and allows it to be more easily adapted or extended at a later date:

```
  10 REM Quiz1 @ Tim Johns, 1982
1983*****************************
  20 REM controller*************
*********************************
  30 GO SUB 600: REM initialise
  40 GO SUB 740: REM setupquiz
  50 GO SUB 90:   REM givequiz
  60 LET g$=INKEY$: GO TO 60-20*
(g$="Y")+10*(g$="N")
  70 STOP
```

The **initialise** subroutine sets up some constants that will be needed throughout the run of the program:

```
 590 REM initialise*************
*********************************
 600 LET number=10
 610 POKE 23658,8
 620 LET w$="
                              "
 630 DIM x$(8,4)
 640 RESTORE 650: FOR n=1 TO 8:
READ x$(n): NEXT n
 650 DATA "at","in","of","for","
to","on","with","from"
 660 PRINT AT 10,7;"Press S to s
tart"
 670 IF INKEY$<>"S" THEN  GO TO
670
 690 RANDOMIZE
 700 RETURN
```

The variable **number** contains the number of questions in the quiz. In this skeletal version there are only ten: if more are added it will be necessary to change **number** in line 600. The POKE in line 610 sets all alphabetic input to upper case in order to simplify the checking of student input. The string variable **w\$** defined in line 620 consists of thirty-two spaces to be used in selectively wiping out lines of the screen display. In lines 660–70 the two-dimensional string array **x\$** is set up and filled with the eight prepositions in the DATA statements in line 650. The resulting array can best be visualised as a numbered list: so that x\$(1) = "at" x\$(7) = "with" and so on.

1	at		3	of		5	to		7	with
2	in		4	for		6	on		8	from

An important point to notice is that string arrays in Sinclair BASIC are so dimensioned that each element in the array is of the same length

106

(here, four characters) – thus "at" is padded out with two spaces, and "for" with one space. This feature has disadvantages. As we shall see later, it may be necessary to 'strip off' the unwanted spaces. But there are also advantages, for example if we dimension each element in the array to thirty-two characters, we can use it to overprint previous text on the screen. Lines 660–70 invite the student to start the quiz. Not only is this a matter of common politeness ('I won't begin until you want me to'), but there is also a hidden technical point. We recommend that the completed program is saved with the direct command:

SAVE "QUIZ" LINE 10

when it will run automatically on being loaded. However, on autorunning the random number 'seed' set by RANDOMIZE will return the same value and the same questions will be set on each run unless a random delay (here, the length of time that elapses before the S key is pressed) is introduced.

While **initialise** sets up each run of the program, **setupquiz** carries out tasks before each presentation of the quiz.

```
730 REM setupquiz**************
*****************************
740 CLS
750 RESTORE 9000
760 LET score=0
770 RETURN
```

Line 750 re-sets the data pointer to the DATA statements from line 9000 onwards that contain the questions:

```
9000 DATA 4,"Smoking is not good
.... you."
9010 DATA 6,"We depend .... your
help."
9020 DATA 2,"I am interested ...
. computers."
9030 DATA 3,"Don't be afraid ...
. the dog."
9040 DATA 1,"Tom is very good ..
.. tennis."
9050 DATA 7,"She is angry .... h
er husband."
9060 DATA 5,"We object .... the
proposal."
9070 DATA 3,"It was kind .... yo
u to help me."
9080 DATA 8,"Apart .... Jim, we
are all here."
9090 DATA 1,"Why are you staring
.... me?"
```

It will be seen that each line contains two data statements: the index number in the **x$** array of a preposition, and a short-gapped sentence thirty-two or fewer characters in length.

The meat of the program is the **givequiz** subroutine, the major part of which is controlled by a loop set to the **number** of questions available (lines 90 and 460). The first part of the loop has the task of preparing the question:

```
 80 REM givequiz***************
***********************************
 90 FOR n=1 TO number
100 READ prep: READ q$
110 PRINT AT 6,10; INVERSE 1;"Q
uestion ";n
120 LET win=1
130 REM z$array****************
140 DIM z$(4,4)
150 LET right=1+INT (RND*4)
160 LET z$(right)=x$(prep)
170 FOR m=1 TO 4: IF z$(m)<>"
" THEN   GO TO 210
180 LET y$=x$(1+INT (RND*8))
190 FOR i=1 TO 4: IF z$(i)=y$ T
HEN   GO TO 180
200 NEXT i: LET z$(m)=y$
210 NEXT m
```

Line 100 copies into **prep** the index number of the preposition, and into **q$** the gapped sentence, while line 130 establishes the initial reward for a correct answer as one point.

The routine in lines 140–210 sets up the two-dimensional string array **z$** for the right answer and three randomly selected distractors from among the other seven prepositions. The right answer having been inserted at a random position in the array in lines 150–160, distractors are inserted in turn in the loop from lines 170 to 210: line 180 checks that the place in the array is not already occupied by the right answer, and the loop in lines 190–200 ensures that no preposition (including the correct answer) is repeated.

The question having been prepared, it is printed out by lines 230 and 240:

```
220 REM printquestion**********
230 PRINT AT 8,0;q$
240 FOR m=1 TO 4: PRINT AT 10,8
*(m-1); INVERSE 1;m; INVERSE 0;"
";z$(m);: NEXT m
```

In line 240 a loop is used to print out the choices: INVERSE 1 prints the number of the choice in white on black, while INVERSE 0 switches the printing back to black on white.

The student's reply must now be obtained and checked:

```
250 REM getanswer**************
260 PRINT AT 12,0; INVERSE 1;"P
ress the number of your choice"
270 LET g$=INKEY$: IF g$<"1" OR
 g$>"4" THEN   GO TO 270
280 LET choice=VAL g$
290 LET c$=z$(choice)
300 GO SUB 550
310 PRINT AT 12,0;w$;AT 12,5;"Y
our answer is ";CHR$ 34;c$;CHR$
34
320 IF choice=right THEN   GO TO
430
```

Notice that we do not in this program use the computer's INPUT function. Since all that the student is required to do is to press a single key, the use of INKEY$ is simpler and more efficient. In line 270 we check that a number 1 and 4 inclusive has been chosen; pressing any other key will produce no effect. A technical point for newcomers to BASIC is that it is possible to use a comparison test such as IF a$ < b$, (literally, if a$ is less than b$) on characters as well as numbers. What is tested is the code of the character (see pages 183–188 in the Spectrum manual). The numeric value of **g$** is obtained by use of the VAL function and copied into the **choice** variable in line 280. The preposition chosen by the student is then copied from the **z$** array into **c$** and passed to the **stripspaces** subroutine which removes any unwanted spaces:

```
540 REM stripspaces************
550 FOR m=4 TO 3 STEP -1
560 IF c$(m)<>" " THEN   RETURN
570 LET c$=c$( TO m-1): NEXT m
580 RETURN
```

so that the choice can be confirmed by line 310 with the student's preposition printed in inverted commas (character 34 in the Spectrum set).

The program branches at line 320 according to whether the student has chosen the correct answer. Wrong answers are dealt with in lines

109

340–410, the student being given the choice of seeing the right answer or trying again:

```
330 REM wronganswer***********
340 PRINT AT 14,8;"That is wron
g";AT 16,0;"Press S to see the r
ight answer"'"Press T if you wan
t to try again"
350 LET g$=INKEY$: GO TO 350+20
*(g$="S")+50*(g$="T")
```

Line 350 shows a technique for branching which is used frequently in the programs in this book. It capitalises on two features of Sinclair BASIC:

1 When the truth of an expression is tested, false = 0 and true = 1.
2 All expressions, including GO TO, GO SUB, and RESTORE line numbers, are evaluated by the interpreter as they are encountered.

Thus, if no key or any other key than S or T is being pressed at the point line 350 is reached, the second instruction in the line is evaluated as:

... GO TO 350 + 20*0 + 50*0   =   GO TO 350

with the effect that the program is caught in a loop until S or T is pressed. If S is pressed, the line is evaluated as:

... GO TO 350 + 20*1 + 50*0   =   GO TO 370

while if T is pressed, we get:

... GO TO 350 + 20*0 + 50*1   =   GO TO 400

Anybody converting the program to another dialect of BASIC will have to substitute for line 350 the more comprehensible but less economical

350 LET g$ = INKEY$
352 IF g$ = "S" THEN GO TO 370
354 IF g$ = "T" THEN GO TO 400
356 GO TO 350

In **seeanswer** the right answer is copied **c$** and passed to **stripspaces** so that it can be printed to the screen:

```
360 REM seeanswer**************
370 LET c$=z$(right): GO SUB 55
0
380 PRINT AT 14,3;"The right an
swer is ";CHR$ 34;c$;CHR$ 34;AT
17,0;w$: GO TO 450
```

Tryagain offers another chance:

```
390 REM tryagain**************
400 LET win=win/2
410 FOR m=14 TO 17: PRINT AT m,
0;w$: NEXT m: GO TO 260
```

In line 400 the reward for a win is halved each time the student makes a further attempt. Since the student's score is finally reported as a whole number with fractions of a point removed, this has the effect that, for example nine answers correct on first attempt and one on second attempt give 9/10, while eight correct on first attempt and two on second also gives 9/10.

Where the test at line 320 shows that the student has chosen the correct answer, control passes to **rightanswer**:

```
420 REM rightanswer***********
430 PRINT AT 14,7;"That is corr
ect"
440 LET score=score+win
450 IF n<number THEN  GO SUB 51
0
460 NEXT n
```

The score is updated in line 440, while line 450, by testing the *number* of available questions ensures that the **nextq** routine offering another question is called only when another question is, in fact, on offer:

```
500 REM nextq*****************
510 PRINT AT 16,0; INVERSE 1;"
Press Q for another question  "
520 IF INKEY$<>"Q" THEN  GO TO
520
530 FOR m=8 TO 16 STEP 2: PRINT
AT m,0;w$: NEXT m: RETURN
```

When all the questions have been answered, **endquiz** prints the student's score and passes control back to the **controller** routine:

```
470 REM endquiz***************
480 PRINT AT 16,2;"Your score i
s ";INT score;" out of ";number
490 PRINT AT 18,6;"Another go?
(Y/N)": RETURN
```

On return to the **controller** routine action is taken in line 60 on the basis of the offer already made in line 480.

Changes and extensions to the program

Data storage and quiz format

The simplest and most necessary change that can be made to the program is to add to the number of examples held in DATA statements. The 48K Spectrum could, in theory, hold over 700 questions of the type used in the quiz, so the patience of both teacher and student is likely to give out long before the memory limits of the machine are approached. It would also be easy to add to the list of prepositions, making sure that the necessary changes were made in lines 640, 650, and 180. If **x$** and **z$** were to be dimensioned to hold prepositions longer than four characters it would be necessary also to adjust the starting point of the **stripspace** loop in line 550.

A drawback of the version of the program as first presented is that there is a limit to the length of contexts that can be used. If contexts longer than thirty-two characters are required, a 'wordwrap' subroutine should be provided to prevent words being split between the end of one line and the beginning of the next (see p. 123).

The general structure of the quiz can, of course, be used to cover a very large range of other language points. Even confined to prepositions, the quiz could be made more interesting and probably more useful pedagogically by requiring the student to provide the context of the preposition rather than the preposition itself. For example, we might define a large **x$** array holding a series of nouns such as *home*, *war* etc. with the contexts held in the DATA statements being:

'In 1941 Britain and Germany were at . . . .'
'When I called Mr Brown was not at . . . .'

A number of different quizzes on related points could be stored in the same program giving the student a 'menu' to choose from (for typical 'menu subroutines' see pp. 135–136). On the basis of the student's choice we would RESTORE the data pointer to a particular block of DATA statements: **r$** would now be a three-dimensional array dimensioned by

DIM x$ (20, 10, 10),

say, for multiple choices for twenty quizzes. The student's choice would be used to specify the first dimension of the array.

One of the many extensions to the quiz format in the specimen program would be to employ a double-gapped context, the program filling one gap from the appropriate array using the method of string-building or **concatenation** shown in later programs in this book, and leaving the other to be completed by the student. Thus from the same **DATA** statement the program could construct either of the following items in a hyponomy quiz:

'When he arrived at work he found that he had left behind his

112

chisels and all his other . . . .'

1 vehicles   2 tools   3 containers   4 papers

or

'When he arrived at work he found that he had left behind his . . . . and all his other tools.'

1 sandwiches   2 bicycles   3 invoices   4 chisels

In addition, clues and remedial material could be stored in DATA statements together with the questions – the first to be offered to students before they make a response, and the second after. Since more than one question might require access to the same 'remedial frame', considerable economy could be achieved by storing in the DATA statement a pointer (for example, the line number of another DATA statement) to where the material can be found.

A problem in adapting the program to run on other computers is that a few dialects of BASIC do not have DATA statements, in which case another method of storing the items must be found. Some computers including the TRS-80, the ZX81 and the Spectrum allow variables and arrays to be saved alongside the program. In this case data can be stored directly in one or more arrays. Some advocate this method on the grounds that the items are hidden from the inquisitive student who finds out how to break into the program and study the listing; others have a sneaking suspicion that anyone who is motivated enough to circumvent the quiz and get at the answers directly may be learning at least as much from the activity as the well-behaved student who uses the quiz in the way the author intended.

Another solution to the problem of data storage is to use subroutines. For a ZX81 version of this program, for example, we would replace line 110 by:

110 GOSUB 8990 + 10*N

and lines 9000 onwards by:

```
9000 LET PREP = 4
9002 LET Q$ = "SMOKING IS NOT GOOD . . . . YOU."
9004 RETURN
9010 LET PREP = 6                    etc.
```

Presentation

Many changes are possible in the presentation of the quiz. The screen display is fairly simple, and some readers might like to experiment with something more elaborate, for example presenting the text within a frame, or using colour to highlight the different choices or the various messages that appear on the screen.

We have experimented with a version of the quiz in which the different prepositions appear for a second at a time in the gap, the player having to 'trap' the correct one by pressing the T key. While such a presentation has an arcade-game element about it that may be motivating for younger learners, we have doubts about it pedagogically since there is a danger that seeing the wrong prepositions appearing within the context may lead the student to learn the wrong answer rather than the right one. For a more justifiable use of animation techniques see WORDSPIN.

The program makes no use of the limited sound facilities of the Spectrum, and some teachers and students would no doubt prefer it to remain silent. Others, however, might appreciate the computer playing a short tune of encouragement on the successful completion of an item, or at the end of the quiz for a high score. The computer might have stored a number of different tunes for random selection stored in a series of subroutines.

Readers bothered by the anomaly in the scoring routine (page 111) may like to experiment with different solutions. Line 400 could be rewritten as LET win = 0 (so the student gets no credit for success after a failure) or the line could be deleted altogether (everybody gets maximum marks if they persevere long enough). The games-minded user might rewrite line 120 as LET win = 400, showing the updated massive-looking score on the screen after each item has been answered.

Selection of items

One obvious development of the program is to generate randomly not only the multiple choices but also the sequencing of the questions. The most efficient method of 'shuffling' the order of presentation is by using a **pointer array**. Since pointer arrays are an essential weapon in the armoury of the CAL programmer, a brief description of how they work may be useful.

First we set up a numeric array – let us call it **S** – which has as its elements a series of numbers from one up to the number of available questions (see illustration (a)). Rather than use a randomly-generated number to select a number directly, we use it to select a position in the pointer array, and then use the element at that position to select that question. After the selection has been made we move all the elements in the array below the selected position up one place. As a result, the element that was used to choose the question disappears and that question cannot be selected a second time.

In making the first selection using array **S**, a random number in the range one to ten is generated. Let us suppose that it is four. The element at that position is itself four, so question four is selected. All the elements below four are then shifted up one place. The second random number generated will be in the range 1 to 9. If it is seven, question eight will be selected and all the elements below position seven moved up. The process will be repeated until all the questions have been selected.

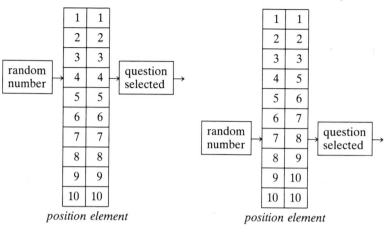

Pointer array 's'

(a) Selection of first question   (b) Selection of second question

position element   *position element*

The explanation above will, it is hoped, make it easier to understand the five additional program lines that are needed to allow random selection.

The pointer array **S** is dimensioned to the appropriate size during **initialise** by

     635   DIM   S(number)

and filled in the SETUPQUIZ routine.

     744   FOR   n = 1 to number: LET   S(n) = n: next n

It is then used to select a question in the main routine

     92   LET   pick = 1 + INT (RND*(number − n + 1))

     94   RESTORE   8990 + 10*(S(pick))

and adjusted to exclude the question from further selection by

     96   IF number > n   THEN FOR   m = pick TO number-n: LET S(m) = S(m + 1):   NEXT m

By changing the place at which the **S** array is adjusted to the **right answer** routine we could ensure that a wrongly-answered question was presented again – though then if we were to be punctilious in our scoring we would also have to mark the question in some way to ensure that it did not carry full marks or second presentation.

Horizon selection and autograding

A random order of presentation, such as that allowed by the changes above, either implies that there is no significant difference in difficulty between the different items, or a view on the part of the program writer that variation and the element of the unexpected

115

outweigh the possible advantages of grading. The best way to resolve the conflict between randomness and grading may be to combine the two approaches, by allowing random selection only within a 'horizon' or 'block' of items at the top of the pointer array: as items are eliminated from the block, others are moved up to take their place in the way we have seen. With graded items this method has the advantage that while difficult items cannot be selected early in the quiz, it is possible for a relatively easy item to remain in the block for some time without being selected, and to turn up late in the quiz offering an agreeable bonus among more difficult material.

Even if we consider grading desirable, we have to admit that it is difficult to carry out accurately. In an ideal world we would not only already know which items will be easy and which difficult, but we would also collect evidence scrupulously as to relative difficulty over a long period when materials are used and constantly re-write in accordance with that evidence. In practice, of course, very few teachers have the time or the inclination to do as much re-grading as they would like. It follows that this is a job which would well be left to the inherently patient and meticulous computer, making the program responsible for keeping a cumulative record of which items students tend to find difficult and which easy, and re-grading the quiz, exercise or drill accordingly. We shall call this technique *autograding*.

In order to add autograding to our simple quiz we shall need two pointer arrays in the place of the one we used previously. The diagram below may help to explain how the two pointer arrays work. One – S – will, as before, organise the top-of-array block of available questions. This time, however, it will point not to a question in a DATA statement, but to a second array in which the questions stored are sorted into order of difficulty, together with the cumulative information (a 'facility value' on a scale of 0 to 1) on the basis of

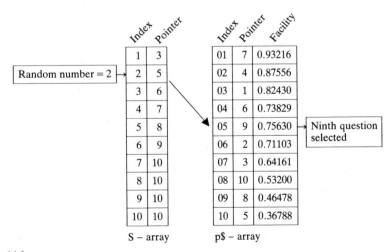

S – array   p$ – array

which the sorting is carried out. This second array – **p$** – will be a string array, the information being sliced out of it as required and converted to numeric form.

It will be necessary to set up the **p$** array, and to ensure that it is saved, along with the information it contains, after the program has been used. The first job will be carried out by a new routine, **programsetup**, which must be RUN once by the command GO TO 3000 before the program is used, and not RUN again since that would destroy the cumulative information. In the present case the array is ready for an eventual fifty questions if needed:

```
3000 REM programsetup***********
3010 LET save=0: LET game=0
3020 DIM p$(50,10)
3030 FOR n=1 TO 50: LET p$(n)=("
0" AND n<10)+STR$ n+" "+"0.00000
": NEXT n
3040 STOP
```

Selection of the question is carried out by the following additions:

```
 92 LET horizon=INT (number/5)-
((INT (number/5)+n-number-1) AND
(number-n<INT (number/5)))
 94 LET pick=1+INT (RND*horizon
)
 96 RESTORE 8990+10*VAL p$(s(pi
ck))( TO 2)
```

Line 92 sets up a block of the top 20 items in the array. Readers who would like to introduce a greater degree of randomness might prefer to divide **number** by 3 or even 2 – the complicated-looking part of the equation after the minus sign is included in order to ensure that at the end of the quiz the block is reduced to match the number of remaining questions.

Line 92 uses **horizon** to select from the pointers at the top of the **s** array, while line 96 restores the data pointer to the chosen question. Notice how in line 96 Sinclair BASIC needs only the expression '(TO 2)' to slice out the first two characters from the array: in most other dialects of BASIC the clumsier LEFT$ would be required.

In order to update the information in the second part of the **p$** array we need to know how many times the quiz has been done using the variable **game**: this is increased, and the **s** array filled, by two additions to the **setupquiz** subroutine:

```
742 LET game=game+1
744 FOR n=1 TO number: LET s(n)
=n: NEXT n
```

The updating is carried out by the **facility** routine.
The lines:

   344 GO SUB 770
   435 GO SUB 770

call it for a wrong answer and a right answer respectively, while the
routine itself recalculates the facility of the question in the light of the
new information:

```
750 RETURN
760 REM adjustindex************
770 LET p$(s(pick))(4 TO )=STR$
(((choice=right)+(VAL (p$(s(pic,
k))(4 TO ))*(game-1)))/game): RE
TURN
```

After the quiz has been completed all the questions are regraded.
There are many methods available for sorting data into order. The
one used here is one of the simpler, and is usually called a 'bubble
sort':

```
780 REM sort*******************
790 LET flag=0
800 FOR n=1 TO number-1
810 IF VAL p$(n)(4 TO )<VAL p$(
n+1)(4 TO ) THEN  LET k$=p$(n):
LET p$(n)=p$(n+1): LET p$(n+1)=k
$: LET flag=1
820 NEXT n
830 IF flag THEN  GO TO 790
840 RETURN
```

At the start of the subroutine a variable **flag** is set to zero (line 790).
In the loop from lines 800 to 820 each adjacent point of items in the
array is tested against each other: if any pair is found with an item
above another with a higher facility value, they are switched round
and **flag** is set to 1. In line 830 **flag** is tested: if it is 1, at least one
switch has been made in the course of the last pass through the loop,
and the procedure is repeated. If it is zero, all the items are in the
correct order, and the sort is completed. While the bubble sort is an
inefficient method of sorting large quantities of disordered data it

works well here since after the first few times the quiz is used the questions will begin to settle down into order of difficulty, and few switches will need to be made.

When the quiz has been done, it may be repeated by the same student or by other students: eventually, however, it will be necessary to save the program with the new data incorporated in it. When the Microdrive becomes available it will be possible for this to be carried out automatically from within the program. At the moment of writing, however, the only medium available for permanent storage is cassette, and much depends on the willingness of students or teachers to undertake part of the work themselves. We replace line 70 in our original program by:

```
70 GO SUB 860: REM save
75 STOP
```

The **save** routine saves two copies of the program in case one copy is corrupted.

```
850 REM save*******************
860 LET save=save+1
870 CLS : PRINT "Please record
the quiz with the"'"questions re
graded:"''"1. The label on the c
assette"'"   should read ";CHR$
34;"QUIZ 1:";save;CHR$ 34;"."''"
   Turn the cassette over and"''
   rewind it to the start."
880 PRINT '"2. Make certain tha
t the EAR"'"   plug on the the c
omputer is"'"   disconnected."''
"3. Press the RECORD button on"'
"   the tape-recorder."''"4. Pre
ss R on the computer."
890 IF INKEY$<>"R" THEN GO TO 890
900 LET j$="QUIZ 1:"+STR$ (save
+1): FOR n=1 TO 2: SAVE j$ LINE
20: NEXT n
910  PRINT '"5. Rewind the cass
ette, and"''"   write ";CHR$ 34;"
QUIZ 1:";save+1;CHR$ 34;" on the
"'"   label."
920 PRINT '"6. Thankyou - and g
oodbye!"
930 RETURN
```

The important point to note here is that in line 900 the program is saved in such a way that when it is next loaded it automatically starts

119

from line 10: this ensures that the user does not attempt to use the RUN command which would clear all variables and arrays, including the crucial **p$** array.

5.3 MONSTER

BOOH programs, that is programs which allow the student to input playful language, can be very simple. This example, INVENT A MONSTER, from an idea by Muriel Higgins, merely invites the student to type in a series of descriptions. The program then assembles them into a prose paragraph. At the end the student can have the paragraph printed (provided a printer has been connected), but there is no other way of preserving the monster. The program is intentionally ephemeral.

The form of the final paragraph will be like this:

```
                THE [NAME]

A [name] is a(n) [size] [colour] creature with [number]
legs which lives in a(n) [noun].   Its favourite food
is [food] but it also eats [food].   When it eats it
sounds like a(n) [noun].   It sleeps in a(n) [noun],
and when it's asleep it looks like a(n) [noun].

Have YOU ever seen an/[name]?
```

The prompts to elicit the descriptions can be either questions or gap-filling, and we have tended to use the latter wherever possible.

```
            What is the name of your creature?
            Size?
            Colour?
            Has .... legs
            Lives in  a ...
            Favourite food ?
            Also eats ...
            Sounds like a ...
            Sleeps in a ...
            Looks like a ...
```

As each prompt is answered, the information is stored but the prompt and the answer are immediately wiped. This is quite deliberate. As in

120

the paper-and-pencil game of CONSEQUENCES, you do not see what has already been written when you write what comes next.

The program can readily be used as a shell for other types of BOOH paragraph, for example the text of a hotel brochure, an advertisement for a second-hand car, or a page from a film star's diary.

INVENT A MONSTER uses the A/AN program described in Chapter 3.8 as a subroutine in order to make the text grammatical. It also needs a way of stopping words from spilling over the ends of lines. This, too, is a general purpose procedure which we also use elsewhere. The only initialisation necessary is to make the keyboard bleep longer and to make sure that the CAPS LOCK is off, so that upper and lower case can be entered.

```
10 REM Invent a monster
20 REM @ Muriel Higgins
30 REM Subroutine @ Tim Johns
40 POKE 23609,70: POKE 23658,0
: REM Keyboard bleep and Caps lo
ck off
50 GO TO 1000
```

The main input routines run from lines 1000 to 1210. **a$** is the variable to hold the text, and since the first word will be 'A' or 'An', it is given a starting value of 'A'. As each input is made, it is added to this string after checking for 'a' or 'an' if necessary. The very first input, the name of the creature, will also be used in the title and in the final sentence, so it is copied into two further variables, **t$** for the title (upper case) and **n$** for its use at the end.

```
 999 REM Input ****************
********************************
1000 LET a$="A"
1010 BORDER 6: CLS : PRINT AT 8,
5;"INVENT A MONSTER"
1020 INPUT "What's the name of
          your creature? ... "
;i$
1030 LET t$=i$: GO SUB 100: LET
n$=i$: LET a$=a$+i$+" is a"
1040 INPUT "Size? ...   ";i$
1050 GO SUB 100: LET a$=a$+i$+"
"
1060 INPUT "Colour? ...   ";i$
1070 LET a$=a$+i$+"creature with"

1080 INPUT "Has ... legs   ";i$
1090 LET a$=a$+i$+" legs which l
ives in a"
1100 INPUT "Lives in a ...   ";i
$
```

```
1110 GO SUB 100: LET a$=a$+i$+".
    Its favourite food is "
1120 INPUT "Favourite food? ..."
    ;i$
1130 LET a$=a$+i$+" but it also
eats "
1140 INPUT "Also eats ...    ";i$
1150 LET a$=a$+i$+".    When it e
ats it sounds like a"
1160 INPUT "Sounds like a ...
";i$
1170 GO SUB 100: LET a$=a$+i$+".
    It sleeps in a"
1180 INPUT "Sleeps in a ...    ";
i$
1190 GO SUB 100: LET a$=a$+i$+",
 and when it's asleep it looks l
ike a"
1200 INPUT "Looks like a ...    "
;i$
1210 GO SUB 100: LET a$=a$+i$+".
```

The article-checking subroutine begins by setting up a variable **p$** to carry either the 'n' of 'An' or else a space, and then makes a copy of the input into a variable **q$** for matching purposes. Line 120 gets rid of a few tricky exceptions. In line 130 the first and third letters of the input are put into variables **x$** and **y$**, and the case of initial 'u' followed by a consonant and a vowel is picked out. Line 140 eliminates all the cases in which the middle consonant is not 'n', for example, words like 'ubiquity' or 'usury'. Line 150 deals with cases like 'unintentional', 'unillustrated', or 'unambitious'. Line 160 provides for other words beginning with vowels, the numerals 8, 11 and 18, and the words with 'silent h'. In line 170 the abbreviations and single-letter prefixes are isolated, and line 180 provides for the ones which need 'an', thus dealing with *X-ray* or *H-bomb* or *M.P.*

```
 99 REM A or An subroutine*****
********************************
100 LET p$=" ": LET q$=i$: FOR
j=1 TO LEN i$: IF CODE i$(j)>64
AND CODE i$(j)<91 THEN    LET q$(j
)=CHR$ (CODE i$(j)+32)
110 NEXT j: LET q$=q$+"     ":
REM standardise to lower case
120 IF q$( TO 2)="eu" OR q$( TO
3)="ewe" OR q$( TO 5)="unani" T
HEN  GO TO 200
130 LET x$=q$(1): LET y$=q$(3):
IF x$<>"u" OR y$<>"a" AND y$<>"
e" AND y$<>"i" AND y$<>"o" AND y
$<>"u" THEN  GO TO 160
140 IF q$(2)<>"n" THEN  GO TO 2
00
150 IF y$<>"i" OR q$(4)="m" OR
q$(4)="n" THEN  LET p$="n ": GO
TO 200
```

```
 160 IF x$="8" OR (q$( TO 2)="11
" OR q$( TO 2)="18") AND (y$=" "
 OR y$="t" OR y$="." OR y$="-")
OR x$="a" OR x$="e" OR x$="i" OR
 x$="o" OR x$="u" OR q$( TO 4)="
hour" OR q$( TO 4)="heir" OR q$(
 TO 4)="hono" OR q$( TO 5)="hone
s" THEN  LET p$="n "
 170 IF q$(2)<>"-" AND q$(2)<>".
" THEN  GO TO 200
 180 IF x$="f" OR x$="h" OR x$="
l" OR x$="m" OR x$="n" OR x$="r"
 OR x$="s" OR x$="x" THEN  LET p
$="n "
 190 IF x$="u" THEN  LET p$=" "
 200 LET i$=p$+i$: RETURN
```

In its present form the subroutine cannot distinguish dates, for example, 'An 1880 penny' v. 'A 1980 penny'. The reader might like to experiment with ways of modifying the program to make that distinction.

The remaining part of the program simply performs the wordwrap operation on **a$** and prints it. Lines 1310 and 1320 convert the title to upper case, and line 1330 centres it on the screen. Lines 1340 to 1360 look for the first space or hyphen occurring at or before the thirty-third character. In lines 1370 to 1400, the substring so identified is printed and then cut from the main text string. Line 1380 removes any leading spaces, while line 1390 checks whether the last line has been reached. Line 1410 prints the punch line.

```
1299 REM Print title **********
*******************************
1300 BORDER 5: CLS : PRINT
1310 FOR j=1 TO LEN t$: IF CODE
t$(j)>96 THEN  LET t$(j)=CHR$ (C
ODE t$(j)-32)
1320 NEXT j
1330 PRINT TAB 13-LEN t$/2;"THE
";t$: PRINT
1339 REM Print text ***********
*******************************
1340 LET fit=33
1350 IF a$(fit)=" " OR a$(fit-1)
="-" THEN  GO TO 1370
1360 LET fit=fit-1: GO TO 1350
1370 PRINT a$( TO fit-1): LET a$
=a$((fit+1) TO )
1380 IF a$(1)=" " THEN  LET a$=a
$(2 TO ): GO TO 1380
1390 IF LEN a$<32 THEN  PRINT a$
: GO TO 1410
1400 GO TO 1340
1410 PRINT : PRINT "Have YOU eve
r seen ";: IF LEN n$>10 THEN PRINT
1420 PRINT "a";n$;"?"
```

Lines 1500 to 1560 round off the program by offering a choice of printing out the text on the Sinclair printer, inventing another monster, or exiting from the program. Notice how, in line 1550, the message line is wiped before the screen is copied so that the printout is 'clean'.

```
1499 REM Delay and instructions*
*********************************
1500 FOR j=1 TO 350: NEXT j
1510 PRINT AT 21,0;"A = again
X = exit    P = print"
1520 LET i$=INKEY$
1530 IF i$="a" OR i$="A" THEN  R
UN
1540 IF i$="x" OR i$="X" THEN  S
TOP
1550 IF i$="p" OR i$="P" THEN  P
RINT AT 21,0;"
                       ": COPY : GO TO 15
10
1560 GO TO 1520
```

The variables used in the program are as follows:
Numeric variables
 j   (counting variable)
 fit   (for formatting)
String variables
 a$ the main text
 i$ input words and phrases
 t$ the name in upper case
 n$ the name in lower case
 p$ to carry the 'n' of 'an'
 q$ copy of i$ used to check 'a' or 'an'
 x$ first letter of i$
 y$ third letter of i$

5.4 Loan

LOAN is a program which will generate requests for money. The student specifies how much is to be borrowed, and from whom. The program is described in Chapter 3.8.

```
10 REM Loan @Tim Johns,1982,19
83
20 REM controller*************
30 GO SUB 1100: REM instruct
40 GO SUB 780: REM drawframes
50 GO SUB 820: REM menuframe
60 GO SUB 870: REM wipeframe
70 GO SUB 250: REM howmuch?
80 GO SUB 980: REM fixmenu
```

124

```
 90 GO SUB 820: REM menuframe
100 GO SUB 380: REM whofrom?
110 GO SUB 470: REM generate
120 GO SUB 910: REM print
130 PRINT AT 19,2;"Another requ
est    - press R"
140 PRINT AT 20,2;"Another situ
ation - press S"
150 LET i$=INKEY$: GO TO 150+10
*(i$="R")+30*(i$="S")
160 GO SUB 870: REM wipeframe
170 GO TO 110
180 GO SUB 950: REM wipeprompt
190 GO SUB 870: REM wipeframe
200 LET paper=6
210 GO SUB 930: REM menumark
220 GO SUB 250: REM howmuch?
230 GO TO 100
```

The first subroutines set up the session:

```
1090 REM instruct***************
1100 CLS : POKE 23658,8: DIM e$(8,27)
1110 LET w$="
                 "
1120 PRINT "It is difficult to b
orrow money."'"It is even more
difficult to"'"know what to say
when we want toborrow money."
1130 PRINT '"This program gives
you an oppor-tunity to study the
 things that"'"English people sa
y in this"'"situation."
1140 PRINT '"The computer will a
sk you how"'"much you want to bo
rrow, and whoyou want to borrow
from.  It"'"will then show you a
 suitable"'"way of making the re
quest."
1150 PRINT '"Experiment with the
 program to"'"discover the diffe
rent ways we"'"have of asking fo
r money."
1160 PRINT #1;AT 0,5; INVERSE 1;
"Press C to continue"
1170 IF INKEY$<>"C" THEN  GO TO
1170
1180 CLS : RETURN
```

The POKE in line 1100 switches all alphabetic input to upper case in order to simplify the checking of input. The instructions have been kept short since the program is intended to be used in conjunction with written materials and probably with a teacher introducing it and suggesting how it could be used.

Three 'housekeeping' routines: **drawframes, menuframe** and **wipe frame** are then called. The last two call further subroutines:

125

```
770 REM drawframes**************
780 PLOT 15,160: DRAW 217,0: DR
AW 0,-66: DRAW -217,0: DRAW 0,66
790 PLOT 15,72: DRAW 217,0: DRA
W 0,-41: DRAW -217,0: DRAW 0,41
800 RETURN
810 REM menuframe**************
820 LET lines=8: LET frame=1: L
ET paper=6: GO SUB 840: RETURN
830 REM fillframe**************
840 FOR n=1 TO lines: PRINT AT
n+frame,2; PAPER paper; BRIGHT 1
;e$(n): NEXT n
850 RETURN
860 REM wipeframe**************
870 LET line=11: GO SUB 890: LE
T lines=5: DIM e$(lines,27): GO
SUB 910: RETURN
880 REM wipeline**************
890 PRINT AT line,0;w$: RETURN
900 REM print****************
910 LET frame=12: LET paper=7:
GO SUB 840: RETURN
```

The effect of these is to draw two frames on the screen, both twenty-seven characters wide. The top frame, eight lines deep, is to hold the menu of potential lenders: this is filled with bright yellow in contrast with the surrounding screen. The bottom frame, four lines deep, will show the requests generated by the program: this is filled with bright white to highlight the language.

The user is then asked how much he or she wants to borrow by the **howmuch?** subroutine:

```
240 REM howmuch?**************
250 PRINT AT 0,1; INK 1;"Borrow
pence=P - or pounds=L? "
260 GO TO 260+10*(INKEY$="P")+2
0*(INKEY$="L")
270 LET x$="p": GO TO 290
280 LET x$="pounds"
290 INPUT "How much? (1-";("99"
AND x$="p");("1000" AND x$<>"p"
);")";z$
300 LET s=LEN z$: IF NOT s THEN
GO TO 290
310 IF CODE z$(s)<48 OR CODE z$
(s)>57 THEN  GO TO 290
320 LET s=s-1: IF s THEN  GO TO
310
330 IF VAL z$<0 OR VAL z$>99 AN
D x$="p" THEN  GO TO 290
340 LET money=VAL z$*(1+99*(x$<
>"p"))
350 LET line=0: GO SUB 890: PRI
```

```
NT AT 0,3-LEN z$/2;"You want to
borrow ";("`" AND x$<>"p");z$;("
p" AND x$="p");" from"
 360 RETURN
```

The user is given the choice of borrowing pence or pounds up to
£1,000. The input routine is written so that it will accept only a string
representing a whole number in numeric form: '3.5' is rejected, as is
'three'. In line 340 the user's decision is used to set the variable
money which represents the amount to be asked for in pence.

The menu of possible lenders now appears. This will remain on
screen throughout the run of the program. **Fixmenu** is called to load
the choices into the string array **e$**:

```
970 REM fixmenu****************
980 DIM e$(8,27)
990 RESTORE 1000: FOR n=1 TO 8:
READ d$: LET e$(n)=" "+STR$ n+"
"+d$: NEXT n
1000 DATA "Your brother or siste
r"
1010 DATA "Your best friend"
1020 DATA "One of your parents"
1030 DATA "An aunt or uncle"
1040 DATA "A colleague at work"
1050 DATA "Your bank manager"
1060 DATA "Your employer"
1070 DATA "A stranger"
1080 RETURN
```

which is then printed by **menuframe**. The user is now asked who the
lender is to be:

```
370 REM whofrom?***************
380 PRINT AT 11,6;"Who do you c
hoose?"
390 LET g$=INKEY$: IF CODE g$<4
9 OR CODE g$>56 THEN  GO TO 390
400 LET paper=7: GO SUB 930: LE
T line=11: GO SUB 890
410 IF g$="8" AND money>10 THEN
 PRINT AT 18,1;"Best to find so
meone you know";AT 19,3;"for tha
t much: try again!": GO TO 440
420 IF g$="6" AND money<1000 TH
EN  PRINT AT 18,0;"You don't nee
d a bank for small";AT 19,6;"cha
nge: try again!": GO TO 440
430 RETURN
440 FOR n=1 TO 300: NEXT n: GO
SUB 960: LET paper=6: GO SUB 930
: GO TO 380
```

127

The user's choice is highlighted by the **menumarks** subroutine which changes the background colour of that line of the menu to bright white:

```
920 REM menumark**************
*
930 PRINT AT 1+VAL g$,2; PAPER
paper; BRIGHT 1; OVER 1;"
                         ": RETURN
```

Two checks on the user's choice are carried out in **whofrom?**. We don't, in the normal course of events, ask the person next to us in the bus queue for a loan of £50, and the program would be hard put to it to generate the language appropriate to such an unusual situation, so line 410 sets a maximum limit of 10p for loans from strangers, and prints a message explaining why a request over that limit has been rejected. We don't ask our bank manager for 5p, or at least not in his capacity as a bank manager, so line 420 sets a minimum limit for overdrafts of £10.

The user's choice having been made, the **generate** subroutine is called. **Generate** consists of four modules: **setvariables**, **setstrings**, **concatenate** and **wordwrap**. The first of these is the heart of the whole program. It sets a number of variables on the basis of the user's choice of amount and potential lender, together with a random factor which introduces an appropriate degree of 'spread' to the requests generated:

```
450 REM generate***************
460 REM setvariables***********
470 LET res=(VAL g$+1)*SQR SQR
money*(1+4*(g$="8"))
480 LET verb=(res>8 OR VAL g$>2
)+INT (RND*(4-(res>8 OR VAL g$>2
))): IF verb=2 AND g$="6" THEN
LET verb=1
490 LET syntax=((RND/res)<.04)+
(res*(0.3+RND)>35)
495 LET matrix=(syntax=2)*(1+(r
es*(0.3+RND)>30)+(res*(0.2+RND)>
50))
500 LET casual=verb AND res*(.5
+RND)<5
510 LET doubt=res*(RND+.25)>10+
12*syntax
530 LET please=(NOT syntax AND
verb AND (res*(.4+RND)>7+8*doubt
))*(2-(RND<0.5 AND NOT doubt))
540 LET short=NOT verb AND NOT
syntax AND res*(.2+RND)<3
545 LET chop=syntax=1 AND res*(
.2+RND)<3
550 LET way=(g$="6" OR g$="7")
AND (verb=1 OR verb=2) AND ((RND
+.25)*res>50+25*doubt)
560 LET loan=res>12+4*RND AND v
erb=1
```

res (line 470) measures the degree of resistance anticipated by the borrower as a function of the amount to be asked for, and the person of whom the request is to be made. The calculation is made using the square root of the square root of **money**, and treating the place in the menu as representing a linear scale from familiarity and equality of relationship towards unfamiliarity and inequality. A special weighting is given where the potential lender is a stranger: in asking for even a small amount of money from someone we do not know we are likely to use the same sort of language that we would use for a much larger sum in the case of someone we do know. The calculation of **res** is open to a good deal of experimentation and fine-tuning, particularly in the way **g$** is incorporated in the equation.

verb(line 480). This variable selects the verb to be used:

0 = 'have got'. For example, *Have you got 5p on you?*
1 = 'let have'. For example, *Could you let me have 5p?*
2 = 'lend'. For example, *Could you lend me 5p?*
3 = 'borrow'. For example, *Could I borrow 5p?*

While it may be felt that there are subtle differences in usage between all four of these, the present version of the program places a restriction only on the first and third. *Have got* is reserved for those cases where there is a close and equal relationship with the potential lender, and only a small amount of money is involved. It is assumed that *lend* is more often used for private than official loans. The second statement line 470 substitutes *let have* for *lend* in the case where the potential lender is a bank manager so that the program will generate requests such as *I wonder if you could possibly let me have an overdraft of £500?* rather than *I wonder if your could possibly lend me £500?*

syntax(line 490) determines the syntax of the request:

0 = Direct question. For example, *Could you lend me 50p?*
1 = Tag question. For example, *You couldn't lend me 50p could you?*
2 = Embedded question. For example, *I wonder if you could lend me 50p?*

These are treated as lying on a scale of mitigation, the first being the least mitigated and the last being the most. The effect is that, while tag questions may appear at all values of **res**, embedded questions cannot appear at the lowest values, nor direct questions at the highest. One effect of this is that **syntax** cannot be set to 3 when the verb is set to 0, so the strange form *I wonder if you have got 10p on you?* is not generated.

casual(line 500) is a flag variable which, when set by lower values of **res**, gives *can* in place of *could*:

0 = *Could you let me have 20p?*
1 = *Can you let me have 20p?*

doubt(line 510). A flag variable which, when set, introduces the mitigating adverbials *possibly*(for the last three verbs) or *by any chance* (for the first). The setting of the flag takes into account not only the value of **res**but also the *verb*and the degree of mitigation already introduced by **syntax**.

please(line 520). A flag variable which, when set, introduces *please* into the request. The way the variable is calculated disallows *please* with any structure other than a direct question, and also with the verb *have got*: it also takes into account the degree of mitigation introduced by **doubt**, so that the appearance of both *possibly*and *please* appearing in the same request is reserved for the higher values of **res**.

place(line 530) is a flag variable which determines the position of *please* in the request:

0 = Final position. For example, *Could you lend me 50p please*?
1 = Medial position. For example, *Could you please lend me 50p*?

The reader may well feel that there are situational factors involved in **place**, medial position being more 'insistent' and final position being more 'polite'. Such distinctions, however, depend crucially on the intonation of the whole utterance, and in the absence of information about intonation the program treats the two positions as equivalent, the only restriction being that medial position is disallowed when **doubt** is set in order to avoid the structurally deviant *Could you possibly please lend me £5*?

short(line 540). A flag variable which, when set by very low values of **res**, gives the form *Got 5p on you*? in place of *Have you got 10p on you*?

way(line 550). A flag variable which when set introduces the highly deferential phrase *see your way to* before the verb:

0 = *You couldn't possibly let me have a loan of £100 could you*?
1 = *You couldn't possibly see your way to letting me have a loan of £100 could you*?

way can be set only where the potential lender is the borrower's bank manager or employer and for the verbs *let have* and *lend*. It also takes into account the value of **doubt**.

loan(line 560) When the verb chosen is **let have** and **res** is not low, this flag variable will introduce the naming expression *a loan of, an advance of* (alternative to *loan* for employers) or *an overdraft of* (alternative for bank managers) before the sum of money asked for.

The variables defined in **setvariables** are then passed to the **setstrings** module which defines most of the strings to be used in constructing the request:

```
570 REM set strings************
575 LET m$=("I'm sorry about th
is, but do you think " AND matri
x=1)+("I wonder if " AND matrix=
2)+("I don't suppose " AND matri
x=3)
580 LET p$=("you" AND verb< >3)+
("I" AND verb=3)
590 LET a$=("could" AND verb AN
D NOT casual)+("can" AND verb AN
D casual)+("have" AND NOT verb)
600 LET n$=("n't" AND NOT casua
l)+("t" AND casual)
610 LET v$=("got" AND NOT verb)
+("let" AND verb=1)+("lend" AND
verb=2)+("borrow" AND verb=3)
620 LET d$=(" possibly" AND dou
bt AND verb)+(" by any chance" A
ND doubt AND NOT verb)
630 LET l$=(" a loan of" AND lo
an): IF loan AND money>1000 AND
res*(0.5*RND)>10 AND (g$="6" OR
g$="7") THEN  LET l$=(" an overd
raft of" AND g$="6")+(" an advan
ce of" AND g$="7")
640 LET h$=("`" AND x$< >"p")+z$
+("p" AND x$="p")
```

The final step in the construction of the request is **concatenate**, which, using the technique of logical operations on strings, employs a single line of BASIC to build up the request in **rs**:

```
650 REM concatenate************
660 LET r$=m$+((p$+" ") AND syn
tax AND NOT chop)+(a$ AND NOT sh
ort)+(n$ AND syntax=1)+((" "+p$)
AND NOT short AND NOT syntax)+(
d$ AND verb)+(" please" AND plea
se=1)+(" see your way to" AND wa
y)+(" " AND NOT short)+v$+("t" A
ND way  AND verb=1)+("ing" AND w
ay)+(" me" AND (verb=1 OR verb=2
))+(" have" AND verb=1)+l$+" "+h
$+(" on you" AND NOT verb)+((" "
+a$+" "+p$) AND (syntax=1 OR mat
rix=3))+(" please" AND please=2)
+(d$ AND NOT verb)+"?"
670 IF r$(1)< >"I" THEN  LET r$(
1)=CHR$ (CODE r$(1)-32)
```

Line 660 is, in fact, a generalised description of a number of apparently very different structures. Notice, for example, how a 'slot' is provided for the pronoun string **p$** both before and after the auxiliary verb string **a$**, the first slot being filled for indirect and tag questions, and the second for direct questions. Line 670 ensures that the first letter in the request is in upper case. The last module in generate is **wordwrap** which fits the request into the **e$** array (the array first used for the menu but now no longer required for that purpose) in such a way that the words do not overlap from one line to the next.

```
690 REM wordwrap**************
700 LET lines=1
710 LET fit=28
720 IF LEN r$<fit THEN  LET e$(
lines)=r$: GO TO 750
 730 IF r$(fit)<>" " THEN  LET f
it=fit-1: GO TO 730
 740 LET e$(lines)=r$( TO fit-1)
: LET r$=r$(fit+1 TO ): LET line
s=lines+1: GO TO 710
 750 PRINT AT 11,8;"You could sa
y"
 760 RETURN
```

On return from the **generate** subroutine, the request is printed to the lower frame by **print**. The only part of the program to add is the short **wipeprompt** subroutine which removes the prompts printed at the bottom of the screen in lines 130 and 140 while a new situation is being selected:

```
940 REM wipeprompt************
950 LET line=11: GO SUB 890
960 FOR n=19 TO 20: LET line=n:
GO SUB 890: NEXT n: RETURN
```

and the program is complete.

Changes and extensions

The present version of LOAN is open to a number of different amendments and extensions.

1 Some fairly simple changes to the **setvariables** subroutine can have a considerable effect on the 'personality' of the program. For example:
   a) To shift the set of requests generated for a particular situation towards greater formality or informality, try changing the criterion values after the comparison symbol. Thus, changing the '5' in line 500 to '10' or '15' will increase the range of situations in which *can* is used instead of *could*.
   b) A question to consider is how far for a particular group of learners or for a particular learning situation the program may be too probabilistic or too deterministic. Does it suggest too wide or too narrow a range of forms for any one particular situation? To make the program more probabilistic, reduce or eliminate the weighting given to the fixed values in the multiplicand for **res**, and make any necessary changes to the criterion value. In 500

132

LET casual = verb AND res *RND < 5

will allow *could* as well as *can* at the lowest values of **res**, and also allow *can* to appear at higher values of **res** than the present version. On the other hand

LET casual = verb AND res* 5 + RND < 27.

will make the program more deterministic, giving a sharper cut-off point between *can* and *could*.

In making changes to the way one variable is calculated in **setvariables** it is important to remember the effect this will have in interaction with other variables. For example, the present version does not generate *I wonder if you can* ... which, to this author, seems slightly odd in the inconsistency between the mitigation expressed by the syntax and that expressed by the auxiliary verb. If the program is not to generate *I wonder if you can* ... any upward shift in the maximum limit for **casual** must be accompanied by an upward shift in the minimum limit for **syntax** = 2. In addition, where the setting of one variable affects the setting of another (for example, **doubt** influencing the setting of **please**) any change in the method of calculation of the first may require changes in the calculation of the second.

2   The language generated by LOAN could be made much richer within the framework of the present program. The reader might like to consider the changes that would have to be made to generate each of the following requests, and the conditions that should be placed on each request:

Couldn't lend me 5p, could you?
Could I trouble you for a loan of 50p?
I wonder whether you could possibly let me have a loan of £10?
I don't suppose you could lend me £1, could you?
I'd be very grateful if you could let me have an advance of £100?

3   There is, inevitably, a degree of artificiality about a request isolated from the total discourse in which it would be used. Extensions to the discourse which the program might generate could include:

Standard prefaces. For example,

By the way, you couldn't let me have 10p could you?
I'm sorry about this, but I wonder whether you could lend me £2?

Indications of repayment. For example,
Could you lend me £1? *I'll let you have it back, tomorrow.*
I wonder if you could see your way to letting me have an overdraft of £200 *for a couple of months?*

Explanations of situation. For example,
Have you got 10p on you? *I need to make a phone call.*
You couldn't possibly let me have an advance of £100 could you? *I'm a bit short until the end of the month.*

133

The last two require information which could be generated by the computer, or selected by the user from a menu of choices. Beyond the individual turn, the request could also be the basis of a three-part exchange:

Couldn't lend me 5p could you?
Sure. Here you are.
Thanks a lot.

Couldn't lend me 5p could you?
Sorry, but I'm out of small change.
Never mind – I'll ask Bill.

It could also be the basis of more complex transactions such as an interview with a bank manager, although that, in this author's view, is at the limit of what a computer might be required to generate by itself, and probably past the limit of what would be most immediately useful for the machine to do for language-learning.

4 As it stands, the program is purely a demonstrator – a tool for investigating how language changes with situation. It could, however, be adapted to other purposes:
   a) Provision of a self-test mode. A simple and effective format would be for the program to select randomly one word from the generated request, and to blank it out, possibly leaving the initial letter as a clue. This could be combined with the 'Swiss cheese' principle so that as the student progressed, further words would be removed until for each request the display would consist only of the initial letters and the sum of money.
   b) The generative techniques employed in the program could be appled to interactive simulations such as ELIZA or ADVENTURE, allowing the computer's output to vary flexibly according to situation.

5.5 WORDSPIN

WORDSPIN was described in Chapter 3.3.

The **controller** subroutine (placed after some initial speed-dependent subroutines) calls the main game subroutines in sequence:

```
 10 REM Wordspin @ Tim Johns,19
81,1983**************************
 20 GO TO 140
130 REM controller*************
********************************
140 GO SUB 1060: REM initialise
150 GO SUB 750: REM menu
160 GO SUB 680: REM extract
170 GO SUB 230: REM trap
180 GO SUB 400: REM bomb
190 IF left THEN   GO TO 160
200 GO SUB 920: REM newgame
210 GO TO 150
```

The **initialise** subroutine draws the frame on the screen and sets up some of the variables to be used in the game:

```
1060 REM initialise*************
******************************
1070 CLS : PLOT 4,171: DRAW 247,
0: DRAW 0,-167: DRAW -247,0: DRA
W 0,167
1080 PLOT 4,156: DRAW 247,0
1090 PLOT 4,34: DRAW 247,0
1100 PLOT 4,19: DRAW 247,0
1110 PLOT 123,170: DRAW 0,-13
1120 PLOT 187,170: DRAW 0,-13
1130 PLOT 127,18: DRAW 0,-13
1140 PRINT AT 1,16;"Word"
1150 PRINT AT 20,1;"HIGH SCORE 0
00";AT 20,17;"YOUR SCORE"
1160 LET w$="
                "
1170 LET q$="??????????????????
??????????"
1180 DIM v(10): DIM b(3)
1190 POKE 23658,8: RANDOMIZE
1200 LET hs=0: RETURN
```

The frame-drawing instructions occupy lines 1070 and 1150. **w$** is a string of spaces to be used in wiping the display: **q$** a string of question marks used to construct the 'blot' which will run from side to side of the word. Two pointer arrays are dimensioned at this stage: **v** to be used in the selection of questions, and **b** which will hold the line numbers of the subroutines to give a version of the game with or without sound effects as required. The variable **hs** will hold the score printed at the bottom left-hand side of the screen, while the POKE in line 1190 ensures that all player input is in upper case.

The **menu** subroutine asks the player to choose:

1 A set of 10 words by name (up to 26 sets possible), the title of the set appearing in the top left hand corner of the screen.
2 Whether to play the game with sound effects.
3 A fast or a slow game (the former demanding faster reflexes in the **trap** phase of the game).

```
 740 REM menu******************
******************************
 750 RESTORE 9000: READ p
 760 FOR n=1 TO p: RESTORE 9000+
10*n: READ t$: PRINT AT n+2-13*(
n>13),1+16*(n>13);CHR$ (n+64);"
";t$: NEXT n
 770 PRINT AT 18,1;"PRESS A LETT
```

```
ER FOR YOUR WORDS"
  780 LET g$=INKEY$: IF CODE g$<6
5 OR CODE g$>64+p THEN  GO TO 78
0
  790 LET file=9000+10*(CODE g$-6
4)
  800 RESTORE file: READ t$: PRIN
T AT 1,1;t$;w$( TO 13-LEN t$)
  810 LET file=file+5: LET left=1
0
  820 FOR n=3 TO 16: PRINT AT n,1
;w$: NEXT n
  830 FOR n=1 TO 10: LET v(n)=n:
NEXT n
  840 PRINT AT 18,1;"  QUIET GAME
OR NOISY? (Q/N)   "
  850 LET g$=INKEY$: IF g$<>"Q" A
ND g$<>"N" THEN  GO TO 850
  860 FOR n=1 TO 3: LET b(n)=30+1
0*n+40*(g$="Q"): NEXT n
  870 PRINT AT 18,3;" FAST GAME O
R SLOW? (F/S)  "
  880 LET g$=INKEY$: IF g$<>"F" A
ND g$<>"S" THEN  GO TO 880
  890 LET f=1+2*(g$="S")
  900 LET score=0: PRINT AT 20,28
;"000"
  910 RETURN
```

The menu reads the DATA statements which are stored from line 9000
on as follows:

```
9000 DATA 4
9010 DATA "Zoo Animals"
9015 DATA "KANGAROO","ELEPHANT",
"GIRAFFE","RHINOCEROS","HIPPOPOT
AMUS","GORILLA","CHIMPANZEE","HY
ENA","ZEBRA","LEOPARD"
9020 DATA "Birds"
9025 DATA "OSTRICH","SPARROW","P
ENGUIN","THRUSH","VULTURE","ALBA
TROSS","EAGLE","PHEASANT","PARTR
IDGE","PEACOCK"
9030 DATA "British Towns"
9035 DATA "LONDON","BIRMINGHAM",
"EDINBURGH","LEICESTER","CARDIFF
","GLASGOW","SOUTHAMPTON","BRIST
OL","PENZANCE","LIVERPOOL"
9040 DATA "Tools"
9045 DATA "CHISEL","SPANNER","SE
CATURS","LATHE","SCREWDRIVER","H
AMMER","PLIERS","SCALPEL","PLANE
","BRADAWL"
```

Line 750 reads the number of sets of words present, and line 760
reads the titles (stored in lines 9010, 9020, 9030 etc.) and prints them
136

out as a menu, each title preceded by a letter from 'A' on. If there are more than thirteen sets of words present, those from fourteen on will be printed in a second column on the right of the screen – so to avoid overprinting, titles should not be more than thirteen characters in length. Line 770 invites the player to choose a set of words by pressing the appropriate letter. Line 780 checks that the player's choice is within the range of titles on offer, and line 790 sets up the variable **file** which is used in line 800 to print the title (padded out with spaces to overwrite any previous title) in the top left-hand corner of the screen. In line 810, five is added to **file** so that it now points to the words in the set chosen, and **left** is set to ten to represent the number of words available. The menu of titles is removed by line 820, and the pointer array **v** filled in line 830.

The choice of a quiet game (without sound effects) or a noisy game (with sound effects) is given in lines 840–860. If the player prefers a noisy game, the **b** array is filled with the line numbers of three subroutines which sound a beep: if a quiet game is preferred, the array contains the line numbers of three subroutines which introduce a similar delay based on a simple loop:

```
30 REM beepdelays*************
40 BEEP 0.1*f,beep: LET beep=5
-beep: RETURN
50 BEEP .02*f,2+1.5*n: RETURN
60 BEEP .01*f,35-m: RETURN
70 REM quietdelays************
80 FOR i=1 TO 10+10*f: NEXT i:
RETURN
90 FOR i=1 TO 1+3*f: NEXT i: R
ETURN
100 FOR i=1 TO f: NEXT i:RETURN
```

Lines 870–890 allow the player to set the speed of the game, the variable **f** used in the calculation of the delays in subroutines 30–60 and 80–100 being set to 1 for a fast game and 3 for a slow game.

The **menu** choices having been made, **extract** is called to select a word from the set chosen:

```
680 REM extract***************
*******************************
690 RESTORE file
700 LET w=1+INT (RND*left)
710 FOR n=1 TO v(w): READ a$: N
EXT n
720 IF left>1 THEN  FOR n=w TO
left-1: LET v(n)=v(n+1): NEXT n
730 GO SUB 970: LET left=left-1
: RETURN
```

The technique used here is to restore the data pointer to the set of words chosen (line 690) and to define a random number **w** on the basis of the number of words left (line 700). The number at place **w** in the pointer array **v** represents the place in the data list of the selected word: line 710 reads along the list copying each word in turn into **a$** until the selected word is reached. Line 720 rewrites the pointer array to eliminate the chosen word from further selection, while line 730 calls the **wordno** subroutine to print at the top of the screen the number of the word, and adjusts the variable **left**:

```
960 REM wordno****************
970 PRINT AT 1,21;("0" AND left
>1);11-left: RETURN
```

With the trap subroutine the game proper starts. The selected word is shown on the screen and may be studied as long as the player wishes. As soon as the B key is pressed the word starts 'revolving' in an endless loop, accompanied (if the sound effects are switched on) by an arcade-game-like warbling on two notes. Pressing T will stop the loop. A successful trap of the word is rewarded by ten points less one point for every unsuccessful attempt.

```
220 REM trap*******************
******************************
230 PRINT AT 14,1;w$;AT 1,25;"T
rap"
240 LET len=LEN a$: LET start=1
6-INT (len/2)
250 PRINT AT 14,start;a$;AT 18,
3;"    PRESS B TO BEGIN    "
260 LET s$=a$: LET win=10: LET
beep=5
270 LET g$=INKEY$: IF g$<>"B" T
HEN  GO TO 270
280 PRINT AT 18,3;" PRESS T TO
TRAP THE WORD "
290 LET s$=s$(2 TO )+s$(1)
300 PRINT AT 14,start;s$
310 GO SUB b(1)
320 IF INKEY$="T" THEN  GO TO 3
40
330 GO TO 290
340 IF s$=a$ THEN  GO SUB 1010:
LET score=score+win: GO SUB 103
0: FOR m=1 TO 100: NEXT m: GO SU
B 1050: RETURN
350 GO SUB 990: LET win=win-(wi
n>1)
360 FOR m=1 TO 50: NEXT m: GO S
UB 1050
370 LET g$=INKEY$: IF g$="T" TH
EN  GO TO 370
380 GO TO 290
```

Lines 240–250 ensure that the word is printed centrally on the screen. In line 260 the word is copied into s$. The revolving effect is obtained by lines 290 and 300 which repeatedly slice and reconstitute s$ so that the first character is placed at the end, and then reprint the string in the same position. A successful trap having being identified in line 340, the subroutines **right** (printing GOOD in white on red), **printscore** and (after a short delay loop) **wipemessage** are called:

```
1000 REM right*****************
1010 PRINT AT 18,3;"          "
; INK 2; INVERSE 1;"GOOD"; INVER
SE 0;"          ": RETURN
1020 REM printscore*************
1030 PRINT AT 20,28;"00"( TO 3-L
EN STR$ score);score: RETURN
1040 REM wipemessage************
1050 PRINT AT 18,1;w$: RETURN
```

and control is returned to the **controller** routine.

An unsuccessful trap is dealt with in lines 350–380. In line 350 the **wrong** subroutine is called:

```
980 REM wrong*****************
990 PRINT AT 18,3;"
"; INK 2; INVERSE 1;"NO"; INVERS
E 0;"          ": RETURN
```

and one point deducted from **win**, providing **win** is greater than one (since it seems only fair to give the player something for a successful trap no matter how many unsuccessful attempts he or she may have made previously). Notice the inclusion of line 370: without it all that would be necessary to make a successful trap would be to keep one's finger pressed continuously on the T key and to wait until the word came around.

When the player has managed to **trap** the word, the **bomb** subroutine is called. A blot (an inverse question mark) appears and runs along the word from side to side, obliterating one letter at a time. The accompanying sound effect rises in pitch as the blot moves right, and falls as it moves left. The blot stops over a randomly-selected letter, when the player is invited to 'bomb the blot'. Pressing the appropriate key will cause a letter to descend from the top of the screen, accompanied by the best imitation achievable in Spectrum BASIC of a bomb-drop whine. If the wrong letter has been selected it will bounce back to the top of the screen, the whine being heard in reverse, and the player loses one point: if the right letter has been selected it appears in the word and a point is won. If the player is successful, the blot multiplies to two inverse question marks, each of which, when it stops, must be bombed; then to four and so on until the point is reached at which the whole word is obscured.

The main body of the subroutine is concerned with the definition and movement of the blot:

```
390 REM bomb*******************
*******************************
 400 PRINT AT 1,25;"Bomb": LET b
lot=1
 410 LET count=len-blot
 420 LET no=20+INT (RND*20)+2*le
n-3*blot
 430 LET x=0: LET y=count-1: LET
 z=1
 440 FOR n=x TO y STEP z: PRINT
AT 14,start;a$( TO n); INVERSE 1
;q$( TO blot); INVERSE 0;a$(blot
+n+1 TO ): GO SUB b(2): LET no=n
o-1: IF NOT no THEN  GO TO 480
 450 NEXT n
 460 IF x THEN  GO TO 430
 470 LET x=count: LET y=1: LET z
=-1: GO TO 440
 480 GO SUB 550
 490 LET blot=blot+blot: IF len>
blot+2 THEN  GO TO 410
 500 LET blot=LEN a$: LET n=0
 510 PRINT AT 14,start; INVERSE
1;q$( TO blot)
 520 GO SUB 550
 530 RETURN
```

The subroutine is best understood as comprising an outer loop (lines 410–430 and 460–470) and two inner loops (line 440 and the **fire** subroutine). The outer loop determines **blot** (the number of question marks to be sliced out of **q$**), **count** (the number of steps left to right and right to left that the blot must move along the string) and **no** (the number of steps to be made by the blot before it stops). Once **blot** approaches the length of the word, the whole word is obscured (lines 510 and 520). The subroutine at line 440 uses string-slicing to give the appearance of the blot moving along the word, and stops when no = 0. At that point **fire** is called:

```
540 REM fire*******************
550 PRINT AT 18,9;"BOMB THE BLO
T";("S" AND blot>1)
560 FOR l=1 TO blot
570 LET g$=INKEY$: IF CODE g$<6
5 OR CODE g$>91 THEN  GO TO 570
```

```
580 LET col=start+1+n-1
590 LET x=3: LET y=13: LET z=1
600 GO SUB 120
610 IF g$=a$(n+1) THEN   PRINT A
T 14,col;g$: LET score=score+1:
GO SUB 1030: GO TO 650
620 LET x=13: LET y=3: LET z=-1
630 GO SUB 120
640 LET score=score-(score>0):
GO SUB 1030: GO TO 570
650 NEXT 1
660 GO SUB 1050
670 RETURN
```

which prints an appropriate prompt on the message line, sets up a loop for the number of letters to be bombed into place, defines **col** as the column on the screen at which the letter obtained at line 570 is to be bombed into the word and calls the **bombswoop** subroutine (placed early in the program to maximise speed). This is responsible both for bombing the letter into the word and for bouncing it back if a match is not found at line 610:

```
110 REM bombswoop**************
120 FOR m=x TO y STEP z: PRINT
AT m,col;g$: GO SUB b(3): PRINT
AT m,col;" ": NEXT m: RETURN
```

At line 190 of the **controller** routine the variable **left** is tested to discover whether there are any words left in the set chosen. If so, control is passed back to **extract**; if not, the **newgame** subroutine is called to adjust the screen display and to check whether the previous highest score has been exceeded:

```
920 REM newgame****************
******************************
930 PRINT AT 1,21;" ";AT 1,25;
"     ";AT 14,1;w$
940 IF score>hs THEN  LET hs=sc
ore: PRINT AT 20,12;"00"( TO 3-L
EN STR$ hs);hs
950 RETURN
```

and control is passed back to **menu**.

Changes and extensions

The program as given here contains only four specimen sets of words

However, the method of data storage should be straightforward enough to allow a teacher without any previous knowledge of programming to prepare a working version with up to 260 words. Sets of words could be defined thematically, as in the specimen sets, or by particular areas of difficulty, for example '-able or -ible?', 'ie or ei?'. Different versions of the program could be made for different groups of students. Alternatively different vocabularies could be merged with the main program using the technique shown later in TEXTBAG. Given a subroutine to define characters (see PORTRAIT) the program could be used with vocabulary lists for languages other than English.

Other adaptations and extensions of the program may be made on the basis of experience and personal preference. For example, some may find the screen format (based on the original version for the ZX81) too sober in view of the obvious roots of the game in arcade-games. Some work on lines 1070–1150 could produce a more colourful display. Others may want to make the noisy version noisier still, for example by replacing the delay loops in lines 340 and 360 by subroutines which play appropriate short musical phrases. Apart from cosmetic changes such as these, there are others which would affect both the playability and the pedagogic value of the game:

1 For some learners – particularly young children – it may be preferable to present words in lower case rather than upper case. In that case the first statement in line 1190 should be POKE 23658,0, and the DATA statements would have to be changed. It would also be desirable to incorporate an upper versus lower case check (see TEXTBAG) at line 610.

2 It may be that for some players the 'slow' version is still too fast. If so, a simple adjustment to line 890, for example:

   LET f = 1 + 4*(g\$ = "S")

will slow things down.

3 In the present version of the game the player's chance of beating the previous high score depends heavily on the set of words chosen: the longer the words, the greater the chance of scoring well. For some teachers this may be an advantage in that the player is motivated to work with the sets of longer (and possibly more difficult) words. Others may prefer to even things out by ensuring that each set of words is similar in length, or by adjusting the scoring system so that additional points are awarded for trapping and successfully bombing words.

4 The original version of the game did not show the word before it started spinning, thus giving the player more to do in 'perceiving' the word in the **trap** phase of the game. Omission of lines 250 and 270 in the present version will produce the same effect. Alterna-

tives would be to present the word for only a short period of time before it starts spinning, or to give the player the choice of whether the words will be shown.

5.6 PORTRAIT-ROBOT (PHOTOFIT)

This is the program for the French version of PHOTOFIT which was described in Chapter 3.7. The bulk of the listing is common to both the English and the French versions, which is why all the variable names are English. In converting the original English version to French, the author had to take account of two problems: providing accented characters, and dealing with gender and adjective agreements.

The first problem is fairly easy to solve with the Spectrum. The following lines of code define graphics E and graphics A as lower case é and à. All input was to be in lower case, and these two turned out to be all that were needed within the vocabulary of the game. In fact the student only needs access to the é. The documentation includes instructions in using the graphics characters, but there are no specific on-screen instructions. If the student, deliberately or accidentally types an unaccented e in place of é, the program simply corrects the letter and continues without comment.

```
10 REM Photofit French version
@John Higgins 1983 ************
20 GO SUB 6500: GO TO 1000
6499 REM Make accented character
s for e and a*******************
********************************
6500 RESTORE : FOR j=1 TO 2: REA
D j$: FOR k=0 TO 7: READ z: POKE
 USR j$+k,z: NEXT k: NEXT j
6510 RETURN
6520 DATA "A",32,16,56,4,124,68,
60,0,"E",4,8,28,34,62,32,30,0
```

We will deal with the problem of gender later. Meanwhile here are the initialisation procedures. We call the villain whose face is shown 'Jean le Terreur' ('Bill Bolt the Burglar' in the English version). First a numeric array is set up which contains the information about the sizes of Jean's features, and a string array to store the word for the feature which is being drawn at any time. Lines 1010 to 1060 give names to line numbers. This is so that one can tell what subsequent instructions are designed to do. For example 'GOSUB mouthout' will erase the mouth that has been drawn. (Using variables instead of line numbers is a Sinclair facility which is not available on many other machines.)

```
 999 REM Initialisation*********
*****************************
1000 CLS : DIM b(9): FOR j=1 TO
9: LET b(j)=INT (RND*3)+1: NEXT
j
1005 DIM e$(9,9): FOR j=1 TO 9:
READ e$(j): NEXT j
1010 LET faceout=100: LET facein
=120: LET hairout=150: LET hairi
n=170
1020 LET browout=200: LET browin
=220: LET eyesout=250: LET eyesi
n=270
1030 LET earsout=300: LET earsin
=320: LET noseout=350: LET nosei
n=370
1040 LET moustacheout=400: LET m
oustachein=420: LET mouthout=450
: LET mouthin=470
1050 LET beardout=500: LET beard
in=520
1060 LET input=1100: LET help=70
0: LET hold=0
1070 GO SUB 900: GO SUB 3000: LE
T x=159
```

The next action is to draw Jean's (or Bill's) face. Since this is done twice, once at the beginning and again at the end, it is put into a subroutine to save having to enter the code twice over. In line 900 we set co-ordinates for the drawing which will place the face on the left (when x is 32). In the line 1070, after this subroutine has been executed, the value of x is re-set to 159, which places the face 'drawn' by the student on the right of the screen. The other named variables, *face*, *hair*, etc, are used to store information about the size of the feature and will be called on in the drawing routines themselves:

```
 899 REM Draw Bill's face*******
********************************
 900 LET x=32: LET y=155
 910 LET face=5*(b(1)-2): GO SUB
 facein
 920 LET hair=b(2): GO SUB hairi
n
 930 LET brow=b(3): GO SUB browi
n
 940 LET eyes=b(4): GO SUB eyesi
n
 950 LET ears=b(5): GO SUB earsi
n
 960 LET nose=b(6): GO SUB nosei
n
 970 LET moustache=b(7)-1: GO SU
B moustachein
 980 LET mouth=b(8): GO SUB mout
hin
 990 LET beard=b(9)-1: GO SUB be
ardin: RETURN
```

The drawing routines are all placed near the beginning of the program in order to enhance speed. They look rather forbidding, but they work sufficiently well to produce recognisable features. Readers may like to try to improve them. Educationally, though, these rather crude drawings are just as effective as lifelike artwork. (See page 68.)

```
 98 REM Drawing routines*******
******************************
 99 REM faceout
100 GO SUB 150: GO SUB 300: PLO
T  INVERSE 1;x-face,y: DRAW  INV
ERSE 1;20+face,-50,1: DRAW  INVE
RSE 1;20,0: DRAW  INVERSE 1;20+f
ace,50,1: RETURN
119 REM facein
120 PLOT x-face,y: DRAW 20+face
,-50,1: DRAW 20,0: DRAW 20+face,
50,1: RETURN
149 REM hairout***************
******************************
150 FOR j=0 TO 18: PLOT  INVERS
E 1;x-5,y+j: DRAW  INVERSE 1;75,
0: NEXT j: RETURN
169 REM hairin
170 PLOT x-face,y: FOR j=0 TO (
62+2*face) STEP 3: DRAW 2,6*SIN
(j/(3*face/5+20))*hair: PLOT x-f
ace+j,y: NEXT j: RETURN
199 REM browout***************
******************************
200 FOR j=1 TO 5: PLOT  INVERSE
1;x+18-brow,y-5-j: DRAW  INVERS
E 1;10+brow*2,0: NEXT j
210 FOR j=1 TO 5: PLOT  INVERSE
1;x+36,y-5-j: DRAW  INVERSE 1;1
0+brow*2,0: NEXT j: RETURN
219 REM browin
220 FOR j=1 TO 10+brow*2: PLOT
x+18-brow*2+j,y-9-SIN ((brow-1)*
j): NEXT j
230 FOR j=1 TO 10+brow*2: PLOT
x+36+j,y-9-SIN (j*(brow-1)): NEX
T j: RETURN
249 REM eyesout***************
******************************
250 PLOT  INVERSE 1;x+18,y-18:
DRAW  INVERSE 1;10,0,eyes: DRAW
 INVERSE 1;-10,0,eyes: PLOT  INV
ERSE 1;x+36,y-18: DRAW  INVERSE
1;10,0,eyes: DRAW  INVERSE 1;-10
,0,eyes: RETURN
269 REM eyesin
270 PLOT x+23,y-18: PLOT x+41,y
-18: PLOT x+18,y-18: DRAW 10,0,e
yes: DRAW -10,0,eyes: PLOT x+36,
y-18: DRAW 10,0,eyes: DRAW -10,0
,eyes: RETURN
```

```
299 REM earsout***************
********************************
300 IF ears=0 THEN  RETURN
310 PLOT  INVERSE 1;x-face/2,14
2: DRAW  INVERSE 1;-ears*PI,0,PI
: DRAW  INVERSE 1;ears*PI+face/P
I,-12: DRAW  INVERSE 1;ears,0: P
LOT  INVERSE 1;x+60+face/2,142:
DRAW  INVERSE 1;ears*PI,0,-PI: D
RAW  INVERSE 1;-ears*PI-face/PI,
-12: DRAW  INVERSE 1;-ears,0: RE
TURN
319 REM earsin
320 PLOT x-face/2,142: DRAW -ea
rs*PI,0,PI: DRAW ears*PI+face/PI
,-12: DRAW ears,0: PLOT x+60+fac
e/2,142: DRAW ears*PI,0,-PI: DRA
W -ears*PI-face/PI,-12: DRAW -ea
rs,0: RETURN
349 REM noseout***************
********************************
350 PLOT  INVERSE 1;x+32,y-22:
DRAW  INVERSE 1;-2*nose,-10: DRA
W  INVERSE 1;4*nose,0: DRAW  INV
ERSE 1;-2*nose,10: RETURN
369 REM nosein
370 PLOT x+32,y-22: DRAW -2*nos
e,-10: DRAW 4*nose,0: DRAW -2*no
se,10: RETURN
399 REM moustacheout***********
********************************
400 FOR j=1 TO moustache+1: PLO
T  INVERSE 1;x+24-moustache,y-34
-j: DRAW  INVERSE 1;16+moustache
*2,0: NEXT j: RETURN
419 REM moustachein
420 IF moustache=0 THEN  RETURN

430 FOR j=1 TO moustache+1: PLO
T x+24-moustache,y-35: DRAW 16+m
oustache*2,0: NEXT j: RETURN
449 REM mouthout***************
********************************
450 PLOT x+24,y-40: DRAW  INVER
SE 1;16,0: DRAW  INVERSE 1;-16,0
,-mouth: RETURN
469 REM mouthin
470 PLOT x+24,y-40: DRAW 16,0:
DRAW -16,0,-mouth: RETURN
499 REM beardout***************
********************************
500 FOR j=1 TO 6*beard STEP bea
rd: PLOT x+31-6*beard+j,y-50: DR
AW  INVERSE 1;0,-beard*j: NEXT j
510 FOR j=-6*beard TO -1 STEP b
eard: PLOT x+32+(6*beard+j),y-50
: DRAW  INVERSE 1;0,beard*j: NEX
T j: RETURN
519 REM beardin
520 IF beard=0 THEN  RETURN
```

146

```
530 FOR j=1 TO 6*beard STEP bea
rd: PLOT x+31-6*beard+j,y-50: DR
AW 0,-beard*j: NEXT j
 540 FOR j=-6*beard TO -1 STEP b
eard: PLOT x+32+(6*beard+j),y-50
: DRAW 0,beard*j: NEXT j: RETURN
```

Lines 30 to 50 contain another subroutine which is used frequently, the one which holds a display constant until the student is ready to move on:

```
29 REM Continue routine ******
*******************************
 30 PRINT "Appuyez sur 'C' pour
continuer."
 40 IF INKEY$<>"c" THEN  GO TO
40
 50 RETURN
```

Instructions for the game are at lines 3000 to 3050. They occupy just one screen, so there is no need to offer an option to bypass them:

```
2999 REM Instructions***********
*******************************
3000 PRINT AT 0,12;"PORTRAIT-ROB
OT";AT 16,0;"Voici Jean La Terre
ur.  Regardezbien son visage.  V
ous m'aiderezplus tard a le dess
iner.": PRINT : GO SUB 30
3010 CLS : PRINT "Indiquez-moi l
a partie du visagea dessiner:"
3020 PRINT : PRINT " visage   ch
eveux    sourcils"," yeux    ore
illes  nez"," bouche    barbe
 moustache"
3030 PRINT : PRINT "Puis dites-m
oi comment la","modifier:"
3040 PRINT : PRINT " plus/moins
grand  large  long"," epais  gro
s  rond"," petit  court  mince
etroit"
3050 PRINT : PRINT "Tapez 'mots'
 pour revoir la","liste des mots
 que je comprends.Tapez 'compare
z' quand le dessinest fini.": PR
INT : GO SUB 30: RETURN
```

Lines 1080 and 1090 complete the initialisation process by re-setting all the size variables to zero, clearing the screen and displaying a

147

reminder to the student about how he or she can get help. The POKE instructions here simply make the keyboard 'click' louder in order to give better feedback to the fingers, and make sure that the CAPS LOCK is switched off, so that keys will show their lower case value:

```
1080 LET face=0: LET hair=0: LET
 brow=0: LET eyes=0: LET ears=0:
 LET nose=0: LET moustache=0: LE
T mouth=0: LET beard=0
1090 POKE 23609,70: POKE 23658,0
: CLS : PRINT AT 19,0;"('mots' p
our l'aide-memoire.)    "
```

The INPUT routine occupies lines 1100 to 1117. In the English version the input is limited to a single word, but in the French version we have to allow for 'plus grand' or 'moins large', so lines 1115 and 1117 allow us to reverse the meaning of a size adjective if 'moins' has been typed. The variable **com** will be used to show if an adjective has the general meaning 'big' or 'small', and the variable **more** is used to reverse it. The input word or phrase is called **d$**, but it has to be at least as long as the longest legal input (because of the way that the Sinclair handles string comparison), and that is why half a line of spaces is added to it:

```
1099 REM Input routine**********
*******************************
1100 INPUT "Vos instructions s.v
.p.",d$: LET d$=d$+"
"
1110 LET com=0: PRINT AT 16,0;"

                        "
1115 PRINT AT 14,0;d$: LET more=
1: IF d$( TO 5)="moins" THEN  LE
T more=-1: LET d$=d$(7 TO )
1117 IF d$( TO 4)="plus" THEN  L
ET d$=d$(6 TO )
```

The next stage consists of scanning the input to see if one of the nouns has been typed in. The variable **hold** is used to keep a record of the last noun recognised in order that we know what we are talking about when the student later wants to modify it. On finding a noun, the program erases that feature, redraws it in the middle size, changes the value of **hold**, and returns to line 1100 (input). Line 1195 covers the case where a student enters an adjective as his or her very first input, before mentioning any noun at all:

```
1119 REM Scan for nouns*********
********************************
1120 IF d$( TO 6)="visage" THEN
 GO SUB faceout: LET face=0: LET
 hold=1: GO SUB facein: GO TO in
put
1130 IF d$( TO 7)="cheveux" THEN
  GO SUB hairout: LET hair=2: LE
T hold=2: GO SUB hairin: GO TO i
nput
1140 IF d$( TO 8)="sourcils" THE
N  GO SUB browout: LET brow=2: L
ET hold=3: GO SUB browin: GO TO
input
1150 IF d$( TO 4)="yeux" THEN  G
O SUB eyesout: LET eyes=2: GO SU
B eyesin: LET hold=4: GO TO inpu
t
1155 IF d$( TO 8)="oreilles" THE
N  GO SUB earsout: LET hold=5: L
ET ears=2: GO SUB earsin: GO TO
input
1160 IF d$( TO 3)="nez" THEN  GO
 SUB noseout: LET nose=2: GO SUB
 nosein: LET hold=6: GO TO input
1170 IF d$( TO 9)="moustache" TH
EN  GO SUB moustacheout: LET mou
stache=1: GO SUB moustachein: LE
T hold=7: GO TO input
1180 IF d$( TO 6)="bouche" THEN
 GO SUB mouthout: LET mouth=2: G
O SUB mouthin: LET hold=8: GO TO
 input
1190 IF d$( TO 5)="barbe" THEN
GO SUB beardout: LET beard=1: GO
 SUB beardin: LET hold=9: GO TO
input
1195 IF hold=0 THEN  GO TO 1370:
 REM No feature specified
```

Scanning for adjectives is a little more complex. The first thing that the computer does in line 1200 is to pass the input to a matching routine in line 6000 to see if the input is one of the legal set of adjectives, and then to check whether the adjective agrees with the noun specified in the hold variable. It also changes intial e to é if necessary. If the adjective does not agree, the correct form is printed to overwrite the student's input. Notice how the computer is designed to behave. A teacher might say 'No, that's wrong. Try again'. In ordinary conversation a Frenchman might ignore your mistake or correct it, but will simply proceed with the conversation after that. In respect of agreements (and accents) the program is designed to behave like a conversational partner rather than like a teacher. The same attitude to correction underlies the 'intelligent spelling checker' used in TEXTBAG and explained in Chapter 5.6.

```
1199 REM Scan for adjectives****
*****************************
1200 LET p$=d$( TO 6): GO SUB 60
00: LET p$=d$( TO 5): GO SUB 600
0: LET p$=d$( TO 4): GO SUB 6000

5999 REM Adjective agreement rou
tine***************************
6000 IF p$(1)="e" THEN  LET p$(1
)="e"
6010 IF p$="etroit" OR p$="court
" OR p$="grand" OR p$="petit" OR
 p$="large" OR p$="mince" OR p$=
"epais" OR p$="long" OR p$="rond
" OR p$="gros" THEN  GO TO 6030
6020 RETURN
6030 FOR j=LEN d$ TO 4 STEP -1:
IF d$(j)=" " THEN  LET d$=d$( TO
 j-1)
6035 NEXT j
6040 LET p$=p$+("u" AND p$="long
" AND (hold=5 OR hold>6))
6050 LET p$=p$+("se" AND p$(LEN
p$)="s" AND (hold=5 OR hold>6))
6060 LET p$=p$+("e" AND p$(LEN p
$)<>"e" AND (hold=5 OR hold>6))
6070 LET p$=p$+("s" AND p$(LEN p
$)<>"s" AND (hold>1 AND hold<6))
6080 IF p$=d$ THEN  RETURN
6090 LET d$=p$: PRINT AT 14,0;d$
;"          ": RETURN
```

Lines 1205 to 1280 identify adjectives and set the variable **com** to correspond to their meanings. The program must decide whether each adjective collocates with the noun in **hold**. (The program bars 'big hair' or 'cheveux grands', for instance.) Assuming that the adjective is legal, the program passes control to one of the lines between 2000 and 2090 in which the new size will be checked against the current size to see if it can be changed. Here we use the facility in Sinclair BASIC to select a line to GO TO by means of calculation involving a variable. In other BASICS this is usually done with the formula on variable GO TO line numbers.

```
1205 IF d$( TO 4)="long" THEN  L
ET com=1*more: IF hold<>1 AND ho
ld<>4 AND hold<>7 THEN  GO TO 20
00+hold*10
1210 IF d$( TO 4)="gran" OR d$(
TO 4)="larg" THEN  LET com=1*mor
e: IF hold<>2 THEN  GO TO 2000+h
old*10
1220 IF d$( TO 4)="epai" OR d$(
```

```
 TO 4)="gros" THEN   LET com=1*mor
e: IF hold<>2 AND hold<>4 THEN
GO TO 2000+hold*10
1230 IF d$( TO 4)="rond" THEN   L
ET com=1*more: IF hold=4 OR hold
=7 THEN   GO TO 2000+hold*10
1240 IF d$( TO 4)="peti" THEN   L
ET com=-1*more: IF hold<>2 THEN
 GO TO 2000+hold*10
1250 IF d$( TO 4)="minc" OR d$(
TO 4)="etro" THEN   LET com=-1*mo
re: IF hold<>2 THEN   GO TO 2000+
hold*10
1260 IF d$( TO 4)="cour" THEN   L
ET com=-1*more: IF hold=2 OR hol
d=8 THEN   GO TO 2000+hold*10
1280 IF com=0 THEN   GO TO 1370



1999 REM Change shapes routines*
*********************************
2010 GO SUB faceout: LET face=5*
com-5*SGN com*(face/5=-com): GO
SUB facein: GO TO input
2020 GO SUB hairout: LET hair=ha
ir+com*((hair<3 AND com=1) OR (h
air>1 AND com=-1)): GO SUB hairi
n: GO TO input
2030 GO SUB browout: LET brow=br
ow+com*((brow<3 AND com=1) OR (b
row>1 AND com=-1)): GO SUB browi
n: GO TO input
2040 GO SUB eyesout: LET eyes=ey
es+com*((eyes<3 AND com=1) OR (e
yes>1 AND com=-1)): GO SUB eyesi
n: GO TO input
2050 GO SUB earsout: LET ears=ea
rs+com*((ears<3 AND com=1) OR (e
ars>1 AND com=-1)): GO SUB earsi
n: GO TO input
2060 GO SUB noseout: LET nose=no
se+com*((nose<3 AND com=1) OR (n
ose>1 AND com=-1)): GO SUB nosei
n: GO TO input
2070 GO SUB moustacheout: LET mo
ustache=moustache+com*((moustach
e>0 AND com=-1) OR (moustache<2
AND com=1)): GO SUB moustachein:
 GO TO input
2080 GO SUB mouthout: LET mouth=
mouth+com*((mouth<3 AND com=1) O
R (mouth>1 AND com=-1)): GO SUB
mouthin: GO TO input
2090 GO SUB beardout: LET beard=
beard+com*((beard>0 AND com=-1)
OR (beard<2 AND com=1)): GO SUB
beardin: GO TO input
```

Other messages, and unsuitable adjective/noun collocations are dealt with between 1300 and 1390. The program reads the noun from the array **e\$**, but must first strip off unwanted spaces included in the array because strings in string arrays have to be of uniform length. The space-stripping is done at line 6100:

```
1299 REM Unsuitable adjective***
********************************
1300 PRINT AT 16,0;"Je ne peux p
as dessiner ";
1310 PRINT ("des" AND (hold>1 AN
D hold<6));("un"  AND (hold=1 OR
 hold>5));("e" AND hold>6)
1320 GO SUB 6100: PRINT f$;d$;".
": GO TO input
1369 REM Other messages*********
********************************
1370 IF d$( TO 4)="mots" THEN  G
O SUB help: GO TO input
1380 IF d$( TO 8)="comparez" THE
N  GO TO 1500
1390 PRINT AT 16,0;"Je ne compre
nds pas.": GO TO input

6099 REM Strip spaces routines**
********************************
6100 LET f$=e$(hold): FOR j=9 TO
 3 STEP -1: IF f$(j)=" " THEN  L
ET f$=f$( TO j)
6110 NEXT j: RETURN
```

A help panel, which reminds students which words the machine is capable of recognising, is called up with the word 'mots'. This prints a

```
699 REM help routine***********
********************************
700 PRINT AT 0,0;"Je comprends:
": PRINT : PRINT "visage  cheveu
x": PRINT "oreilles yeux": PRINT
 "sourcils  nez": PRINT "bouche
barbe": PRINT "moustache": PRIN
T "plus  moins"
710 PRINT "long  court": PRINT
"large  etroit": PRINT "epais  m
ince": PRINT "grand  petit": PRI
NT "rond  gros": PRINT : PRINT "
mots  comparez"
720 PRINT AT 19,0;"
                    ";AT 18,0;: GO
SUB 30
740 PRINT AT 0,0;: FOR j=1 TO 1
9: PRINT "                   ": NEX
T j: PRINT AT 18,12;"
        ","('mots' pour l'aide-me
moire.)   ": RETURN
```

list of words over the left half of the screen, in order not to obliterate the working drawing, and is wiped off again when the student presses C. The listing for this is from lines 700 to 740.

The end of the game occurs when the student types 'comparez'. This passes control to line 1500, where, feature by feature, the student's drawing is compared with Jean's face. A message is generated for each difference. The problem of pronoun selection is dealt with in lines 60 to 90. The first message will be printed on line 12. Before printing a message the program looks up the cursor position (PEEK 23689), and selects the name 'Jean' if it is 12, and the pronoun 'il' if it is more than 12. The same technique is used at the end. Once all the comparisons have been made, if the cursor position is still 12, it follows that no messages have been printed and therefore no differences found. This leads the machine to print out the congratulatory message 'Une ressemblance parfaite.' Finally the user is offered the chance to play again.

```
1499 REM End of game************
********************************
1500 PRINT AT 14,0;"            "
;AT 18,0;"
         ";AT 12,0;: IF face<5*(
b(1)-2) THEN  GO SUB 60: PRINT "
le visage plus grand."
1510 IF face>5*(b(1)-2) THEN  GO
 SUB 60: PRINT "le visage plus p
etit."
1520 IF hair<>b(2) THEN  GO SUB
60: PRINT "les cheveux ";("plus
longs" AND hair<b(2));("plus cou
rts" AND hair>b(2));"."
1540 IF brow<>b(3) THEN  GO SUB
60: PRINT "les sourcils ";("plus
 epais" AND brow<b(3));("plus mi
nce" AND brow>b(3));"."
1560 IF eyes<>b(4) THEN  GO SUB
60: PRINT "les yeux ";("plus gra
nds" AND eyes<b(4));("plus petit
s" AND eyes>b(4));"."
1580 IF ears<>b(5) THEN  GO SUB
60: PRINT "les oreilles ";("plus
 grandes" AND ears<b(5));("plus
petites" AND ears>b(5));"."
1590 IF nose<>b(6) THEN  GO SUB
60: PRINT "le nez ";("plus grand
" AND nose<b(6));("plus petit" A
ND nose>b(6));"."
1610 IF mouth<>b(8) THEN  GO SUB
 60: PRINT "la bouche ";("plus g
rande" AND mouth<b(8));("plus pe
tite" AND mouth>b(8));"."
1630 IF moustache=0 AND b(7)>1 T
HEN  GO SUB 60: PRINT "une moust
ache.": GO TO 1670
```

153

```
1640 IF moustache<(b(7)-1) THEN
 GO SUB 60: PRINT "la moustache
plus grande.": GO TO 1670
1650 IF moustache>0 AND b(7)=1 T
HEN  GO SUB 80: PRINT "de mousta
che.": GO TO 1670
1660 IF moustache>b(7)-1 THEN  G
O SUB 60: PRINT "la moustache pl
us petite."
1670 IF beard=0 AND b(9)>1 THEN
 GO SUB 60: PRINT "une barbe.":
GO TO 1800
1680 IF beard<b(9)-1 THEN  GO SU
B 60: PRINT "la barbe plus longu
e."
1690 IF beard>0 AND b(9)=1 THEN
 GO SUB 80: PRINT "de barbe.": G
O TO 1800
1700 IF beard>b(9)-1 THEN  GO SU
B 60: PRINT "la barbe plus court
e."
1800 GO SUB 900
1810 IF PEEK 23689=12 THEN  PRIN
T : PRINT : PRINT "Une ressembla
nce parfaite."
1850 PRINT : PRINT : PRINT "Appu
yez sur 'R' pour jouer","encore
une fois."
1860 IF INKEY$="" THEN  GO TO 18
60
1870 IF INKEY$="r" THEN  RUN
1900 STOP

  59 REM Report routine*********
********************************
  60 IF PEEK 23689=12 THEN  PRIN
T "Jean a ";: RETURN
  70 PRINT "Il a ";: RETURN
  80 IF PEEK 23689=12 THEN  PRIN
T "Jean n'a pas ";: RETURN
  90 PRINT "Il n'a pas ";: RETURN
```

Here is a checklist of the variables used in the program:

Variables used to identify lines

faceout, facein, hairout, hairin, browout, browin, eyesout, eyesin, earsout, earsin, noseout, nosein, moustacheout, moustachein, mouthout, mouthin, beardout, beardin, input, help

Flag variables

com, more

Graphics co-ordinates

x, y

Drawing variables for feature and size

hold, face, hair, brow, eyes, ears, nose, mouth, moustache, beard

154

Counting variables
    j, k
Numeric array
    b(9)
String variable
    d$ – input drawing instructions
    p$ – adjective checked for agreement
    f$ – current feature, read from e$ and stripped of spaces
String array for reporting on current feature
    e$(9, 9)

The program as presented runs on the 48K Spectrum, and is too long to fit the 16K model. It is just possible to squeeze it in by the following means:

1   Delete all REM statements.

2   Shorten all the long variable names to one or two letters.

3   Combine lines wherever possible into multi-statement lines.

4   Replace the numbers, 0, 1, 2, 3, 4, 5, 6, 7, 8, 9, 12 and 50 by variables. (Each number used in a program occupies five bytes of memory, whereas a short variable uses only one, so it is possible to save memory by giving a variable name to a frequently occurring number.)

The outcome of these measures will be a program which is much more difficult to read and harder to de-bug, but there is no other solution if memory is short.

5.7 TEXTBAG

TEXTBAG is a program which invites the student to restore a masked text by 'buying' or guessing the hidden words. The procedure was described in Chapter 3.6. It is long and fairly complex and should be typed with care. Two cassettes are needed – one for the main program (lines 10 to 1810) and another for the texts (line 9000 onwards).

Starting Routines

```
  10 REM TEXTBAG      @Tim Johns
1981,1983************************
  14 BRIGHT 1: CLS : PRINT ;AT 8
,12;"TEXTBAG": GO SUB 1440
  20 GO SUB 1520: GO SUB 1580: G
O SUB 1460: CLS : GO TO 1010
```

Line 14 sets the screen to bright in contrast with the surrounding border. Subroutine 1440, called in the same line, warns the player to stop the tape:

```
1430 REM stoptape **************
1440 PRINT  FLASH 1;AT 12,9;"STO
P THE TAPE": RETURN
```

Line 20 calls three subroutines placed at the end of the program:
- 1520 **Initialisation**
- 1580 **Instructions**
- 1460 **Get file**

We shall look at each of these in turn.

```
1510 REM initialisation*********
********************************
1520 DIM a$(21,33): DIM b$(21,33
): LET y=1: LET x=y
1530 RESTORE 1540: FOR n=1 TO 2:
 READ u$: FOR m=0 TO 7: READ r:
POKE USR u$+m,r: NEXT m: NEXT n
1540 DATA "A",0,0,0,40,20,0,0,0
1550 DATA "B",195,129,129,129,12
9,129,129,195
1560 POKE 23658,0: LET stock=250
: LET s$="
           ": GO SUB 1210: RETURN
```

The two-dimensional string arrays **a$** and **b$** are set up: **a$** to hold up to 21 lines of text, each line being thirty-two.characters long plus an extra character to simplify the checking routines, and **b$** to contain a copy of **a$** with the letters obliterated. The coordinate variables **y** (line of text) and **x** (character in line) are also defined early in the program, since it is important that the BASIC interpreter should have rapid access to them in order to enable the cursor movement and word identification routines to run smoothly.

There are two user-defined graphics in the program: USR 'A' (character 144) is a centrally-placed tilde used to obliterate the characters in the text, and USR 'B' (character 145) is the text cursor – a pair of square brackets – which can be moved around the screen to identify the words to be bought or guessed.

In line 1560 **s$** is a string of thirty-two spaces to be used in 'wiping out' words and text, while **w$**, defined in subroutine 1210:

```
1200 REM wstring****************
1210 LET w$="????????????????????
????????????????": RETURN
```

is a 'dummy' string into which the player's guesses and answers will be copied. All that remains to be done before returning is to give the player an initial stock of 250 points, and to POKE a zero into the FLAGS2 systems variable to ensure that CAPS LOCK is switched off.

The **instructions** require little comment:

```
1570 REM instructions**********
******************************
1600 PRINT AT 12,1;" Do you want
 instructions? y/n"
1610 LET g$=INKEY$: IF g$="n" TH
EN  CLS : RETURN
1620 IF g$<>"y" THEN  GO TO 1610
1630 CLS : PRINT  ´´"This is a ga
me in which you willhave to rebu
ild texts and to"´"find informat
ion which is hiddenin them."´´"T
he computer will choose a text"´
"and remove all the letters,"´"l
eaving only the spaces and the"´
"punctuation."
1640 PRINT ´"To BUY one of the w
ords in the"´"text costs three p
oints: all you"´"have to do is m
ove the cursor "; INK 2;CHR$ 145
´ INK 0;"so that it is over the
word you"´"want and then press t
he ~B~"´"key."
1650 GO SUB 1790: PRINT  ´"If you
 think you can GUESS a"´"word, p
lace the cursor over it,"´"and p
ress the ~G~ key, when a"´"flash
ing cursor ~"; INK 2; FLASH 1;"
"; INK 0; FLASH 0;"~ will appear
,"´"ready for you to type in you
r"´"guess."
1660 PRINT ´"A successful guess
gets you 10"´"points, and the wo
rd will flash"´"green."´´"The pr
ogram will try to"´"recognize a
wrongly spelled word"´"but it wi
ll then flash purple"´"and you m
ay get less than 10"´"points."´´
"If you make a wrong guess you"´
"lose 5 points."
1670 GO SUB 1790: PRINT  ´"At the
 bottom of the screen"´"there wi
ll be a question which"´"can be
answered from the text -"´" one
word only is needed."
1680 PRINT ´"When you think that
 you can"´"ANSWER the question,
press the"´"~A~ key. After compl
eting your"´"answer, press ENTER
."
1690 PRINT ´"At the start you ca
n get 100"´"points (less any poi
nts for a"´"mis-spelling) for a
```

```
          correct"'"answer: this goes down
      as more"'"words appear in the t
      ext.  A"'"wrong answer loses 50
      points."'''When you have answere
      d the"'"question another one wil
      l"'"appear."
1700 GO SUB 1790: PRINT "You can
      make any corrections"'"when you
      are typing your GUESS"'"or your
      ANSWER by pressing the"'"back a
      rrow key ~5~"
1710  PRINT '"If you change your
      mind and"'"decide not to GUESS
      or to ANSWER"'"press the back ar
      row key when it"'"is at the star
      t of the word."
1720 PRINT '"If you want to QUIT
      the text you"'"are working on,
      press the ~Q~"'"key."
1730 PRINT '"The texts are loade
      d from a"'"separate cassette lab
      elled"'"TEXTS.  When you are pla
      ying the"'"game you will see at
      the top of"'"the screen the numb
      er of texts"'"that remain before
      you must load"'"a new cassette.
      "
1740 GO SUB 1790: PRINT "Finally
      , here are two tips for"'"playin
      g TEXTBAG -"'''1. In rebuilding
      the text, it"'"   is a good idea
       to BUY the"'"   longer words an
      d to try to"'"   GUESS the short
      er ones"'"   between them."
1750 PRINT '"2. Remember that th
      e sooner you"'"   answer the que
      stion at the"'"   bottom of the
      screen, the"'"   higher your rew
      ard will be."'"   So, from the s
      tart, decide"'"   where the info
      rmation you are"'"   looking for
       is likely to"'"   be, and let t
      hat guide you"'"   in rebuilding
      the text."
1760 PRINT '"  Would you like to
      read the"'"  instructions again
      ?  (y/n)"
1770 LET g$=INKEY$: GO TO 1770-1
40*(g$="y")+10*(g$="n")
1780 CLS : RETURN
1790 PRINT #1; BRIGHT 1;AT 1,0;"
      Press the ~C~ key to continue
      "
1800 IF INKEY$<>"c" AND INKEY$<>
"C" THEN  GO TO 1800
1810 CLS : RETURN
```

Notice that lines 1600–10 give the player the choice to avoid the instructions and lines 1760–1770 give an opportunity to read them again.

The **get file** routine asks the player to choose and load a cassette of texts, which will be merged with the main program as DATA statements from line 9000 onwards:

```
1450 REM getfile****************
********************************
1460 PRINT AT 2,0;"  Choose a ca
ssette of texts,"'"  place it in
 the tape-"'"  recorder, make ce
rtain that"'"  it is rewound to
the start,"'"  and press the PLA
Y button."''"  Then press any ke
y on the"'"  Spectrum."
1470 IF INKEY$="" THEN  GO TO 14
70
1480 PRINT AT 12,9; FLASH 1;"TEX
TS LOADING"
1490 RANDOMIZE : MERGE "TEXTS"
1500 RESTORE 9000: READ nt: DIM
t(nt+1): FOR n=1 TO nt: LET t(n)
=n: NEXT n: RETURN
```

In line 1500 the number of texts present in the merged text file is read into the variable **nt**, and a pointer array **t** is set up to select them.

It will help in understanding the rest of the program to see at this stage how the texts are stored. Here is a short specimen file of three texts:

```
9000 DATA 3
9005 DATA "AN AMBITIOUS LAD"
9010  DATA "Having left his home
 town of Coventry, Jack came up
to London to make his fortune.
After seeking work for two month
s, he was taken on as an apprent
ice to a barber.  He was given t
he princely wage of three pounds
, and could now begin to explore
 the pleasures of the great metr
opolis.  He was particularly fon
d of the theatre, and almost eve
ry evening of the week could be
found in the gallery or hanging
round the stage door waiting for
 a glimpse of one of his favouri
```

te actresses. One day, he thoug
ht, he would be a famous author,
 and all England would know his
name."
9015 DATA 6,"1432Jack came from"
,"1Coventry*","1732Jack worked f
or a","2barber*hairdresser*","11
18Jack earned   pounds a we
ek","1three*","2032Where did Jac
k work?","1London*","1032Jack li
ked","2actresses*theatres*","243
2Jack wanted to become an","1aut
hor*"
9020   DATA "THE NAUGHTY GNOME"
9025 DATA "Once upon a time ther
e was a little gnome whose name
was Gabble. He lived in a foxho
le which the previous owner had
deserted and earned his living b
y stealing milk from the neighbo
uring farm and turning it into b
utter, which he sold to the elve
s in the Big Wood. One day the
farmer caught sight of him and c
hased him waving a large stick.
  ~Stop!~ he shouted. ~If I catc
h you I'll skin you alive and fr
y you for breakfast!~ But Gabbl
e managed to run away and hide i
n a ditch until night came, when
 the farmer got tired of looking
 for him and went home for his s
upper."
9030   DATA 7,"2032The gnome's na
me was","1Gabble*","1432The gnom
e sold","1butter*","1832The gnom
e hid in a","1ditch*","1626The f
armer liked   gnomes","7e
ating*frying*skinning*fried*catc
hing*chasing*dead*","2032The gno
me lived in a","1foxhole*","1832
The farmer waved a","1stick*","0
311The   lived in the Big W
ood","1elves*"
9035 DATA "THE SAD PRINCESS"
9040 DATA "Once there was a beau
tiful princess called Alice who
lived in a tall tower. She was
eighteen years old, and had gree
n eyes and long golden hair whic
h hung down her back. Her lover
 was a handsome prince called Be
rthold who was away in France fi
ghting for the King. Before he
left she had given him a ring to
 remember her by, and he had giv
en her a red, red rose. She pre
ssed the rose between the pages
of her bible, and whenever she t
hought of him she opened the boo
k and the scent of the faded flo

```
wer filled the room."
9045  DATA 7,"2332Alice gave the
 prince a","1ring*","2132The pri
nce's name was","1Berthold*","16
32Alice lived in a","1tower*","2
432Alice kept a rose in her","1b
ible*","0928Alice had
         hair","2long*golden*","1
732Alice's eyes were","1green*",
"1732The prince was in","1France
*"
```

The DATA statement in line 9000 contains an index to the number of texts in the file: this must, of course, be updated every time new texts are added.

Each text is prefaced by a title: this is not used in this version of TEXTBAG, but is needed for programs such as STORYBOARD and CLOSE-UP.

The text itself is stored as a single DATA string. It would save time later in setting it up to store each screen line separately: that would, however, make it more difficult to use the same file for a program such as JUMBLER, which involves the re-ordering of the whole text before it is printed.

The text is followed by the questions and answers. It will be seen that these are stored with the index to the number of questions first, and the questions and answers stored alternately. Each question string contains two two-digit numbers which will be sliced off later to show where the player's answer will appear, and the space available for it. For example,

"1432Jack came from"

shows that the initial text is fourteen characters long, and that there is space available for the answer up to the thirty-second column on the screen.

While many questions on a text will have only one 'correct' answer, others may allow a number which are equally plausible – see, for example, the fourth question on the second text. The way answers are stored allows up to nine alternatives: an initial one-digit number shows the number of answers stored, and an asterisk is used as a final delimiter for each one.

In setting up a new text file, or adding texts to a new one, it is important to follow exactly the method of line-numbering shown in the specimen file, since the sequence is used within the main program to restore the data pointer to the selected text (see line 1020 on p.162.)

Each text and accompanying material takes up a little over 900 bytes, which allows the 48K Spectrum to load approximately thirty texts in addition to the main program.

Setting up text

Having merged the text data, the program jumps to the **newtext** routine:

```
 990 REM newtext****************
****************************
1000 GO SUB 1360: IF NOT nt OR g
$="c" THEN   GO SUB 1460: GO SUB
1350
1010 GO SUB 1420
1020 LET text=t(1+INT (nt*RND)):
 RESTORE 8995+15*text
1030 FOR n=text TO nt: LET t(n)=
t(n+1): NEXT n: LET nt=nt-1
1040 GO SUB 80: GO SUB 40: GO SU
B 1190
1050 LET done=0: LET words=0: LE
T check=1: LET x=1: LET y=1
1060 GO SUB 1380: GO SUB 1400: F
OR n=1 TO lines: PRINT b$(n)( TO
 32): NEXT n: GO SUB 1320: GO SU'
```

There are two entry points to the routine:

Line 1000, to be used on subsequent calls to the routine, calls the wipe subroutine to remove previous text from the screen:

```
1350 REM wipe*******************
1360 PRINT AT 0,0: FOR n=1 TO 21
: PRINT s$: NEXT n: PRINT #1;AT
1,0; BRIGHT 1;s$: RETURN
```

and checks whether a new cassette of texts is to be loaded, in which case the appropriate subroutines are called. Control then passes to Line 1010, used as the entry point on the first call to the routine. This line calls a subroutine to print a 'wait' message, since the preparation and manipulation of the text take a little time (on average fifteen seconds):

```
1410 REM wait*******************
1420 PRINT AT 9,6;"Please wait a
 moment": RETURN
```

A text is then selected: line 1020 sets the data pointer, and 1030 adjusts the pointer array **t** to ensure that the text is not selected again.

Line 1040 calls three important subroutines: **loadarrays, manipulate, and pickquestion.**

```
 70 REM loadarrays************
 80 READ t$: LET lines=1
 90 LET fit=33
100 IF LEN t$<fit THEN  LET a$(
lines)=t$: GO TO 150
110 IF t$(fit)<>" " AND t$(fit-
1)<>"-" THEN  LET fit=fit-1: GO
TO 110
120 LET a$(lines)=t$( TO fit-1)
: LET t$=t$(fit TO ): LET lines=
lines+1
130 IF t$(1)=" " THEN  LET t$=t
$(2 TO ): GO TO 130
140 GO TO 90
150 READ nq: DIM q(nq+1): DIM q
$(nq,36): DIM r$(nq,60)
160 FOR n=1 TO nq: LET q(n)=n:
READ q$(n): READ r$(n): NEXT n:
RETURN
```

The text is read into **t$** and in 90–140 is copied into the **a$** array in such a way that the words do not 'spill over' from one line to the next. At the end of the routine the variable **lines** contains the number of lines of text.

In line 150 the variable **nq** is set to the number of available questions, and the question pointer array **q** and the question and answer string arrays – **q$** and **r$** respectively – are set up. In line 160 the arrays are filled, the questions and answers being copied from the data statements in the next file.

The **manipulate** subroutine accounts for most of the delay in preparing the text, so it is, along with the previous subroutine, placed as early in the program as possible:

```
 30 REM manipulate************
 40 FOR n=1 TO lines: LET b$(n)
=a$(n): NEXT n
 50 FOR n=1 TO lines: FOR m=1 T
O 32: LET z$=a$(n,m): IF (z$>="A
" AND z$<="Z") OR (z$>="a" AND z
$<="z") THEN  LET b$(n,m)=CHR$ 1
44
 60 NEXT m: NEXT n: RETURN
```

Each character in the **a$** array is checked to see whether it is a letter of the alphabet: if not, it is copied into the corresponding position in the **b$** array: if so, that position is filled with the obliteration character.

The **pickquestion** subroutine is fast, and can be placed later in the program:

```
1180 REM pickquestion***********
1190 LET qu=1+INT (RND*nq): LET
p$=q$(q(qu)): LET lmar=VAL p$(1
TO 2)+2: LET rmar=VAL p$(3 TO 4)
: LET p$=p$(5 TO ): RETURN
```

The question to be answered is randomly selected using the pointer array, and is copied into **p$**: the variables **lmar** and **rmar**, sliced out from the start of the string, will be used to identify the space for the player's answer.

All is now ready to print the screen for the playing of the game. This is done in line 1050. Subroutines **printnt** and **printstock** print in blue (INK 1) at the top of the screen the number of texts left, and the player's current stock of points:

```
1370 REM printnt***************
1380 PRINT AT 0,0; INK 1;("LAST"
 AND NOT nt);(STR$ nt AND nt);"
TEXT";("S" AND nt>1);(" LEFT" AN
D nt);"  ": RETURN
```

It is worth studying how line 1390, by testing the variable **nt**, will print as required:

$$(nt = 2)$$
$$(nt = 1)$$
$$(nt = 0)$$

Notice also how line 1390 ensures that the player's stock of points, no matter how small or how large, will always be printed flush with the right hand side of the screen.

Having dealt with the top line of the screen, the program then proceeds, by means of a simple loop, to print the obliterated text from the **b$** array. The space available for the text is from the second to the twenty-second lines, while the prompts (reminding the player what choices are available) and the question are printed on the twenty-third and twenty-fourth lines respectively. These lines are normally reserved on the Spectrum for INPUT and for error messages:

they can, however, be used from within a BASIC program by means of the command PRINT #1 (PRINT #2 printing on the normal upper screen).

```
1270 REM banner****************
1280 IF LEN p$>31 THEN  GO TO 13
00
1290 LET p$=p$+s$( TO 32-LEN p$)
1300 FOR n=1 TO 32: PRINT #1; BR
IGHT 1;AT 1,32-n;p$( TO n): FOR
m=1 TO 5: NEXT m: NEXT n: RETURN
1310 REM prompt1****************
1320 PRINT #1;AT 0,0;"B=buy  A=a
nswer  G=guess  Q=quit": RETURN
1330 REM prompt2****************
1340 PRINT #1;AT 0,0;"  Press E
NTER when finished   ": RETURN
```

1280–1300 show a simple technique for 'padding out' the question with spaces, and then sliding it into position, billboard-fashion, from the right of the screen.

The routine
The central routine for moving the text cursor around the screen and for distributing control to the **buy**, **guess**, **answer**, and **quit** routines is shown below:

```
420 REM game*****************
*******************************
430  PRINT AT y,x-1; OVER 1; IN
K 2;CHR$ 145
440 LET g$=INKEY$
450 GO TO 460+20*(g$="5")+30*(g
$="8")+40*(g$="6")+50*(g$="7")
460 GO TO 440+90*(g$="b")+150*(
g$="g")+260*(g$="a")+510*(g$="q"
)
470 REM movecursor************
480 PRINT AT y,x-1;b$(y,x): LET
x=x-(x>1): GO TO 430
490 PRINT AT y,x-1;b$(y,x): LET
x=x+(x<32): GO TO 430
500 PRINT AT y,x-1;b$(y,x): LET
y=y+(y<lines): GO TO 430
510 PRINT AT y,x-1;b$(y,x): LET
y=y-(y>1): GO TO 430
```

The cursor is printed in red in line 430 using OVER 1 so that the character underneath shows through. Lines 450 and 460 show to good advantage the ability of Sinclair BASIC to evaluate GO TO statements: this allows a more immediate response to INKEY than would a series of conditional statements of the form:

IF g$ = "5" THEN GO TO 480
IF g$ = "6" THEN GO TO 490   etc.

A point worth noticing is that the text columns are numbered 1–32 in the **a$** and **b$** arrays, and 0–31 for printing to the screen. Thus x in the array corresponds to x−1 on the screen. Since the first line of text is the second line on the screen, a similar conversion is not required for the y-coordinate.

Buy routine

```
520 REM buy*********************
*******************************
530 IF b$ (y,x)<>CHR$ 144 THEN
GO TO 470
540 GO SUB 1080: LET ink=2: LET
stock=stock-3
550 LET inv=1: GO SUB 1250: GO
SUB 1400: FOR n=1 TO 50: NEXT n:
LET b$(y,start TO end)=a$(y,sta
rt TO end): GO SUB 1150: LET ink
=0: LET inv=0: GO SUB 1250
560 IF done THEN  GO TO 960
570 LET x=end: LET words=words+
1: GO TO 430
```

Line 530 deals with the case of the player who has attempted to buy a space or a punctuation mark or a word that is already on the screen. If all is well, subroutine **startend** is called in line 540 to identify the start and the end of the word:

```
1070 REM startend***************
1080 PRINT AT y,x-1;b$(y,x): LET
 end=x
1090 IF x=1 THEN  GO TO 1110
1100 IF b$(y,x-1)=CHR$ 144 THEN
 LET x=x-1: GO TO 1090
1110 LET start=x
1120 IF b$(y,end+1)=CHR$ 144 THE
N  LET end=end+1: GO TO 1120
1130 RETURN
```

ink is then set to 2, and **inv** to 1 so that the bought word will appear, fairly dramatically, in white on a red background when the **showword** subroutine is called:

166

```
1240 REM showword**************
1250 PRINT  INK ink; INVERSE inv
;AT y,start-1;a$(y,start TO end)
1260 GO SUB 1140: RETURN
```

The player's stock of points having been reduced by 3 in line 540, the **printstock** subroutine is called, and the bought word is copied into the appropriate position in the **b$** array. Throughout the game **b$** holds a copy of what is on the screen, so that when **b$** corresponds exactly to **a$** the program can recognise that the text has been completed. The ongoing comparison between the two arrays is carried out by the **checkscreen** subroutine; the **check** variable holding the line number of the point before which the text has been reconstituted:

```
1140 REM checkscreen***********
1150 IF a$(check)<>b$(check) THE
N  RETURN
1160 IF check=lines THEN  LET do
ne=1: RETURN
1170 LET check=check+1: GO TO 11
50
```

which sets the flag variable **done** if the text has been completed.

After a short pause loop, **showword** is called again, this time printing the word more soberly in black on white, **done** is checked, the variable **words** (used in calculating the reward for a successful answer) is updated, and x is set to **end** so that, on return to the main game routine, the text cursor will appear over the last letter of the bought word.

Guess Routine

```
580 REM guess*****************
*******************************
590 IF b$(y,x)<>CHR$ 144 THEN
GO TO 470
600 GO SUB 1080: LET d$=CHR$ 14
4: LET screen=2: GO SUB 180
610 IF change=1 THEN  PRINT AT
y,start-1;CHR$ 144: LET x=end: G
O TO 430
620 LET c$=a$(y): GO SUB 300
630 IF NOT gotit THEN  GO TO 67
0
640 REM rightguess************
```

167

```
650 LET stock=stock+10-INT (7*s
ub/(1+end-start)): LET ink=3+(NO
T sub): GO TO 550
 660 REM wrongguess*************
 670 FOR n=start-1 TO end-1: PRI
NT AT y,n;CHR$ 144: NEXT n
 680 LET stock=stock-5: GO SUB 1
390: GO TO 430
```

Having checked that the player has selected an obliterated word, **startend** is called. **l$** (the 'replacement character' for use when the player backspaces the input cursor) and **screen** are defined, and the **input** subroutine is called:

```
170 REM input*****************
180 LET change=0
190 FOR n=start TO end
200 PRINT #screen;AT y,n-1; OVE
R 1; BRIGHT 1; FLASH 1; INK 2;"
"
210 IF INKEY$<>"" THEN  GO TO 2
10
220 LET g$=INKEY$: IF (g$>="A"
AND g$<="Z") OR (g$>="a" AND g$<
="z") THEN  PRINT #screen; BRIGH
T 1;AT y,n-1;g$: LET w$(n)=g$: G
O TO 270
230 IF CODE g$=53 AND n=start T
HEN  LET change=1: RETURN
240 IF CODE g$=53 THEN  PRINT #
screen; BRIGHT 1;AT y,n-2;d$;d$:
LET n=n-1: GO TO 200
250 IF screen=1 AND CODE g$=13
THEN  RETURN
260 GO TO 220
270 NEXT n
280 RETURN
```

This subroutine illustrates the greater flexibility from using a custom-made input routine in place of the standard INPUT provided by the BASIC interpreter. Most obviously, it is possible to arrange for input to be made within the text rather than – as is always the case with the Sinclair INPUT – at the bottom of the screen. The programmer is free to design an input cursor to taste – in this case (line 200) a flashing red block, which contrasts nicely with the non-flashing open brackets of the text cursor. Most important of all, it is possible to check each key depression and take action accordingly.

210 Guards against unintentional 'double entries'.
220 Checks that entries are alphabetic.
230 Allows the player to change his or her mind about making a guess by pressing the left-arrow key when the cursor is at the

168

start of a word. The **change** flag variable is set to enable the main routine to recognise that a guess has not been made.

240 Allows the player to backspace the cursor by pressing the left-arrow key when it is at any place in the word other than the first letter.

250 To understand this line it is necessary to know that the same subroutine is used for input for a 'guess' (screen = 2) and for in 'answer' (screen = 1). For a **guess** the player does not have to press ENTER when the word is completed: the length of the required word is apparent from the screen display, and, the input loop having been set to that length, input is automatically terminated when the last letter is typed. For an **answer**, however, the length of expected response is not given, and the input loop is set to the length of the available space. Accordingly, the player must press ENTER (CODE 13) when the word is finished.

On return from **input**, the **change** flag is tested and control returned to the **game** routine if it is set. If not, a guess has been made which must be checked against the word in the **a$** array. The relevant line is copied out of **a$** into **c$**, and the **checkword** subroutine called:

```
290 REM checkword**************
300 LET sub=0: LET back=sub
310 FOR m=start TO end: IF w$(m
)=c$(m) THEN   GO TO 370
320 IF ABS (CODE w$(m)-CODE c$(
m))=32 THEN   LET sub=sub+0.4: GO
TO 370
330 IF w$(m)=c$(m+1) AND w$(m+1
)=c$(m) THEN   LET w$(m+1)=w$(m):
LET sub=sub+2: GO TO 370
340 IF w$(m+1)=c$(m) THEN   LET
w$(m TO )=w$(m+1 TO ): LET back=
back+1: LET sub=sub+2: GO TO 370
350 IF w$(m)=c$(m+1) THEN   LET
w$(m+1 TO )=w$(m TO ): LET back=
back-1: LET sub=sub+2: GO TO 370
360 LET sub=sub+2.5
370 NEXT m
380 IF screen=1 THEN   GO SUB 40
0
390 LET gotit=sub<=(end-start):
RETURN
400 IF len-1mar-back>end THEN
LET sub=sub+2*(len-1mar-back-end
)
410 RETURN
```

This subroutine is worth studying in detail to see how it works and how it might be adapted and possibly improved for other programs where 'semi-intelligent' checking of student input is required. The basis for such a routine is that simple matching of input against target response produces results which have helped to give computer-assisted learning a bad name among language teachers. A human teacher, seeking the answer 'America' is able to recognise that 'France' is wrong, while 'Amerika' or 'america' or 'Ammerica' are attempts at the right answer that have been let down by spelling or typing mistakes. Simple matching treats all the responses as equally bad. For the machine to behave in a more 'human' way it will have to do at least the following:

1 Measure the extent of deviance between input and target, and compare the proportion that is deviant with the proportion that is non-deviant. Thus we would expect the machine to recognize that 'cat' is not an attempt to spell 'dog' (3/3 mismatches), while 'defelupmemt' is quite possibly an attempt to spell 'development' (3/11 mismatches).

2 Have the ability to weight deviances differentially. To take a simple example, we would expect the machine to recognize that the degree of similarity between 'The' and 'the' is very much greater than that between 'The' and She'.

3 Have some ability – however primitive – to go beyond simple one-to-one matching by looking for disturbances in pattern between input and target. For example, the human being, recognizing the matching pattern of letters after the second 'm' would judge 'Ammerica' to have one mismatch: character-by-character matching would show six mismatches. There are three fundamental sources of pattern-disturbance:

a) reversal of letters – for example, 'colunm'
b) insertion of letters – for example, 'Ammerica'
c) omission of letters – for example, 'agression'

The **checkword** subroutine should not be too difficult to understand in the light of the above discussion. The variable **sub** is set up to accumulate an estimate of the extent of deviance between target and input, and the flag variable **gotit** (no explanation necessary) set in line 390 on the basis of a comparison of the final value of **sub** and the length of the target word. Within the loop, line 310 checks for one-to-one correspondence between characters, 320 for upper v. lower case, 330 for reversal, 340 for insertion, and 350 for omission.

Where input is obtained from the 'answer' routine it may – even after adjustments made to **w\$** for insertion and omission – be different in length from the target. Since the checking loop is defined on the length of the target, this presents no problem as long as input is shorter than the target: the non-alphabetic 'padding' in the copy string **w\$** will trigger the appropriate increments of **sub** at line 360. The case where student input remains **longer** than target is covered by subroutine 400: notice the use of the **back** variable which records any changes made in lines 340 and 350 to the initial length of input. Logically, of course, **sub** should also take account of the value of **back** for 'guess' input: however, trial and error suggests that any consequent improvement in the performance of the subroutine would be negligible except for a few highly idosyncratic mis-spellings.

On return from **checkword** the **gotit** flag is tested: if it is set, the player's reward is estimated on the basis of the extent of deviance from the target word, and the colour for the display of the word determined (magenta – INK 3 – deviance: green – INK 4 – no deviance). Return to the **game** routine is then made via line 550 of the **buy** routine.

Where **gotit** is not set, the player's guess is unceremoniously removed from the screen, five points deducted from his or her stock of points, and control returned to the **game** routine.

Answer Routine

```
 690 REM answer****************
*******************************
 700 IF NOT nq THEN   GO TO 430
 710 PRINT AT y,x-1;b$(y,x): GO
SUB 1340: GO SUB 1210
 720 LET start=lmar: LET end=rma
r-1: LET yy=y: LET y=1: LET scre
en=1: LET d$=" ": GO SUB 180: LE
T len=n
 730 PRINT #1;AT y,n-1; BRIGHT 1
;" ": IF change THEN  LET y=yy:
GO SUB 1320: GO TO 430
 740 LET x$=w$(lmar TO )
 750 REM extract****************
 755 LET e$=r$(q(qu))
 760 LET na=VAL e$(1): LET e$=e$
(2 TO )
 770 FOR n=1 TO na: LET start=1:
LET end=1
 780 IF e$(end+1)<>"*" THEN  LET
end=end+1: GO TO 780
 790 LET c$=e$( TO end)+"*": LET
w$=x$: GO SUB 300: IF gotit THE
N  GO TO 840
 800 LET e$=e$(end+2 TO ): NEXT
n
 810 REM   wronganswer**********
 820 FOR n=lmar-1  TO rmar-1: PR
INT #1;AT 1,n; BRIGHT 1;" ": NEX
T n: LET stock=stock-50: GO SUB
1390: GO TO 880
 830 REM rightanswer***********
 840 LET stock=stock+100-words-I
NT (50*sub/(1+end-start)): LET f
lash=1: LET ink=3+(NOT sub): GO
SUB 1230: GO SUB 1400
 850 FOR n=0 TO 200: NEXT n: LET
```

```
flash=0: LET ink=0: GO SUB 1230
860 FOR n=qu TO nq: LET q(n)=q(
n+1): NEXT n: LET nq=nq-1: IF NO
T nq THEN    GO TO 900
870 GO SUB 1190: GO SUB 1280
880 LET y=yy: GO SUB 1210: GO S
UB 1320: GO TO 430
890 REM lastquestion***********
900 GO SUB 1320: LET p$="    Tha
t's your last question": GO SUB
1280
910 FOR m=1 TO 100: NEXT m: LET
p$="Continue with the same text
? y/n": GO SUB 1280
920 LET g$=INKEY$: GO TO 920+10
*(g$="y")+30*(g$="n")
930 LET p$="": GO SUB 1280: LET
y=yy: GO TO 430
```

The **answer** routine should be relatively easy to understand for anyone who has managed to follow how the **guess** routine works.

In the **extract** section (lines 750 to 800) answers are extracted one by one from the alternatives stored in the **r$** array and passed to the **checkword** subroutine until a match is found with the player's input or there are no alternatives left. The delay involved in checking a number of alternatives is noticeable with the present form of the **checkword** subroutine (up to two or three seconds), which is why the program does not allow for the storage of more than nine.

The only new subroutine called from this routine is **printword** which gives a flashier display of the correct answer than **showword**:

```
1220 REM printword**************
1230 PRINT #1;AT 1,lmar-1; INK i
nk; FLASH flash;   BRIGHT 1;c$(1
TO end); FLASH 0;s$( TO rmar-lma
r-end): RETURN
```

Lines 900 to 980 cater for cater for players who have completed all the questions on a text, and would either like to continue reconstituting the text, or would like to move on to a new one.

Quit Routine

```
940 REM quit*******************
950 PRINT AT 1,0;: FOR n=1 TO l
ines: PRINT a$(n, TO 32): NEXT n
960 LET p$="   t=new text    c=n
ew cassette": GO SUB 1270
970 LET g$=INKEY$: IF g$='t' OR
g$="c" THEN   GO TO 1000
980 GO TO 970
```

There are two entry points to this routine: 960 (used when the text has been completed) and 950 (when it has not).

Changes and extensions

Being a very flexible type of program, TEXTBAG is open to a number of alterations and improvements. Some possibilities are outlined below: others will no doubt occur to the reader.

1   Small 'cosmetic' changes might make the game more attractive for some players. Experiment with different coloured borders (yellow – BORDER 6 – is quite effective). Try the effect of changing the length of the pauses during word display, or filling the pauses with short fanfares using the BEEP command. You may find the rewards and penalties too mean, or too generous: if so, try changing the formulae for calculating stock in lines 540, 650, 680, 820 and 840.

2   The program obliterates letters only. To obliterate numbers also, it is necessary to extend the conditional statement in line 50:

   IF(z$ > = '0' AND z$ < = '9') OR (z$ > = 'A' AND z$ < = 'Z') OR (z$ > = 'A' AND z$ < = 'z') THEN LET b$ (n,m) = CHR$ 144

   and to make a similar change in line 220. The resulting small gain in flexibility – you will now, for example, be able to ask questions about dates concealed in the text – will, however, be bought at the expense of an increased delay in setting up the text and a slightly less crisp response to the input cursor.

3   A problem with the present program is that, to make the maximum amount of space available for the text, the space for question + answer is restricted to one line. It might well be worth while rewriting the relevant parts of the program so that two lines are available for this purpose, with a corresponding reduction to twenty lines in the space for text.

4   In this version the program will only handle texts written in the character set for English normally available on the Spectrum. To enable it to handle texts in a range of different languages, include an index number at the start of the text file (for example 0 for English, 1 for French, 2 for German, 3 for Russian). Insert a line immediately after the file is merged with the main program which will use the index to branch the program to a subroutine that loads the appropriate user-defined graphics: for example:

   1495 READ lang: GO SUB 2000 + 100*lang

   Alternatively the UDG subroutine would be merged at a fixed location along with the text data. In either case, it would be possible in the same subroutine to define the various screen prompts and messages in the language of the text file, while in line 1050 **lang** could be used to branch to subroutines for French,

German etc. corresponding to **printstock** for English.

5   Having chosen a suitable cassette of texts, the player, in this version of TEXTBAG, is given no control over the order in which texts are selected. Players may well prefer to select texts for themselves, choosing topics that interest them, or avoiding or looking again at texts that they have worked with previously. To make this change it will be necessary to delete line 1020 and replace it with a section of code – half-a-dozen lines will do the trick – which will:

   a) Read the titles of the texts directly from the file and print them as a numbered menu.
   b) Ask the student to select one of the texts by typing in its number. More ambitiously, you could design a special cursor which would be moved up and down alongside the menu to indicate a selection.
   c) Check the player's choice and use it to restore the data pointer to the text chosen.

   An elaboration of this idea – and in the authors' view a very desirable one – is to ask players whether they want to select texts themselves or let the computer do it. A flag variable would be set on the basis of that choice, and used to direct the program to the appropriate routine around line 1020.

6   The routine that offers most scope for further development is **checkword**.
   a) The only character-to-character correspondence recognised by the routine is upper v. lower case. It measures 'Cat' as being closer to 'cat' than 'mat', but cannot recognise that 'kat' is also closer to 'cat' than 'mat'. Checks of frequently-confused letters that could tune the routine more finely would include:
      i)   Specific sound-spelling correspondences – for example 'c' and 'k'.
      ii) More general sound-spelling correspondences – for example that both target and input characters are vowels.
      iii) Mirror-image reversals – for example 'b' and 'd'.
      iv) Voiced versus unvoiced consonants – for example 'p' and 'b'.

      For maximum efficiency, the choice of possible correspondences and the weighting given to them should take into account the language background of the user. Thus a check for iii) is likely to give greatest improvement in the sensitivity of the routine for children learning English as a first language, while iv) will be most use for learners of English as a foreign language: 'p' and 'b', for example, represent a particular difficulty for Arabic-speaking learners.

b) The checks for inserted and omitted letters might be improved in several ways. For example, if presented with 'Ammirica' the routine will not recognize that an insertion has been made on the third pass through the routine – though it will be recognized on the fourth pass. Fine-tuning in this area could use one or more of the following techniques:
   i) Adding a check for repetition or non-repetition of the previous character.
   ii) Incorporation of checks on possible correspondences in examining the context (in the example given both 'i' and 'e' are vowels).
   iii) Extension of forward search for a one-to-one match in context.

   In making extensions such as those outlined above it is important to keep in mind the trade-off between the sophistication of the routine and the speed at which it will execute. Where only one target word is to be checked against input, a number of extensions could be made and processing time kept within reasonable limits. For programs such as TEXTBAG where a number of target words may have to be checked it is best to keep the routine relatively simple.

c) An expanded version of the routine could be used as the basis of a program which would train spelling. Features of such a program might be:
   i) Animated display of corrections of the student's input.
   ii) Storage of information about the categories of error made by the student in order that the program can decide whether to switch into appropriate remedial material.

7 As has been mentioned, the major delay in playing the game is caused by the manipulation of the **b$** array. The **manipulate** subroutine is simple in structure: it is slow because each character in **a$** has to be checked using the codes for upper and lower case characters. This subroutine can be considerably speeded up if we use machine code rather than BASIC: the version below reduces the overall waiting time between texts to two or three seconds, and also, incidentally, obliterates numeric as well as alphabetic characters. It requires only the addition of the following lines to the program to POKE 57 bytes into the area of the Spectrum normally used as a buffer by the printer: it is relocatable, so the code could also be placed in a REM statement at the start of the program.

With lines 1551 to 1557 in place, lines 30 to 60 can be deleted; GOSUB 40 in line 1040 replaced by LET xx = USR 23296; and the alteration on page 173 made to the **input** routine in order to allow for numeric input. There is also no need now for the **wait** routine.

```
1550>DATA "B",195,129,129,129,12
9,129,129,195
1551 FOR n=23296 TO 23352: READ
r: POKE n,r: NEXT n
1552 DATA 42,75,92,17,8,0,25,229
,17,189
1553 DATA 2,25,235,225,213,1,181
,2,197,237
1554 DATA 176,193,225,126,254,48
,56,22,254,58
1555 DATA 56,16,254,65,56,28,254
,91,56,8
1556  DATA 254,97,56,6,254,123,4
8,2,54,144
1557 DATA 35,11,120,177,32,223,2
01
```

For those who would like to have some idea of how the routine works, the assembler program that will generate the code is given below. Note that the structure of the program is considerably simplified by the fact that the **a$** and **b$** arrays, having been defined first in the initialisation routine, will come at the start of the variables area.

	LD	HL,(23627)	; Find start of variables area
	LD	DE,8	; find location of the first character
	ADD	HL,DE	; in a$ array
	PUSH	HL	; and save it.
	LD	DE,701	; Find location of first character
	ADD	HL,DE	; in b$ array
	EX	DE,HL	; and make DE point to it.
	POP	HL	; Get back start of a$,
	PUSH	DE	; save location of 1st character in b$,
	LD	BC, 693	; load BC counter to move 21 × 33 characters from a$ to b$,
	PUSH	BC	; save counter,
	LDIR		; and copy whole of a$ to b$.
	POP	BC	; Get back counter
	POP	HL	; and start of b$.
LOOP	LD	A,(HL)	; Identify character in b$.
	CP	48	; Code less than 48 (="0")?
	JR	C, NEXT	; If so, leave alone and on to next.
	CP	58	; Code less than 58 (=":")?
	JR	C, TILDE	; If so, obliterate.
	CP	65	; Code less than 65 (="A")?
	JR	C, NEXT	; If so, leave alone and on to next.

176

```
CP       91          ; Code less than 91 (=" ")?
JR       C, TILDE    ; If so, obliterate.
CP       97          ; Code less than 97 (="a")?
JR       C, NEXT     ; If so, leave alone and on to next.
CP       123         ; Code less than 123 (=" ")?
JR       NC, NEXT    ; If not, leave alone and on to next.
TILDE   LD       (HL), 144   ; Replace character by "~".
NEXT    INC      HL          ; Point to next character.
DEC      BC          ; Decrease counter:
LD       A,B         ; is it
OR       C           ; zero?
JR       NZ, LOOP    ; If not, continue.
RET                  ; If so, return to BASIC.
```

5.8 JOHN AND MARY

JOHN AND MARY was described in Chapter 3.9. The version listed here is one which was developed on the 16K Spectrum, and is therefore unambitious in the range of language it can produce or analyse. It is not, strictly speaking, an example of artificial intelligence, since it operates in a rule-bound way, with no facility for learning or for reacting to unforeseen inputs. It is offered as a basis on which the reader may wish to build if he or she has a machine with more than 9K of usable memory. Owners of the 16K Spectrum should be able to enter a simplified version of the program, deleting all the REM statements, using short variable names and reducing the amount of vocabulary.

The recognition vocabulary is all stored in DATA statements at line 5000 ff. The first group, line 5000, consists of items which will be treated as 'verbs', the second group (line 5050) as 'nouns' and the last

```
  10 REM John and Mary    @ John
Higgins 1983 ********************
  15 BORDER 5: RESTORE
  20 GO TO 4000

4999 REM Vocabulary
5000 DATA "open","shut","bring",
"send","is","are","whois","where
is","whereare","ask","help","tha
nk","hello"
5050  DATA "johnandmary","maryan
djohn","they","them","mary","she
","her","john","he","him","thedo
or","it"
5100 DATA "here","inthekitchen",
"inthelounge","together","intoth
ekitchen","intothelounge","in","
out","open","shut"
```

group (line 5100) as 'places'. Any change in the number of items will entail changes in the loops which read them at lines 410, 1050, 1100 and 1200, as well as changes in the messages that the program will issue when it recognises them. We will point these out when we come to them.

Initialisation takes place from lines 4000 to 4100. The POKE statement simply lengthens the keyboard beep. Next in line 4000 an array, x (**3**), is set up to store the machine's knowledge of its universe. This simply amounts to three flag variables which carry the following meanings:

x (**1**) set to 0 when John is in the lounge,
set to 1 when he is in the kitchen

x (**2**) set to 0 when Mary is in the lounge,
set to 1 when she is in the kitchen

x (**3**) set to 0 when the door is shut,
set to 1 when the door is open

The initial state of the world is JOHN IN LOUNGE, MARY IN KITCHEN, DOOR OPEN.

```
3999 REM Initialisation
4000 POKE 23609,70: DIM x(3): LE
T x(2)=1: LET x(3)=1: LET s$=" a
lready."
```

The machine's next task is to draw the room outline, lines 4010–4020, and to label subroutines with variable names, line 4030. It then sets the four grammar variables, draws the initial state of John, Mary and the door, and goes to the input routine:

```
4009 REM Draw room
4010 CLS : PLOT 20,60: DRAW 30,2
0: DRAW 95,0: DRAW 0,45: DRAW -4
0,0: DRAW 0,-45: DRAW 93,0: DRAW
 30,-20: PLOT 50,80: DRAW 0,54:
DRAW -30,20
4020 PLOT 50,134: DRAW 150,0: DR
AW 30,20: PLOT 200,134: DRAW 0,-
54
4030 LET input=1000: LET questio
n=1500: LET answer=2000: LET giv
eup=900: LET movedoor=100: LET m
ovejohn=200: LET movemary=250: L
ET standardise=300
4050 LET verb=0: LET noun=0: LET
 place=0: LET pronoun=0
4100 GO SUB movedoor: GO SUB mov
ejohn: GO SUB movemary: GO TO in
put
```

Quite deliberately there is no initial presentation of instructions. The program waits to be explored. Typing the word 'help', however, brings up a short description of the program. This is at line 3000:

```
2999 REM Response to help
3000 PRINT AT 16,0;"You can give
me commands or ask questions.
 If you just press  'Enter', I w
ill ask a question. Press 'Enter
' again and I will  answer it."
3010 GO TO input
```

The main input loop is at line 1000. The variable **check** is a flag which labels the user's input as a 'question' (value 0) or an 'answer' (value 1). On getting input, the program wipes out the words of the last exchange and checks to see if the input was null or contained words. If null, it passes control to a question generator in line 1500. Otherwise it sets about parsing the input, the first step being to standardise the input to lower case without punctuation or spaces so that it can be matched with the data. The standardisation takes place in a subroutine at line 300.

```
999 REM Main input
1000 LET check=0: INPUT a$: LET
a$=a$+" ": FOR j=16 TO 20: PRIN
T AT j,0;"
           ": NEXT j: PRINT AT 16
,0;: LET b$="": IF a$(1)=" " THE
N  GO TO question
1010 LET t$=a$: GO SUB standardi
se

299 REM Standardise input to lo
wer case
300 FOR j=1 TO LEN t$: LET a=CO
DE t$(j): IF a>96 AND a<123 THEN
  LET b$=b$+CHR$ a
310 IF a>64 AND a<91 THEN  LET
b$=b$+CHR$ (a+32)
320 NEXT j: RETURN
```

The process of parsing consists of reading each word of the data in turn and trying to match it to the beginning of the input string. The input string is **a$**; the standardised form of it is **b$**; the data to be matched is **c$**; a part successfully matched with a 'verb' element is **d$**; a part matched with a 'noun' is **e$**; finally a part matched with a 'place' is **f$**. Each of **d$**, **e$** are printed as they are parsed. A failure to match sends the program to the **giveup** routine which prints 'I don't understand'. In between each stage of the parsing the program checks to see whether there is an interpretation for what it has got so far. If it finds a complete interpretation, it calls up the **answer** routine at line 2000. If it finds no interpretation it goes to **giveup**.

```
1049 REM Parse first element
1050 RESTORE : LET verb=0: FOR j
=101 TO 113: READ c$: IF LEN c$>
LEN b$ OR verb>0 THEN  GO TO 107
0
1060 IF b$( TO LEN c$)=c$ THEN
LET verb=j: LET d$=a$( TO LEN c$
+1+(j>106 AND j<110)): PRINT d$;
: LET b$=b$(LEN c$+1 TO )
1070 NEXT j: IF verb=0 THEN   GO
TO giveup
1075 IF verb=113 THEN  PRINT AT
16,0;a$;AT 18,0;"Hello!": GO TO
input
1080 IF verb=112 THEN  PRINT AT
16,0;a$;AT 18,0;"You're welcome.
": GO TO input
1085 IF verb=111 THEN  GO TO 300
0
1090 IF verb=110 THEN  GO TO que
stion
1099 REM Parse second element
1100 LET e$="": LET noun=0: FOR
j=201 TO 212: READ c$: IF LEN c$
>LEN b$ OR noun>0 THEN   GO TO 11
30
1110 IF b$( TO LEN c$)=c$ THEN
LET noun=j: LET e$=a$(LEN d$+1 T
O LEN d$+LEN c$+2*(noun=201 OR n
oun=202)+(verb=108 OR verb=109)+
(noun=211)): PRINT e$;: IF LEN b
$>LEN c$ THEN  LET b$=b$(LEN c$+
1 TO )
1120 IF b$=c$ THEN  LET b$=""
1130 NEXT j: IF noun=0 AND verb<
>107 THEN  GO TO giveup: REM No
noun
1140 IF verb<103 AND noun>210 TH
EN  GO TO answer: REM Open/Shut
door
1150 IF verb<103 OR ((verb=103 O
R verb=104) AND noun>210) THEN
GO TO giveup: REM Open/Shut with
out door or vv
1160 IF (verb=105 OR verb=108) A
ND noun<205 THEN  GO TO giveup:
REM Singular verb with plural no
un
1170 IF (verb=106 OR verb=109) A
ND noun>204 THEN  GO TO giveup:
REM Plural verb with singular no
un
1180 IF verb>107 THEN  GO TO ans
wer: REM Where question complete
1190 IF b$="" THEN  GO TO giveup
```

```
                 : REM Sentence complete but no s
                 ense found
                 1199 REM Parse third element
                 1200 LET place=0: FOR j=301 TO 3
                 10: READ c$: IF LEN c$>LEN b$ TH
                 EN   GO TO 1230
                 1210 IF b$=c$ THEN   LET place=j:
                  LET f$=a$(LEN d$+LEN e$+1 TO ):
                  PRINT f$;: LET b$=""
                 1230 NEXT j: IF place=0 THEN   GO
                  TO giveup: REM No element recog
                 nised
                 1250 IF verb=107 AND noun=0 AND
                 place<304 THEN   GO TO answer: RE
                 M Who question with place
                 1260 IF verb=103 AND (place=301
                 OR place=304 OR place=306 OR pla
                 ce=307) THEN   GO TO answer: REM
                 Bring and inward sense
                 1270 IF verb=104 AND (place=305
                 OR place=308) THEN   GO TO answer
                 : REM Send and outward sense
                 1280 IF (verb=105 OR verb=106) A
                 ND (place<305 OR place>308) THEN
                   GO TO answer: REM Y/N question
                  plus location
                 1300 GO TO giveup: REM No sense
                 recognised
```

The question generator at line 1500 creates a random question whenever the user has pressed ENTER on its own and prints it on the screen. It then has its own input routine to collect an answer. A null input (ENTER on its own) makes the machine find and print an answer. Any other input sets the **check** flag to 1, which means that the machine will find its own answer and compare it with the user's.

```
                 1499 REM Create question
                 1500 LET verb=105+INT (5*RND): L
                 ET verb=verb-(verb=106)
                 1505 LET r=RND
                 1510 IF verb=105 THEN   IF r<.35
                 THEN   LET noun=208: PRINT "Is Jo
                 hn ";: GO TO 1540
                 1520 IF verb=105 THEN   IF r<.7 T
                 HEN   LET noun=205: PRINT "Is Mar
                 y ";: GO TO 1540
                 1530 IF verb=105 THEN   LET noun=
                 211: LET place=309: PRINT "Is th
                 e door open?": GO TO 1580
                 1535 IF verb=107 THEN   PRINT "Wh
                 o is ";: LET noun=0
                 1540 IF verb<108 THEN   LET place
                 =301+INT (3*RND): RESTORE 5100:
                 FOR j=301 TO place: READ c$: NEX
                 T j: PRINT c$( TO 2);: IF LEN c$
```

```
<10 THEN  PRINT c$(3 TO );"?": G
O TO 1550
1545 IF verb<108 THEN  PRINT " "
  ;c$(3 TO 5);" ";c$(6 TO );"?"
1550 IF verb=108 THEN  LET r=INT
  (RND*2): LET noun=205+3*r: PRIN
T "Where is "+("Mary?" AND r=0)+
("John?" AND r=1)
1560 IF verb=109 THEN  LET noun=
202: PRINT "Where are Mary and J
ohn?"
1580 INPUT z$: LET t$=z$: GO SUB
  standardise: IF b$="" OR b$="an
swer" THEN  GO TO answer
1590 PRINT AT 18,0;z$: LET check
=1
```

The 'answer' routine at line 2000 begins by assigning a default value of 'OK' to the answer it will give. It then checks on pronouns. If a full noun has been used, it copies that noun into a temporary variable called **pronoun**, which therefore always holds the last noun mentioned. It then tries to match any pronoun it finds with the noun in **pronoun**, and, if it fails, calls up a subroutine at line 400, which asks 'Who?' or 'What?'

```
1999 REM Find answer
2000 LET r$="OK": IF noun=201 OR
  noun=202 OR noun=205 OR noun=20
8 OR noun=211 THEN  LET pronoun=
noun: REM noun used
2010 IF ((noun=203 OR noun=204)
AND pronoun>202) OR ((noun=206 O
R noun=207) AND pronoun<>205) OR
  ((noun=209 OR noun=210) AND pro
noun<>208) THEN  PRINT AT 18,0;"
Who?": GO SUB 400: IF noun=0 THE
N  GO TO giveup
2015 IF noun=212 AND pronoun<>21
1 THEN  PRINT AT 18,0;"What?": G
O SUB 400: IF noun=0 THEN  GO TO
  giveup

 399 REM Pronoun reference
 400 LET noun=0: INPUT w$: LET t
$=w$: LET b$="": GO SUB standard
ise
 410 RESTORE 5050: FOR j=201 TO
212: READ c$
 420 IF c$=b$ THEN  LET noun=j
 430 NEXT j: PRINT AT 18,0;"
": RETURN
 900 PRINT AT 18,0;"I don't unde
rstand."
```

182

The answer-finding process begins at line 2020, and goes through each 'verb' element in turn, replacing the 'OK' of r$ with other words as it finds appropriate responses.

```
2020 IF verb<105 THEN  GO TO 250
0: REM input was command
2030 IF verb<>105 THEN  GO TO 20
80: REM process 'is' questions
2040 IF noun=208 OR (noun=209 AN
D pronoun=208) THEN  GO TO 2045:
 REM John is subject
2042 GO TO 2050
2045 IF ((place=301 OR place=303
) AND x(1)=0) OR (place=302 AND
x(1)=1) THEN  LET r$="Yes.": GO
TO 2400
2047 LET r$="No.": GO TO 2400
2050 IF noun=205 OR (noun=206 AN
D pronoun=205) THEN  GO TO 2055:
 REM subject is Mary
2052 GO TO 2060
2055 IF ((place=301 OR place=303
) AND x(2)=0) OR (place=302 AND
x(2)=1) THEN  LET r$="Yes.": GO
TO 2400
2057 LET r$="No.": GO TO 2400
2060 IF (noun=211 OR (noun=212 A
ND pronoun=211)) AND (place=309
OR place=310) THEN  GO TO 2065:
REM subject is door
2062 GO TO 2078
2065 IF (place=310 AND x(3)=0) O
R (place=309 AND x(3)=1) THEN  L
ET r$="Yes.": GO TO 2400
2070 LET r$="No.": GO TO 2400
2078 LET r$="Is what?": GO TO 24
00
2080 IF verb<>106 THEN  GO TO 21
00
2085 IF (x(1)=0 AND (place=301 O
R place=303 OR place=304) AND x(
2)=0) OR (x(1)=1 AND x(2)=1 AND
(place=302 OR place=304)) THEN
LET r$="Yes.": GO TO 2400
2090 LET r$="No.": GO TO 2400
2100 IF verb=107 AND (place=301
OR place=303) THEN  LET r$=("Joh
n " AND x(1)=0)+("and " AND (x(1
)=0 AND x(2)=0))+("Mary " AND x(
2)=0)+("Nobody " AND (x(1)=1 AND
 x(2)=1))+("is." AND (x(1)<>0 OR
 x(2)<>0))+("are." AND (x(1)=0 A
ND x(2)=0)): GO TO 2400
2110 IF verb=107 THEN  LET r$=("
John " AND x(1)=1)+("and " AND (
x(1)=1 AND x(2)=1))+("Mary " AND
 x(2)=1)+("Nobody " AND (x(1)=0
AND x(2)=0))+("is." AND (x(1)<>1
 OR x(2)<>1))+("are." AND (x(1)=
```

183

```
1 AND x(2)=1)): GO TO 2400
2120 IF verb=109 THEN  LET r$=("
In the " AND x(1)=x(2))+("Mary i
s in the " AND x(1)<>x(2))+("kit
chen" AND x(2)=1)+("lounge" AND
x(2)=0)+("." AND x(1)=x(2))+(" a
nd " AND x(1)<>x(2))+("John is i
n the " AND x(1)<>x(2))+("lounge
." AND x(1)=0 AND x(1)<>x(2))+("
kitchen." AND x(1)=1 AND x(1)<>x
(2)): GO TO 2400
2130 LET r$=("Here." AND (((noun
=208 OR (pronoun=208 AND noun=20
9)) AND x(1)=0) OR ((noun=205 OR
 (pronoun=205 AND noun=206)) AND
  x(2)=0)))+("In the kitchen." AN
D ((noun=208 AND x(1)=1) OR (nou
n=205 AND x(2)=1)))+("Between th
e kitchen and the      lounge." A
ND noun>210)
2150 IF r$="" THEN  GO TO giveup
```

When an input has been identified as a command rather than a question, it is handled by lines 2500 to 2630. These check on the state of the 'world', and either report why an instruction cannot be obeyed, or else call up drawing routines which redraw the figures to correspond to the current variables in the array x().

```
2499 REM Obey instruction
2500 IF verb=101 AND x(3)=1 THEN
   LET r$="It's open"+s$: GO TO 2
400
2510 IF verb=101 THEN  LET x(3)=
1: GO SUB movedoor: GO TO 2400
2520 IF verb=102 AND x(3)=0 THEN
   LET r$="It's shut"+s$: GO TO 2
400
2530 IF verb=102 THEN  LET x(3)=
0: GO SUB movedoor: GO TO 2400
2535 IF x(3)=0 THEN  LET r$="The
 door's shut.": LET pronoun=211:
 GO TO 2400
2540 IF verb=103 AND (noun=208 O
R noun=210) AND x(1)=0 THEN  LET
 r$="He's here"+s$: GO TO 2400
2550 IF verb=103 AND (noun=208 O
R noun=210) THEN  LET x(1)=0: GO
 SUB movejohn: GO TO 2400
2560 IF verb=103 AND (noun=205 O
R (noun=207 AND pronoun=205)) AN
D x(2)=0 THEN  LET r$="She's her
e"+s$: GO TO 2400
2570 IF verb=103 AND (noun=205 O
R (noun=207 AND pronoun=205)) TH
EN  LET x(2)=0: GO SUB movemary:
 GO TO 2400
```

```
2580 IF verb=103 AND x(1)=0 AND
x(2)=0 THEN  LET r$="They're her
e"+s$: GO TO 2400
2590 IF verb=103 THEN  LET x(1)=
0: LET x(2)=0: GO SUB movejohn:
GO SUB movemary: GO TO 2400
2600 IF (noun=208 OR noun=210) A
ND x(1)=1 THEN  LET r$="He's the
re"+s$: GO TO 2400
2605 IF noun=208 OR noun=210 THE
N  LET x(1)=1: GO SUB movejohn:
GO TO 2400
2610 IF (noun=205 OR (noun=207 A
ND pronoun=205)) AND x(2)=1 THEN
  LET r$="She's there"+s$: GO TO
 2400
2615 IF (noun=205 OR (noun=207 A
ND pronoun=205)) THEN  LET x(2)=
1: GO SUB movemary: GO TO 2400
2620 IF x(1)=1 AND x(2)=1 THEN
LET r$="They're there"+s$: GO TO
 2400
2630 LET x(1)=1: LET x(2)=1: GO
SUB movejohn: GO SUB movemary: G
O TO 2400
```

The drawing routines themselves are from lines 100 to 290:

```
 99 REM Shut door
100 IF x(3)=1 THEN  GO TO 150
110 PLOT 145,125: DRAW   INVERSE
1;20,-30: DRAW   INVERSE 1;0,-45
: DRAW   INVERSE 1;-20,30: DRAW 2
0,0: FOR j=144 TO 106 STEP -1: P
LOT j,125: DRAW   INVERSE 1;0,-44
: NEXT j
120 RETURN
149 REM Open door
150 PLOT 145,125: DRAW 20,-30:
DRAW 0,-45: DRAW -20,30: DRAW  I
NVERSE 1;19,0: GO SUB movejohn:
GO SUB movemary: RETURN
160 RETURN
199 REM Erase John from kitchen
200 IF x(1)=0 THEN  CIRCLE  INV
ERSE 1;135,118,3: PLOT  INVERSE
1;135,115: DRAW   INVERSE 1;-4,-1
0: PLOT  INVERSE 1;135,115: DRAW
  INVERSE 1;4,-10: PLOT  INVERSE
1;135,115: DRAW   INVERSE 1;0,-1
8: DRAW   INVERSE 1;-4,-17: PLOT
 INVERSE 1;135,97: DRAW   INVERSE
1;4,-17
209 REM Erase John from lounge
210 IF x(1)=1 THEN  CIRCLE  INV
ERSE 1;70,105,3: PLOT  INVERSE 1
;70,102: DRAW   INVERSE 1;-4,-10:
```

185

```
    PLOT  INVERSE 1;70,102: DRAW   I
NVERSE 1;4,-10: PLOT  INVERSE 1;
70,102: DRAW  INVERSE 1;0,-18: D
RAW  INVERSE 1;-4,-17: PLOT  INV
ERSE 1;70,84: DRAW  INVERSE 1;4,
-17
 219 REM Draw John in lounge
 220 IF x(1)=0 THEN  CIRCLE 70,1
05,3: PLOT 70,102: DRAW -4,-10:
PLOT 70,102: DRAW 4,-10: PLOT 70
,102: DRAW 0,-18: DRAW -4,-17: P
LOT 70,84: DRAW 4,-17
 229 REM Draw John in kitchen
 230 IF x(1)=1 THEN  CIRCLE 135,
118,3: PLOT 135,115: DRAW -4,-10
: PLOT 135,115: DRAW 4,-10: PLOT
 135,115: DRAW 0,-18: DRAW -4,-1
7: PLOT 135,97: DRAW 4,-17
 240 RETURN
 249 REM Erase Mary from kitchen
 250 IF x(2)=0 THEN  CIRCLE  INV
ERSE 1;115,118,3: PLOT  INVERSE
1;115,115: DRAW  INVERSE 1;-4,-1
0: DRAW  INVERSE 1;4,10: DRAW  I
NVERSE 1;4,-10: DRAW  INVERSE 1;
-4,10: DRAW  INVERSE 1;0,-12: DR
AW  INVERSE 1;-4,-14: DRAW  INVE
RSE 1;8,0: DRAW  INVERSE 1;-4,14
: PLOT  INVERSE 1;113,89: DRAW
INVERSE 1;0,-8: PLOT  INVERSE 1;
117,89: DRAW  INVERSE 1;0,-8
 259 REM Erase Mary from lounge
 260 IF x(2)=1 THEN  CIRCLE  INV
ERSE 1;90,105,3: PLOT  INVERSE 1
;90,102: DRAW  INVERSE 1;-4,-10:
 DRAW  INVERSE 1;4,10: DRAW  INV
ERSE 1;4,-10: DRAW  INVERSE 1;-4
,10: DRAW  INVERSE 1;0,-12: DRAW
  INVERSE 1;-4,-14: DRAW  INVERS
E 1;8,0: DRAW  INVERSE 1;-4,14:
PLOT  INVERSE 1;88,76: DRAW  INV
ERSE 1;0,-8: PLOT  INVERSE 1;92,
76: DRAW  INVERSE 1;0,-8
 269 REM Draw Mary in kitchen
 270 IF x(2)=1 THEN  CIRCLE 115,
118,3: PLOT 115,115: DRAW -4,-10
: DRAW 4,10: DRAW 4,-10: DRAW -4
,10: DRAW 0,-12: DRAW -4,-14: DR
A. 8,0: DRAW -4,14: PLOT 113,89:
 DRAW 0,-8: PLOT 117,89: DRAW 0,
-8
 279 REM Draw Mary in lounge
 280 IF x(2)=0 THEN  CIRCLE 90,1
05,3: PLOT 90,102: DRAW -4,-10:
DRAW 4,10: DRAW 4,-10: DRAW -4,1
0: DRAW 0,-12: DRAW -4,-14: DRAW
 8,0: DRAW -4,14: PLOT 88,76: DR
AW 0,-8: PLOT 92,76: DRAW 0,-8
 290 RETURN
```

Finally the answer is either printed out or matched at line 2400, before returning control to the input routine:

```
2399 REM Print or compare answer
s
2400 IF check=0 THEN  PRINT AT 1
8,0;r$: GO TO input
2410 LET b$="": LET t$=r$: GO SU
B standardise: LET w$=b$: LET b$
="": LET t$=z$: GO SUB standardi
se: IF w$=b$ THEN  PRINT AT 18,2
4;"I agree.": GO TO input
2420 PRINT AT 19,0;"My answer wa
s: ";r$: GO TO input
```

Here is a summary of the variables used in the program:

Variables used as labels for subroutines
  input, question, answer, giveup, standardise, movejohn, movemary, movedoor

Numeric variables
  check, verb, noun, place, pronoun
  a – ASCII code used in standardise routine
  r – random number

Counting variable
  j

Numeric array
  x (3)

String variables
  a$ – input command or question
  b$ – standardised input
  c$ – vocabulary for matching
  d$ – matched verb
  e$ – matched noun
  f$ – matched place
  z$ – user's answer
  r$ – machine's answer
  s$ – "already"

187

Notes and further reading

Chapter 1

On computers in education there are three studies which are worth reading:

Coburn et al (1982), *Practical Guide to Computers in Education*. Massachusetts, Addison Wesley.
Maddison (1982), *Microcomputers in the Classroom*. London, Hodder and Stoughton.
Rushby (1979), *An Introduction to Educational Computing*. London, Croom Helm.

Another important book is:

Papert (1980), *Mindstorms: Children, Computers and Powerful Ideas*. Brighton, The Harvester Press.

from which we have quoted in 1.1.

Developments in many relevant areas are reported in the journal *Educational Computing*, available from:

Magsub,
Oakfield House,
Perrymount Road,
Haywards Heath,
West Sussex.

A newsletter for language teachers is CALLBOARD, edited by Graham Davies and obtainable from:

Editorial:
Graham Davies and David Steel
School of Language Studies
Ealing College of Higher Education
St Mary's Road
London W5 5RT

Subscriptions:
CALLBOARD
19 High Street
Eccleshall
Stafford
ST21 6BW

1.2
The best known introduction to the approaches discussed in this section is:

Widdowson (1978), *Teaching Language as Communication*. Oxford, Oxford University Press.

Krashen's theory of second language acquisition is presented in:

Krashen (1982), *Principles and Practice in Second Language Acquisition*. Oxford, Pergamon Press.

1.3
A useful anthology of significant articles is:

Taylor (1980), *The Computer in the School: Tutor, Tool, Tutee?* New York, Teacher's College Press, Columbia University.

This collection includes the article *Should the Computer Teach the Student or Vice Versa?* by Arthur Luehrmann, discussed on page 18.

The evaluation study by Kemmis is:

Kemmis et al (1977), *How Do Students Learn?* Working papers in computer-assisted learning: UNCAL Evaluation Studies, Norwich. Centre for Applied Research in Education, Occasional Publications No 5.

The original report is difficult to get hold of but it is summarised and discussed by Rushby (1979) and Maddison (1982). (See notes to Chapter 1.)

Chapter 2

There are many books available, and more being published all the time, which describe how a computer system works and discuss computer applications. Among the best known are:

Evans (1979), *The Mighty Micro*. London, Gollancz.
Bradbeer et al (1982), *The Computer Book*. London, BBC Publications.

In a field where developments are so rapid, the best way to find out what devices are available is to look at recent issues of a journal. Among the hundreds published, at least a dozen are very widely distributed through newsagents, among which we would recommend:

Your Computer
Practical Computing
Personal Computer World

and, for a view of the American scene, *Byte*.

2.1
We are indebted to Chris Harrison for drawing our attention to the *scrolling* versus *paging* distinction.

Chapter 3
The teacher whose comment was reported in 3.1 is Pam Fiddy, in the discussion of her paper *High Technology Teaching for Low Technology Teachers* published in the proceedings of the Educational Computing Conference, Polytechnic of North London, 1982.

3.2
The only book so far on the preparation of instructional material specifically for language teachers is:

> Davies and Higgins (1982), *Computers, Language Learning and Teaching*. CILT Information Guide No 22. London, Centre for Information on Language Teaching and Research.

An article which is worth reading is *Answer-processing and error correction in foreign language CAI* by James Pusack, which appears in:

Wyatt (ed) (1983). *Computer-assisted Language Instruction*. Special issue of *System*, Vol 11 No 1, Oxford, Pergamon Press.

Dakin's account of 'meaningful drills' can be found in:
Dakin (1973). *The Language Laboratory and Language Learning*. London, Longman.

Brian Farrington's work is described in Farrington (1982). *Computer-based Exercises for Language Learning at University Level*. Computers and Education No 6. pp. 113–116.

3.3
Leon and Martin's work is described in their article *Machines and Measurement* in:

Bolinger (ed) (1972). *Intonation, Selected Readings*. London, Penguin Books.

3.4
Chris Jones's games for the Sinclair ZX81 are published by the author under the title WORDPACK and are available through:

Wida Software,
2, Nicholas Gardens, London W5.

3.5
For an account of programmed learning and its applications in language teaching see:

Howatt (1969). *Programmed Learning and the Language Teacher* London, Longman.

3.6
Several ideas in this chapter and in Chapters 3.8 and 3.11 are taken up in:

Chandler (ed) (1983). *Exploring English with Microcomputers* MEP Readers 1. National Association of Teachers of English and Micro-Electronics Education Programme.

Also see:

Johns (1982). *The uses of an analytic generator: the computer as teacher of English for specific purposes*. ELT Documents No 112. London, The British Council, pp. 96–105.

Higgins, (1982). *How real is a computer simulation?* ELT Documents No 113. London, The British Council, pp. 102–109.

The testing technique devised by Alan Davies is illustrated by Rebecca Valette in:

Vallette (1967). *Modern Language Testing; A Handbook*. Harcourt, Brace and Jovanovitch, New York

Daniel Chandler's STORYMAKER is described and listed in Chandler (1982). *Great Expectations*. Educational Computing No 30 pp. 24–25. (See notes to Chapter 1.)

Winograd's SHRDLU program was published in:

Winograd (1972). *Understanding Natural Language*. Edinburgh, The University Press.

The suggestion that students' own compositions can be used as text in games like STORYBOARD and JUMBLER was made by Judith Pierpoint of the City University, New York.

3.7
The most authoritative book on

simulations for EFL teaching is

Jones (1982). *Simulations and Language Teaching*. Cambridge, Cambridge University Press.

3.9

A book which contains some interesting programs in the field of artificial intelligence, together with an account of their origins, is:

Krutch (1981). *Experiments in Artificial Intelligence for Small Computers*. Indianapolis, Howard W Sams.

One of the programs listed is a version of Weizenbaum's ELIZA (DOCTOR). The best general textbook of artificial intelligence is

Winston, (1981). *Artificial Intelligence*. Reading, Mass, Addison Wesley.

The most thorough and up-to-date account of language and artificial intelligence is contained in

Winograd (1983). *Language as a Cognitive Process, Vol 1: Syntax*, Reading, Mass, Addison Wesley.

For a full account of the JOHN AND MARY program, see Richard Power, *A Computer Model of Conversation*, unpublished PhD dissertation, University of Edinburgh, 1974.

3.10

Muriel Higgin's article, *Computer EFL Practice: Student power and the BOOH factor*, was a prize-winning entry in the 1982 English Speaking Union language competition, but is not yet published. It is included in a collection of articles, *Computers and ELT: British Council Inputs* which is held in British Council offices and in the BC/CILT Language Teaching Library, 20 Carlton House Terrace, London.

The program ANIMALS is described in an article by David Ahl (as ANIMAL) in Ahl (1976).

Learning, Innovation and Animals. The Best of Creative Computing Vol I pp. 197–201.

Nick Bullard's simulations are described in an article, *The Role of the Microcomputer in the Language Classroom*, to appear in Practical English Teacher. London, Mary Glasgow.

The program Castaway is based on SHIPWRECKED which forms part of the first simulation in:

Jones (1974). *Nine Graded Simulations*. First published by the Inner London Education Authority; soon to be published by Max Hueber Verlag, West Germany.

Chris Harrison's TOWN PLAN is described and listed in:

Harrison (1982). *Town Planning and Shopping and Language Learning*. Practical Computer, pp. 78–83.

David Ahl's article, *Computers in the Language Arts*, which first proposed the use of MADLIBS as learning activities, appeared in:

Lecarme and Lewis (eds) (1975). *Computers in Education*. Amsterdam, North Holland Publishing Company.

3.11

Bright and McGregor (1972). *Teaching English as a Second Language*. London, Longman.

Chapter 4

Computers in linguistic research are dealt with by:

Hockey (1980). *Computer Applications in the Humanities*. London, Duckworth.

4.2

See notes to Chapter 3.9.

INDEX

Major references are given in **bold**.
Alphabetical order is letter-by-letter, compound headings of two or more words being treated as single entities alphabetized all through (except for a word or words in parenthesis).